THE SOVIET MILITARY

THE SOVIET MILITARY

Political Education, Training and Morale

E. S. Williams
Air Commodore (retired), Royal Air Force
Research Associate, Royal United Services Institute, London

with chapters by C. N. Donnelly and J. E. Moore

Foreword by
Sir Curtis Keeble

St. Martin's Press   New York

First published in the United States of America in 1986

Printed in Great Britain

ISBN 0–312–74835–3

Library of Congress Cataloging-in-Publication Data
Williams, E. S., 1924–
The Soviet military.
Bibliography: p.
Includes index.
1. Military education—Soviet Union—History—20th
century. 2. Soviet Union—Armed Forces. I. Donnelly,
C. N. (Christopher N.) II. Moore, John Evelyn.
II. Title.
U601.W55 1986 355.5′0947 86–6556
ISBN 0–312–74835–3

Contents

List of Plates

All photographs are by courtesy of TASS

Notes on the Contributors

Air Commodore E. S. Williams, CBE, MPhil learned Russian at London University and, later, living with an *émigré* family in Paris (1952–54). He has been closely connected with Soviet studies ever since. In 1964 he went to serve for three years in the Soviet Union as Assistant Air Attaché. He spent another four years there as the UK Defence Attaché (1978–81). At present he is Soviet Studies Associate at the Royal United Services Institute for Defence Studies, London.

Christopher Donnelly is Head of the Soviet Studies Centre at the Royal Military Academy, Sandhurst. A Russian speaker, he has studied in the Soviet Union and travelled extensively in Eastern Europe. He lectures widely on the Soviet Army.

Captain John Moore, RN(retired), a former head of British analysis of Soviet Naval Affairs, is the Editor of *Jane's Fighting Ships*. He is the author of *The Soviet Navy Today, Seapower and Politics* and *Warships of the Soviet Navy*.

Foreword

In 1591, Giles Fletcher wrote in his book *Of The Russe Commonwealth*:

> If the Russe soldier were as hardy to execute an enterprise as he is hard to bear out toil and travail, or were otherwise as apt and well trained for the wars as he is indifferent from his lodging and diet, he would far excel the soldiers of our parts. Whereas now he is far meaner of courage and execution in any warlike service, which cometh partly of his servile condition that will not suffer any great courage or valor to grow in him, partly for lack of due honour and reward which he hath no great hope of, whatsoever service or execution he do.

My professional concern has been primarily with Soviet foreign policy, and in that policy the Soviet successor to Fletcher's 'Russe soldier' has his part. Air Commodore Williams and his colleagues have performed an important task in helping us to understand him better.

The foreign policy of any major power must have defence policy as a substantial component, but, in the case of the Soviet Union, the linkage is more than usually close. It is practical, doctrinal and personal. Soviet foreign policy is based upon a mixture of national interest and Marxist–Leninist doctrine. Doctrinally, it requires the preordained victory of socialism in an unremitting struggle against capitalism. Its tactics are formulated in accordance with a Soviet perception of the changing correlation of forces, both political and military. The power of the Soviet state has its source and its repository in the doctrine and the structure of the Communist Party. It has the armed forces as a primary instrument and in any assessment of the effectiveness of that instrument, the morale and the will of the officers and men of the Soviet forces, must be a key component.

The linkage of the military and political elements has been

crucial to the survival of the power of party and state from 1917
onwards. Fletcher's unflattering description did the Russian
soldier less than justice. There was no lack of courage in the
Russian armies of World War I, but it was the breaking of the
Imperial Army of 1917 which gave Lenin the decisive grasp on
power and the lesson was not lost. Having consolidated and
sustained Communist power with the Red Army in the Civil War,
having survived and triumphed by military strength in 1941–45,
the Soviet Union can now claim Superpower parity with the
United States only by virtue of military power. Only by the use of
military power to sustain political doctrine can it maintain its
imperial structure in Europe and Asia.

This whole complex of Soviet foreign and defence policy is the
subject of continual, exhaustive and authoritative analysis in the
West. Much less, however, has been written about the men and
women upon whom the structure of Soviet military power rests.
The Soviet soldier is at one and the same time a descendant of the
Russian soldier and a creature of the Soviet state. It has been a
constant preoccupation of the Party to remedy the weaknesses
which Fletcher identified and to ensure that the Soviet armed
forces are not only fully equipped and fully trained, but inspired
by a total, unquestioning loyalty to party and state. Upon their
success depends not merely the strength of the armed forces, but
also, to a certain degree, the stability of the political structure of
the Soviet state itself. At the level of the individual citizen and at
the level of the higher military and political leadership the threads
come together and as history has demonstrated, their
interrelationship is crucial to the control, the direction and the
execution of the power of the state.

A major concern of the current Soviet leadership is to instil into
the people a sense of civil discipline. The linkage between the
political indoctrination of the child and of the soldier is close and
for many the foundation of that discipline, laid down from the
earliest years, is reinforced during the period of compulsory
military service. But how sound is it? In the years from 1941 to
1945, the discipline and morale of the armed forces and of the civil
population commanded respect as they ensured the survival and
enhancement of Soviet power in the face of an attack upon the
Soviet Union itself. I saw at first hand the frightening power of
Soviet military discipline at one point during the war and I saw
what happened when that discipline was absent. Subsequently,

the conduct of Soviet servicemen has been tested in operations in Eastern Europe and it is currently being tested in the very different circumstances of offensive operations in Afghanistan. This book suggests that, not surprisingly, the ideological armour is already being penetrated by the shafts of reality. There is no reason to suppose that if the Soviet Union itself were again under threat the response would be less positive than in 1941. Yet, for all that the propagandist may try to simplify the world into the forces of light and of darkness, the real challenges which now confront the Soviet Union are far more subtle. Not only the military capability of the state and its international posture, but its whole evolutionary process will reflect the way in which a new generation of Soviet citizens – whether as soldiers or as civilians – react to a complex and changing environment.

There can be no confident predictions. As Air Commodore Williams writes in his preface, the Soviet soldier is still an enigma. He may even in certain respects be an enigma to his own leaders. This is a closed sector of a closed society. The direct evidence of those Soviet citizens who for one reason or another have left their country is bound to be unrepresentative, but it can usefully supplement and illustrate the material available from published Soviet sources as well as from the limited direct access available to a Western observer. Fortunately, a careful study of all these sources, carried out by a team with first-hand experience of the Soviet Union, a feel for the way in which it functions and a sympathetic understanding of its people can reveal much. The value of this work in terms of the formulation of our defence policy is clear. It is not less relevant to our broader understanding of the Soviet Union and to the conduct of relations with it.

CURTIS KEEBLE

Preface

At the beginning of World War II the opposing armies knew their enemy or their allies well. The belligerent nations were closely interrelated by history. Both Britain and France were connected with Germany through many cultural, academic and commercial ties. There was also a broad familiarity and facility of language among them. Above all, these three countries had been locked together in the intimacy of World War I barely twenty years earlier. There was thus no particular clamour on either side to 'know thine enemy'. He was known well enough. Cross-cultural perceptions did not give rise to serious problems of understanding until the Soviet Union and Japan entered the war in 1941.

The characteristics of Japanese fighting men were virtually unknown to the Allies and knowledge of them was acquired only slowly and painfully. Likewise to the Germans, the Soviet soldier was an enigma. There had been their long experience of Russians on the Eastern Front, 1914–18, but there was little to indicate how twenty-four years of communist dictatorship had affected soldiers' attitudes. Logic suggested that collectivisation, forced labour, the terror and the purges would have turned their stomachs against fighting for the Soviet regime and their showing in the Spanish Civil War and in Finland (1940) seemed to validate this logic. But the Germans also had to learn the hard way that conventional logic was an untrustworthy guide. Had Hitler in 1941 possessed any real knowledge of the Soviet soldier's psyche it is unlikely that he would ever have launched 'Barbarrossa'.

Forty-five years on the Soviet soldier is still an enigma. In the 'Great Fatherland War' he proved a most formidable enemy both in actuality and in mythology. The Germans used to say that he had to be killed at least twice before he would die. Is he still so formidable? Would he still perform in the traditions of his father – or grandfather – the legendary hero of Stalingrad, Kursk and Berlin? Or is he softer, or as generally cynical towards the Marxist ideology as many young Soviet people profess to be? Faced with a major war would he be willing to die for his 'Homeland' as were those millions of his ancestors? Is he still 'twelve feet tall'?

This book cannot answer these questions, but it does attempt to provide some background against which they can be pondered. It does not set out to paint a complete portrait of the Soviet serviceman, illustrating every facet of his training and style of life. Neither can it pretend to be a comprehensive assessment of morale, nor predict the quality of performance in war of the individual soldier, airman or sailor. It can claim only to throw some light on the education that all young Soviet men receive; education – or, pejoratively perhaps, indoctrination – designed as much to prepare them for military service as to school them for life generally in the wider socialist community. Without some understanding of this educational system it is scarcely possible to draw up a complete net assessment of the relative strengths of Warsaw Pact and NATO forces.

The authors present a view of this human dimension in the hope that it will assist those whose duty it is to make net assessments. It is hoped also that it will serve to inform the perceptions of other readers, service and civilian, who concern themselves seriously with matters of peace and war.

Part I confines itself to a consideration of the military aspects of the Soviet education system both as it operates in the state schools and as it is refined and developed in the youth organisations and, later, among the ranks of the Soviet Armed Forces. It is related to features and problems of morale.

Part II comprises three sketches of the Soviet soldier, the airman and the sailor respectively, providing some visual context for Part I. These chapters (4, 5, and 6), by three different authors, approach the subject from several directions and emphasise different formative influences. Taken together they form a composite impression of the serviceman in the framework of his particular parent service. Unlike the British Armed Forces and those of most other nations, the Soviet Armed Forces are not the traditional three separate arms but five. In addition to the Army, the Air Forces and the Navy there are also the Strategic Rocket Forces and the Air Defence Force, both these latter being quite independent organisations from the other three. Since however they are raised from the same human resource pool, nurtured, educated and trained politically and generally in the same manner, it was judged unnecessary to treat them separately here. The reader will find some instances of overlap in these separate service chapters. They have been retained to emphasise common, fundamental features by illuminating them from different angles. Chapter 7 examines some current aspects of morale among the Soviet Armed Forces.

E.S.W.

Part I
Education and Morale

1 Political Education and Training

INTRODUCTION

People are not born soldiers. They become soldiers. Both in wartime and peacetime military tasks require a great expenditure of effort from a man. And this is why the education of the soldier is no easy matter. The process should not begin at that moment when the new recruit joins the ranks, but much earlier, at the time of the first signs of maturity, during the time of adolescent dreams.

Red Star, 22 March 1973

It is a commonplace to say that Soviet servicemen are politically indoctrinated. Although an impressive number of authors have written at varying length on the subject there is still no widespread understanding in the Western world of the scope, extent and content of the indoctrination programme. Seven years of working in the Soviet Union, first as an Assistant Air Attaché in the 1960s and later from 1978–81 as Defence Attaché, has convinced this author that the education of Soviet soldiers has a far greater significance for future international relations than is generally realised.

No full examination of the indoctrination pattern has been made recently. There have been many references to it in articles on the Soviet military forces and a chapter devoted to it in Goldhamer's excellent book *The Soviet Soldier*, but not since Louis Nemzer's *Basic Patterns of Political Propaganda Operations in the Soviet Armed Forces* (1953) has there been anything like a full treatment. Compared with Soviet strategy and military hardware, about which whole libraries have been written, the morale and motivation aspects of the total Soviet military capability have been studied only cursorily. Thirty years on it is surprising to find

3

that so much of what Nemzer wrote in 1952 holds good in 1986. He discerned a dual pattern of inculcating blind patriotism on the one hand and blind hatred for the nation's enemies, real, supposed or potential, on the other. The pattern has not fundamentally changed and the larger part of his work retains its validity. His research was carried out in the early days of the Cold War period when the possibility of an armed clash of Soviet and Western forces seemed more imminent than we care to think it is at present. His concern was to meet the immediate requirement for a possible psychological campaign directed at the military personnel of the USSR, a ludicrous notion today perhaps but the field of knowledge Nemzer ploughed for the first time is still an essential element of our Western assessment of the USSR's total military posture. The essence lies in the question, 'Do the Soviet armed forces possess the necessary quality of morale to enable them to press forward their attack on Day One of World War III?' Perhaps there is the even more important question, 'Will they have that touch of *un petit peu* to sustain them on Day Two?'

Marshal Grechko, the Soviet Minister of Defence until he died in 1976, had little doubt of the answer. He wrote:

> Our Soviet Armed Forces are being constantly supplied with diverse modern weapons and military equipment. The strength of the Army and Navy does not however lie solely in the capability of these modern weapons. The main thing, the most important thing, is the people in whose hands these weapons rest. Under present-day conditions of war, even as ever before, will victory depend ultimately upon the state of the combat morale of the warring armies. Men who have mastered their equipment and who are strong in political conviction will be the victors. Our Soviet forces consist of such men.[1]

Grechko was undoubtedly right, even if not original, about morale as the prime ingredient of victory in war but, given the continuance of the long peace between East and West, uneasy though it might be, does his confidence in the superiority of Soviet morale continue to be justified? These chapters will present the results of some research into the education of the soldier and the likely effect on his morale of the incessant indoctrination practised by the Soviet authorities. They will go on to hint at the wider influence that the indoctrination of servicemen undoubtedly has upon the Soviet nation as a whole. More than one million men are conscripted annually into the Soviet forces. Each year the same number of men are released into civilian life at the end of two years during which 30 per cent of their military training time has been allocated to political studies. The Soviet Armed Forces may thus be seen as a vast seminary where the education of Soviet youth is consolidated and set in a framework of military reality. In this way the Armed Forces must have an enormously persuasive and pervasive effect on Soviet society as a whole and by logical extension, upon the climate of international relations.

This is the crucial point. It is arguable if a corporate public opinion can exist in the truly totalitarian state but, ultimately, this is of small concern to the rulers of the Soviet Union. It is however necessary for the government there to ensure that public attitudes are uniformly and unquestioningly approving of its policies and this docile unanimity is in all probability the fundamental aim of the national indoctrination programme, or in Soviet terminology, the 'political enlightenment' programme. In earlier Soviet times the programme was no less strident and all-pervading than it is today but there were large sectors of the population then who were actively anti-Soviet and as such were a direct threat to the government, indeed to the communist system, with the result that coercion of a more violent kind in the shape of the purges and the terror weapon was employed to produce general acquiescence. Nowadays the terror weapon is used only rarely and selectively. It is a tribute to the political enlighteners that this state has been reached, that their long years of opinion moulding or attitude forming have produced such a reliable conformity.

The basis of this conformity is the set of perceptions that Soviet citizens have first, of themselves and, second, of the nature of the world beyond their frontiers. Formation of these perceptions will be examined in some detail. In essence they see Soviet society as the triumph of the workers' struggle against exploitation and, although their society has not yet fully blossomed and there is some wry cynicism about the slow rate of burgeoning, there is nevertheless a dynamic spirit about their hopes for the future. It is still a mistily discerned future but utopian all the same, a time of universal peace on earth with man's prime occupation the exploration of the cosmos. Delaying their progress along this golden road is the capitalist world, the reactionary, predatory enemies who seek to destroy socialism by subversion and war.

These are the general themes of the 'enlightenment'. Only good is ascribed to the Communist Party and only bad to the bourgeois capitalist nations. Individual office-holders may be criticised but never the Party, not even in the softest whisper while, on the other hand, nothing said or done in the non-communist world is presented other than as totally evil.

The military 'enlighteners' are certainly as active in this work as their civilian counterparts in *Agitprop*, probably more so considering the highest degree of zeal they are expected to engender in their flock. In all major military units, air force regiments and naval ships the man responsible for political indoctrination is the Deputy Commander for Political Affairs or, to use the Russian contraction, the *Zampolit*. He is assisted by politically trained personnel operating at sub-unit levels and his activities are directed and coordinated by the Main Political Administration (MPA) in the Soviet Ministry of Defence. The Military Publishing House prepares and produces most of the materials used by the *Zampolit*, books, pamphlets, posters, etc.

It is necessary first to look in some detail at the political education a young man has received before joining the Armed Forces. The *Zampolit* does not exactly start with an empty page. Soviet authorities claim that political instruction is not given to children under the age of seven. While this could be true in the direct sense it is certainly not so in the round. From his first days in the nursery school the child is surrounded by the aura of Lenin. He is encouraged to revere and adore him for his immortal, Christlike qualities and to respect the Party as his church militant. As the child progresses upwards through the kindergarten, the primary school and the parallel spare-time educational organisations, the Little *Oktobrists*, the Pioneers and the KOMSOMOL, so does his instruction become closely refined as the principles of Marxism–Leninism are wrought in him. Reference is made in these pages to the books he reads in the several phases of his school life, many of them foreshadowing the *Zampolit*'s twin strands of instruction in service to the homeland and implacable hate for its capitalist enemies. After such a lengthy preparation it is scarcely surprising that new recruits to the armed forces are generally receptive of the *Zampolit*'s message. Although there is evidence of apathy and indeed some opposition to the doctrines expressed, this is not judged to pose any serious problems of command or discipline within the ranks.

Following the survey of pre-military political education this part of the book will concentrate on the *Zampolit*'s indoctrination curriculum, the unchanging themes of the perceived ideological struggle between capitalism and communism. The question will then be asked, 'why do they do it?' To non-communist eyes the whole programme appears preposterous and, insofar as the recipients of the indoctrination are deliberately denied the full facts on most topics, it is patently chicane. But it has been operating on successive generations of Soviet citizens for almost seventy years and would surely have been abandoned along the way had it not proved effective. Above all else it has done much to foster the notion that the Soviet armed forces and the Soviet people are a single entity, united in a mystical trinity comprising the peasant, the worker and the soldier. This union is the foundation of the state, in fact it is the state itself, the MPA's task being to ensure that the soldier is seen as its firmest pillar, greatly respected and not simply a tax burden that could be lightly discarded. All branches of Soviet propaganda continue to emphasise World War II and the high price of victory. One of the main reasons for this is to help create this popular regard for the armed forces and to convince the soldiers of today that they are part of a continuum, that they stand now in their father's or grandfather's boots, waiting for the successors of Napoleon, and Hitler to attack their homeland. To the extent that there appears to be no generation gap, no crisis of identity between young and old, it must be judged successful but whether it can be maintained for many years longer remains a matter for speculation.

There is little doubt that the preaching will continue for as long as a military threat can be credibly presented – or longer. In the present setting, Soviet philosophy holds that nuclear war, unless forced upon them by an aggressor, can never be a practical course, ethically or strategically. It would appear to be policy therefore to wage a purely ideological struggle with the non-communist world without resort to destructive physical war, rather as Lenin directed when he wrote that the soundest strategy is to delay operations until the moral disintegration of the enemy renders the delivery of the mortal blow both possible and easy. To win this waiting game the cohesion of the armed forces is a prime factor. A healthy hate – or a healthy fear – of the perceived capitalist enemy would seem from the nature of their political teachings to be the mainstay of this cohesion and it can be expected therefore that the

Zampolit will support and reinforce it until all opposing political systems and alliances have collapsed from the strain of internal dissension. As an early Soviet strategist, General Svechin,[2] wrote in 1926, 'The task of the Red Army is to shake trees bearing fruit which is already rotten'.

Part I leads finally to some necessarily speculative comment on the extent of the *Zampolit*'s influence not only on servicemen but on public opinion[3] as a whole in the Soviet Union although no definitive work in the field can be expected while the government there maintains its traditional tight security. At present there is not even a remote prospect of its relaxation. In spite of it, several studies have appeared over the past years based largely on the evidence of defactors and émigrés[4] but the massive population transfers of the immediate post-war years have dwindled to a trickle and almost the only data available to researchers now are the Soviet open media. Conclusions drawn from these sources must be oblique and inferential but until the doors are opened to foreign social scientists they will remain tentative and the opinions of the Soviet comrade-in-the-street will continue to be an enigma.

There are, of course, travellers tales, frequently supportive to media inferences but by nature they tend to be subjective, reflecting many of the traveller's own prejudices and wishful thoughts. The religious, for example, will report that God is very much alive and his church healthy in spite of state oppression, while the atheist or agnostic will contend the opposite, that the old forms of worship are disappearing rapidly and Christianity will not survive another generation. Defectors' evidence though extremely valuable is nevertheless similarly flawed, their stories inspired all too often by a desire to tell Western audiences what they would like to hear. In any case the security system denies the foreigner unfettered access to Soviet citizens and samples of public opinion will therefore be so small as to defy correlation and any conclusion they support should be treated with enormous reservation.

It is not surprising therefore that comparatively few studies of Soviet public opinion have been attempted. What is surprising is that the West scarcely notices the deficiency, assuming after nearly seventy years of Party rule that all policy is decided centrally by a small oligarchy in the Kremlin and that public opinion is irrelevant. That the Party itself does not judge it so is quite evident from the scale of the enlightenment effort. This study is primarily concerned with the armed services contribution to the programme but this is recognised only as a part, however significant, of the whole. All sectors of Soviet society have their own 'enlighteners', propagandists and agitators working in industrial enterprises, public administration and utilities, under the overall control of the state's *Agitprop* organisation.

Agitprop trains the agitators (variously estimated to total between 200 000 and 400 000 over the whole USSR), finances and establishes the 'agitation points', provides the materials, posters, films, tracts and books, and monitors the content of the propagated messages. Agitators are either full-time workers or part-time volunteers. In either case, theirs is a noble profession, the terms 'propagandist' and 'agitator' having none of the perjorative associations normal in the Western world. The military variant, the *Zampolit*, is *primus inter pares* with civilian agitators. He is entrusted with the political education of all servicemen under his superior's command and responsible for the state of their morale.

NOTE ON SOURCES

Soviet military publications can be purchased by foreigners in the military bookshops found in most Soviet towns. Quality varies and certainly a rigorous censorship ensures that none of the books or pamphlets on sale contains information on anything that could be remotely classed as a state secret. They are predominantly technical, historical, or political in content, very much devoted to matters of morale, motivation and the 'communist world outlook' on current affairs. The writer collected some four or five hundred examples of these works during his years of residence in Moscow and has drawn heavily upon them for this book. They range in weight and scope from the eight-volume *Soviet Military Encyclopaedia* down to a twenty-paged tract on *Bourgeois Culture in the Service of Reaction*.

These publications and the periodic military press represent the typical reading of a Soviet serviceman. Thick and serious journals such as *Military Herald, Communist of the Armed Forces, Supply and Logistics* and the *Military History Journal* are directed at the senior levels and those with great promotion ambitions.

Somewhat lighter, illustrated journals, *Soviet Warrior*, *Sergeant Major*, *The Banner Carrier* and others are directed to lower ranks and all read the Ministry of Defence's daily newspaper *Red Star*. There is little doubt that these journals are influential.

From time to time in the West one hears the suggestion that such publications are spurious, an elaborate ruse designed to create false impressions of Soviet strategic thought and the state of military training. In the writer's view this suggestion is without much substance. He has seen all these publications in the hands of run-of-the-mill officers and soldiers and knows they are regarded seriously. To claim that they constitute merely a gigantic disinformation scheme to dupe Western observers is to presuppose a double bluff of a magnitude beyond even the capabilities of the Soviet propaganda machine. Experience and intuition suggest that they may be taken at face value as genuine educational influences although it is acknowledged that certain obliquities in exposition need careful interpretation even by the experienced reader. *Mountain Warfare* illustrates this point. During the first three years following the invasion of Afghanistan nothing of any substance concerning the war was directly reported in the media. But an inordinate weight of articles published in the military press throughout this period was devoted to the subject of 'mountain warfare'. Readers tacitly understood that they referred to the conduct of the campaign, though explicit mention of the fact was never made, the argument being confined to theoretical precepts with reference to 'troop exercises'. Soviet servicemen are accustomed to these allegorical presentations. Security training convinces them of their necessity and they are accepted as natural.

Another set of books on various branches of general education and the inculcation of the 'communist world-outlook' in children was collected in the civilian book shops. These have been heavily consulted for the section on pre-service education. Appropriate Western books have been consulted where necessary, especially those written by *émigrés* or defectors.

The author was able to visit a considerable number of military barracks and training schools as well as a cross-sectional variety of educational establishments in most of the fifteen republics of the USSR. An invaluable insight into the relation between political enlightenment and education generally was gained from these visits and they provided much confirmation of inferences drawn from the literature.

A special debt of gratitude is owed to R. A. Gabriel for his pioneer sociological study of the Soviet Army, *The New Red Legions*, and to E. Wimbush and A. Alexiev for their impressive work, *The Ethnic Factor in the Soviet Armed Forces*, published by the Rand Corporation. Other sources consulted have been acknowledged in the notes.

THE PRE-SCHOOL PHASE

The education of a future soldier begins in childhood.
G. Bardaschuk, 'Commissioned as an Officer' – *Naval Digest*
(Moscow: Military Publishing House, 1972)

The Nursery School

Revolutionary enlightenment has its roots in the nursery. Traditional Russian child-rearing practices have persisted in the Soviet age and children spend most of the first year of life tightly swaddled parcel-like, in blankets. Tradition would also place them in the care of their maternal grandmother (*babushka*) leaving mothers free to toil in the fields alongside fathers. Initially, the Revolution changed little. Urban wives became workers equally with their rural sisters, following their husbands into professions, trades and public service on parity terms with the males except for their right to paid maternity leave after the confinement. With mothers thus occupied, the *babushka* became as important an educational factor in the cities as she had always been in the villages.

Pleasing though this might have been to the Soviet authorities insofar as it allowed vast resources of female labour to be harnessed to the Five-Year Plans, it nevertheless presented them with a formidable ideological problem. The *babushka* was the fount of religious knowledge and ritual and, by the nature of things, she implanted in her charges, at their most impressionable age, the idea of God and the wonder of his works. Total anathema to the new communist regime, it had to be accepted while economic factors took precedence. In spite of intense and continuous atheistic propaganda throughout the seventy years since the Revolution, God is still alive in the Soviet Union, terminally ill though perhaps he is, and he owes his survival thus far to the powerful influence of the *babushka*. He cannot however rely on her support for much longer.

For several reasons, one being the inadequacy of old-age pensions in a time of rising consumer expectations, the *babushka* is being forced out of the child-minding business by the need to work on past the pensionable age into those years when her daughter would normally require her services. An all-Union shortage of *babushkas* has arisen, no doubt a pleasant prospect for the state which has already largely replaced her with a truly vast number of nursery schools. These have been established in every hamlet and collective-farm village, most apartment blocks in cities and very often at factories and other places of work. Each morning mothers dump their offspring here, blanket parcels or toddlers up to the age of three, before they go to work. In the evening they collect them again, sometimes quite late, depending upon the length of journeying involved. Infants can spend up to ten hours a day at the nursery school. The routine is as might be imagined – playing and sleeping under the direction of qualified child nurses. The author visited such nursery schools in places as far apart as Archangel and Yakutsk. They are much of a muchness, adequately but not lavishly provided, with cots or beds for approximately fifty children, playrooms, a kitchen and bathrooms.

The nursery school curriculum as might be expected is mainly feeding, sponging and pacifying and it would be fatuous to suggest that any coherent political aims are pursued with such young children. Nevertheless it is here that a child is first introduced to the personage of Lenin. Impressive pictures of him hang on the walls, silver busts also abound wherever they can be placed, alongside those well-known Lenin associated sayings and slogans with their New Testament overtones. Lenin did not say, 'Lo, I am with you always', but probably the most common slogan in the Soviet Union today is, 'Lenin lived, is still living and will always live.' Nor did he say, 'suffer the little children to come unto me . . .' but he did say, 'Our only privileged class – the children.' Heeding the reverent tones of his nurses the child thus learns unconsciously himself to revere Lenin, uncritically in this early age. In years gone by Lenin's vicar on earth received a similar degree of adoration but nowadays the cult is purely monotheistic. As Hedrik Smith reports, 'Unlike the Stalinist era, no living leader is idolised; all affection is focused on Lenin'. Two- and three-year-olds, teachers are taught in their manuals, should be taught to recognise, love and respect Lenin's portrait . . . The innumerable songs about Lenin give him the aura of a combined George Washington, Santa Claus and Christ figure, the most perfect human who ever lived and in the words of one tune 'always the best friend of children'. Some songs imagine him coming back to life, playing hide-and-seek, picking strawberries, bouncing children on his knee and the children love him better than their own grandfather, telling him, 'We want to be like you in every way.'[5]

Beyond this establishing of Lenin in the child's mind, staking it out for the communist mythology rather than for the *babushka*'s discredited Orthodox Christian superstitions, the nursery school can contribute little more to what could be termed political education. Vladimirov[6] has pointed to another function of the nursery school – to accustom the child to the idea of 'collective' rather than 'individual' society.[7] No doubt this is true in that the child thrown into the collective deep-end at the age of one is less likely to develop strong individual characteristics than he would if allowed three or four years of his grandmother's undivided attention. On the other hand it is probably going too far to claim, as Vladimirov does that nursery school children quickly develop a 'political antennae', a very valuable faculty in Soviet society he says, since it gives an understanding of which questions it is permitted to ask and which it is not. While this may be true, it would be difficult to distinguish these 'political antennae' from the conditioned reactions of what in the Western world is called the socialisation process.

THE KINDERGARTEN

It is in the kindergarten (*dyetsky sad*) that Soviet education begins positively to show its ideological colours. The children are now between the ages of four and seven and well past the need for nursing. They have reached the reading stage and in addition to Lenin by osmosis they can begin to absorb definite elements of the communist ideology. The kindergarten premises are not noticeably superior to those of the nursery school, larger perhaps, to accommodate more children and usually with an outside playground, but essentially the same except that the staff are teachers rather than nurses and the book has replaced the cuddly toy as the medium of diversion. The kindergarten is, like the nursery school, very much a child-dumping centre enabling mothers to do a full day's work and consequently the child's day is long and the routine still includes sleeping periods.

First reading books used in kindergartens appear to fall into two broad categories, books about animals and toys, not dissimilar to children's books elsewhere in the world and, a quite different category, intensely patriotic books about soldiers and the children of soldiers, about Lenin and other Party heroes, and about child-heroes of the Civil War or the Great Patriotic War of 1941–45.

An example of this second category is a thin volume called, *Father's Old Army Tunic*. A mother intends to cut up her father's old tunic to make an overcoat for her son. In the process she tells the child the story of the tunic, of her father's great deeds during the war, of the heroism that the whole nation displayed in the victorious struggle against the fascist invaders. When the overcoat is finished the young boy dons it and immediately feels himself possessed of a new courage, confident that if such a testing time should come again he would be as steadfast and self-sacrificing as his grandfather was in defending the homeland.[8]

In another book of the genre a border guard and his dog successfully prevent some saboteurs from crossing into Soviet territory, the dog proving himself as zealous a communist as his master.[9] This recurrent theme of an embattled and besieged Soviet nation defending its long frontier from an army of spies and saboteurs, who sit waiting for any relaxation on the part of the border guards as their opportunity to penetrate, is played at all levels of Soviet education and no doubt contributes greatly to the distrust the citizen instinctively feels for foreigners.

Foreigners are given visual form and dimension in a popular story of the child-hero type called *Malchish Kibalchish and the Tale of the Military Secret*.[10] There is a war on in this book. The Red Army or the Soviet Army – and it is carefully not specified which – is fighting the 'Bourzhins', as the bourgeois capitalist enemies are usually known by children. It is timeless war, having had no beginning and no end is in sight. Successive generations of Soviet people go off in turn to fight the ever-pressing Bourzhins and in turn are killed defending their homeland. The Bourzhins are depicted as tall, hook-nosed people with pince-nez, wearing morning dress and top hats in the style of bankers of a bygone age, with sufficient traces of Stars and Stripes, Union Jack and Rising Sun incorporated in their haberdashery to indicate their true origins. The Bourzhins never win but neither do they lose, so the struggle continues. The time comes eventually for the boy Malchish himself to join the war. He is captured by the hateful Bourzhins, interrogated and tortured to make him reveal the whereabout of the Red or Soviet Army. Brave and true little boy that he is, Malchish resists all their attempts and in the end dies at the hands of his torturers and takes the great military secret with him to the grave. Not that this is a tragedy. On the contrary all praise and honour are then bestowed on Malchish and he is advanced as the model of youthful military virtue for emulation by all young Soviet people.

Times change and so do heroes. *Malchish*, to judge by the number of copies sold, is a popular book and he appears to have replaced an earlier juvenile hero, one Pavlik Morozov[11] who gained immortality at the time of collectivisation by reporting his own father to the police for keeping back grain that should have been declared to the authorities. Pavlik's martyrdom was made possible by his late father's farmer friends who simply murdered him. At least Malchish offends no Thomas Arnold standards.

By the time he is seven the child is reading Malchish fluently and is acquainted with the notion of the bourgeois enemy. He has also acquired equally vague notions of a benevolent 'Party', of the Great October Revolution, the Great Patriotic War and a firm idea that the communists are 'goodies'. It is time for him now to make the transition into school proper and begin the formal education programme which is known as the 'Eight-Year School'.

THE 'EIGHT-YEAR SCHOOL' PHASE

'School children and students! Study and acquire knowledge and the habit of work persistently! Love the Soviet Homeland ardently! Be active fighters for the cause of Lenin and for Communism!'

Pravda, May Day Slogan, 14 April 1982

1 September is a great landmark in the Soviet calendar. Schools reopen on this day and seven-year-olds from the kindergarten enter upon their formal education in the state school system. The children receive greeting cards from their parents and families on this very special occasion and set off for school in their new uniforms, suits and berets for the boys, blue blazers, skirts, white blouses and berets for the girls. In contrast to current Western trends, Soviet parents consider uniforms to be democratising.

Eight-year schools are divided for convenience into 'primary' and 'middle' classes. There is no segregation by intelligence or 'streaming' but a small number of schools do now exist for the especially gifted. The quality of school premises varies throughout the country, from ramshackle wooden huts in the more unfortunate villages to the recently-built, two- or three-storey masonry buildings found in cities or on the larger collective and state farm complexes. To the author they seemed to be reasonably well-equipped, the schools that he saw comparing closely with below-average, British equivalents. Teachers are dedicated, active communists mostly, although ideology is kept very much in the background during the early drilling in mathematics, science and language. This cannot quite be said of geography or history where tuition very closely reflects the 'world-communist outlook' aim, the central core of Soviet education. Monoszona[12] has described the process more than fully. She examines the content and the methods to be followed in all schools, youth organisations and in the family for ensuring the development of the Marxist–Leninist 'outlook'.

Monoszona's manual is for teachers and emphasises again the seamless robe character of Marxist–Leninist education, relating all of life's experience in one general scientific combination with a quotation from an address at the Twenty-Fifth Party Congress:

> The strength of our front lies in the awareness of our masses. The Party therefore concerns itself constantly with inculcating communist awareness, the will and the knowledge needed for the building of communism.

She introduces the concept of 'Soviet Man', explaining that he was created and tempered in the trying time of the revolutionary struggle for freedom, in the days of 'socialist construction' and in the frightful experience of the Great Fatherland War. This 'Soviet

Man' by his prodigious feats of labour and his unselfish concern for his class brothers in all parts of the world has proved his deep devotion to the ideals of communism and demonstrated his 'burning patriotism and internationalism'.

Soviet Man is driven by Marxism–Leninism, a unified scientific world outlook revealing the regulated development of the world's natural resources, of society and of man's understanding of his environment. Marxism–Leninism points the way of transition from a society based on the exploitation of man by man to one based on socialism and communism. It is characterised by its dialectic–materialist approach to the phenomena of nature and social behaviour and by a purposeful social activity founded upon a firm faith in the eventual victory of communism. This driving force is expressed in Soviet patriotism, in socialist internationalism, in the attitude to work and working people, in social humanism, in the daily pursuit of just socio-political ideals and, above all, in an uncompromising stand against bourgeois ideology and those remnants of it which still survive in Soviet society. The communist world-outlook ensures a correct orientation to the processes of socialist development, illuminating the perspectives of the future and facilitating the true interpretation of events, both internal and international.

Monoszona goes on to claim that the builder of communism will be equipped with an accurate understanding of the present epoch in terms of the class and Party approach to every facet of social life. Such an understanding helps to maintain that total opposition necessary in the struggle against reactionary bourgeois concepts and against all the contemporary revisionists and apologists for capitalism. She suggests furthermore that a mature Marxist–Leninist communist world-outlook will clearly expose the false nature of the bourgeois ideology, its mysticism and nationalism, its attempts to glorify capitalism as the only possible economic system for mankind, its repudiation of social equality and justification of aggressive wars.

There is an abundance of books available to expand Monoszona's typical advice to Soviet teachers but her distillation serves admirably to highlight Soviet political educational aims. These it seems are to inculcate[13] a love of the communist system supported by patriotism and internationalism, the latter apparently meaning friendship and cooperation with those countries ruled by governments of similar political persuasion.

Equally important is the need to generate an active animus towards the bourgeois defenders of non-communist systems. As a corollary to this strictly scientific approach to knowledge and life it seems necessary to preach also an active form of atheism.

If there is to be progress in science and technology, a prerequisite according to Monoszona is the communist education of the work force in scientific principles. The teaching of these among the masses will discredit religion and guarantee the spread of atheism in the USSR. She includes this encouragement of atheism as one of the primary tasks in the school curriculum.

The seven-year-old child on the 1 September will be unaware of these aims and the curriculum he will follow for at least the next eight years though the reading of kindergarten books such as *Malchish* will have made him receptive to the main thrust of the arguments now to be put before him. As his powers of comprehension increase so will these arguments expand in scope and detail. His notions about the Party and communism will be shaped to a more definite form and he will be given opportunities himself actually to take part in the work of the party.

'Eight-Year School'[14] allowing some regional differences, operates daily from 8.30 a.m. to 1 p.m. or 2 p.m. in the afternoon with rest and meal breaks. Teachers would therefore have their work cut out to teach fundamental subject-matter without having to teach communist ideology or atheism as well, nevertheless, at least one hour every week is allocated to 'social studies', the collective label for all social, political and morality studies. The amount of time devoted to them increases as the pupil progresses through the school.

Since 1977, the new Soviet Constitution is used, it would seem, as a convenient pick-up from the kindergarten. *A Word about a Great Matter*[15] is representative of the books on the Constitution currently in use in the first school year. The 'great matter' is indeed the Constitution itself and the book explains how fortunate Soviet infants are to be born under its all-protective shield. They are entitled to free medical care, free education, the guaranteed right to work, to housing and to financial succour in old age. This messsage is conveyed in the first place by pictures mostly, but more words will be added later. When the child is getting near to the end of the Eight-Year School he will have absorbed the coherent idea that:

The new Constitution of the USSR[16] is an embodiment of the collective wisdom of the entire Soviet people. It has confirmed once again that the ultimate aim of all the transformations that are being effected in the country is the provision of truly human conditions of existence to every person. It shows clearly that the concepts of freedom, human rights, democracy and social justice are filled with a real content only under socialism.

No other society that has ever existed on earth has done so much, or could do as much, for the people and for every working-man as socialism has. The greatest achievement of socialism is the affirmation of the principle of social equality. Every Soviet citizen enjoys a wide range of rights and freedoms enabling him to take an active part in social and political life, to choose a life path conforming to his interests and capabilities, to be useful to his country, to his people.

The Soviet citizen never experiences the humiliating feeling of fear of the morrow, of being left without work, shelter and medical assistance. The USSR Constitution protects his rights and interests, his dignity as a citizen and a human being. It firmly guarantees to him the achievements of developed socialism recorded in it and confidently leads him along the road of further progress.

Likewise will the pupil have learned that this wonderful Constitution must be defended against any aggression from outside. The Bourzhins will have been transformed into real life characters as the USA, its allies, NATO, or simply as the bourgeois western states. History is presented to him in Marxist class terms, the successive epochs superseding each other until 7 November 1917 ushered in the new and final epoch of socialism and communism. The Great October Revolution put an end to the possibility of exploitation of one class by another. But, he is told, the Revolution was immediately in danger from bourgeois elements and from foreign interventionists who were trying to strangle it at birth.

The first history book[17] puts an outline on the emotional foundation laid by the *Malchish* type of tales. Baruzgin clearly sets out the lines for all subsequent refinement of the historical factors of the 'communist world-outlook', in particular of the military element. His book is for seven- to nine-year-olds and announces to the young reader that it is a story about 'soldier heroes, his grandfather and his father'. In line with most popular versions of Soviet military history World War I is ignored altogether. In spite of the great Russian efforts and sacrifices made over four years, it was a bourgeois war fought for capitalist aims and except for its significance as the crisis which created the conditions for a successful revolution, it is inconvenient to recall.[18] So the first character on the scene is the 'Red Guard', the immortal prototype Soviet soldier from the actual time of the Revolution.

Baruzgin introduces his subject:

> This is the story of a hero, an extraordinary hero. It is about a man who fought in a thousand battles and emerged victorious from all of them. It is about a man who perished a hundred times and yet did not perish, a man who defended and still defends our country from its enemies.

And the Red Guard's triumph is told in a befitting heroic style, its opening scene is the storming of the Winter Palace on the night of 6–7 November 1917, a bitter all-night battle against tremendous odds.[19] By morning the Red Guard was allowed a few moments to warm himself at the bonfires outside Lenin's headquarters in the Smol'niy Institute before leaving to do battle with those still to be defeated enemies, the White Guards and the foreign interventionists.

He returns victorious at the end of the Civil War, no longer a Red Guard simply but a soldier of the Red Army with a red star in his cap to prove it. He sees all around him the destruction these wars have wrought. He experiences the consequent famine and hunger. Its enemies had tried to annihilate Soviet power but, thanks to the Red Army, they did not succeed. He reports to his son about the great battles at Pskov and Narva, about the fighting in the north and in the south, on the Volga, in the Urals, in the Far East and on the sands of Central Asia. Wherever the White Guards had appeared the Red Army had fought and beaten them.

The son becomes the soldier in his turn – as did Malchish – and serves first as a frontier guard, on watch for any attempt those interventionists might again make to violate his country. But soon he appears once more on the streets of his home town wearing two medals for bravery; one recognising his part in the action against the Japanese aggressors at Lake Hassan (1939) and the other, the battle on the Karelian Isthmus (1939) against the Finns.

'We defended our glorious city of Leningrad', he tells his friends. 'Good', they say. Baruzgin avoids any references to the causes of the Finnish Winter War but then so do most Soviet writers, and schoolchildren are not encouraged to pursue their enquiries in this direction.

Now we meet the soldier again in World War II, fighting in front of Brest and Moscow, at Stalingrad, Leningrad, Sebastopol, Kiev and the other hero-cities. As he fights he is upheld by his cry of, 'For the Fatherland'. It could have been that same soldier who fought at the Winter Palace and in the Civil War or Lake Hassan, but perhaps not. No matter; sons, grandsons, even mothers and grandfathers are united through the ages by the battle cry, 'For the Fatherland'. The Soviet soldier beat the fascists to a standstill in Berlin and, writes Baruzgin, the liberated German inhabitants cried, 'Glory to the Soviet soldier!' Not only did he liberate the Germans but he also liberated the Yugoslavians, the Poles, Romanians, Hungarians, Bulgars and Czechs in passing. Memorials were raised to him in all these countries so that people would never forget who saved the world from the fascists. Baruzgin is careful not to mention allies in this war, probably for fear of diluting the glory.[20]

The World War II episode closes with the great victory parade in Red Square when the standards of the infamous fascist regiments are piled up in an ignominious heap in front of Lenin's tomb, the Square echoing with the soldiers' unison cry of, 'Glory, glory, glory!'

But the end of that great war did not mean an end to the need for military vigilance. Study of the new Constitution soon familiarises the child with the concept of 'peaceful coexistence'. When he is old enough to read the actual Constitution for himself – and his mentors make sure that he does – Article 28[21] informs him that:

the foreign policy of the USSR is aimed at ensuring international conditions favourable for building communism in the USSR, safeguarding the state interests of the Soviet Union, consolidating the positions of World socialism, supporting the struggle of peoples for national liberation and social progress, disarmament and consistently implementing the principle of the peaceful coexistence of states with different social systems.

Considering the military emphasis in his education so far, he could be excused some puzzlement over peaceful coexistence and forgiven for asking why the glorious Soviet forces cannot put paid to the Bourzhins once and for all. In a non-nuclear world they probably would, but this cannot be told in a direct way. His teacher has to go back to Lenin and his 1917 'Decree on Peace' for a legitimate explanation and to prove that Soviet policy is always consistent. Lenin it certainly was who first enunciated the principle of peaceful co-existence but not much was heard of it between the wars. It was the nuclear-realistic Khrushchev who exhumed the principle and suggested that a final Armageddon-type shooting war between the two opposed systems might not now be inevitable. Khrushchev, of course, is no longer a quotable source but his teacher can speak of Lenin's boundless wisdom and point out that a communist society can be built only gradually by the creative efforts of the whole people and these must not be destroyed by war. It could not rise on ruins poisoned by radioactivity. This is why the Soviet Union is foremost in the struggle for peace in the world and Soviet forces are strong only in order to deter the capitalist aggressor. They are in fact peace forces rather than war forces. Unfortunately the 'cold war' unleashed by the West after the end of World War II dictates that these defensive 'peace' forces must remain large.

The first glimpses of Baruzgin's post-World War II Soviet soldier show him very much in this defensive role, but the glory is there just the same. Again he is walking down the street in his home town with yet another medal on his chest. Again the children ask about it, particularly as there is no war on. But the soldier explains that there is a war on, that an aircraft from a foreign country had been flying over the Soviet Union, so high that it could not be seen or heard from the ground. The pilot had been instructed to uncover Soviet military secrets, to photograph factories, military installations and airfields. But Soviet air defences are not penetrated with impunity; rockets were launched and brought the enemy intruder down. The successful missile crew were awarded medals for their performance in defence of the homeland.[22]

Other soldiers also serve courageously in clearing away vast stores of explosives left lying around dangerously by the Germans as they retreated from the Soviet Union. Disposers of these devilish stockpiles are awarded medals to mark the gratitude of the whole population.

But these specific successes only serve to remind the Soviet people that their armed forces are eternally vigilant, ready in their submarines, their rocket silos, their tanks and their aeroplanes, waiting to repulse the invader whenever he should be so foolish as to risk an attack against the Soviet Union.

Finally, Baruzgin reminds his readers that though they possess these mighty forces, the real Soviet strength lies in the qualities of the individual soldier and the population supporting him. Together they make the nation invincible.

An attempt has been made to encapsulate the general and military indoctrination of schoolchildren in primary and middle schools up to the age of about fifteen years. These themes are greatly reinforced by the several youth organisations whose function is considered in the next section. Problems of communist morality are very much the concern of the schools but for convenience these are also more appropriately reviewed in later pages. Speculation on the effectiveness of military–political education as a whole is left until the concluding sections.

SOVIET YOUTH ORGANISATIONS

Arming our young people with knowledge and experience of the preceding generations has always been one of the Party's principal concerns. It must strive always to exert its ideological influence on all sectors of youth, nurturing them in the revolutionary, military and labouring traditions of the Party and in the spirit of communist morality.[23]

The *Oktobrists* and *Pioneers*

School does not really finish at 1.30 p.m. each day. After the primary or middle school sessions end the pupils continue their education during the afternoons and evenings in the youth organisations, as *Oktobrists* for the 7–9-year-olds, as *Pioneers* from 9 to 14. Every town and village has its Pioneer Palaces, schools in effect, but where the activity is art and craft rather than the 'three Rs' and where classroom discipline is a little more relaxed. The staff are fully qualified teachers working under a director or headmaster as in the formal schools. The children are divided into groups by age and activity, working through the day according to a set programme. Music, wood and metal work, sewing and drama are just a few examples of the pursuits on offer. Equipment and materials appear to be provided on a very adequate scale and the children produce good work. Even more time is allocated to ideological, political and military studies than in the formal schools. The pride of every Pioneer Palace is its 'Lenin Room', an assembly hall devoted to the memory of the great man. Usually these Lenin Rooms are finished in highly polished timber and furnished to a much better standard than the rest of the building. A large bust or statue of Lenin is always prominent and there is much red bunting about the walls and windows. Showcases contain the Palace's trophies and there is often a 'Heroes' Corner' with a display of photographs of those former members who were killed in the Great Fatherland War. Lenin Rooms are treated with great reverence as chapels of religion, which indeed they are.

Oktobrists and *Pioneers* wear the same uniform. At its simplest this is a red cap and red neckerchief worn with ordinary school uniform but there is a parade order with blue shirts or blouses on which badges and insignia are worn boy-scout fashion.

The Soviet Youth organisations have indeed frequently been compared with the scout movement but this is misleading.[24] It has been speciously argued by some that the scouts have been every bit as ideological in their aims as their Soviet counterparts but it is impossible to sustain the comparison. Even in their most imperialist, chauvinistic early days the scout movement never possessed the minds of the nation's youth in the way that the Soviet organisations do. It is a simple matter of scale. All Soviet children become *Oktobrists* and *Pioneers*. Kassoff estimated the membership to be 35 million. There is no way of avoiding membership. Not that children seek to avoid membership since, outside the system, there would be only the most limited opportunities for any form of sport, hobby or pastime. And nowadays, the full advantages of the *Pioneer* Palace are open to the great majority of children. Kassoff observed that in 1960 only in the show palaces of Moscow and Leningrad were the facilities representative of those the authorities wished to establish universally, that the serious and chronic housing shortage was postponing the provision of *Pioneer* Palaces in most other regions. No longer is this so. The housing shortage has largely been redressed and local authorities everywhere are not able to allocate buildings for the *Pioneers* on such a lavish scale.

Not only are the Palaces provided but also sport facilities, children's theatres, and *Pioneer* summer camps in the countryside away from the cities or on prime sites near health resorts where children spend a month or perhaps more during the longer summer holiday. These camps ensure that the Young *Oktobrist* or *Pioneer* does not escape from the youth organisation's direction for many days or weeks of the year. In some cities the *Pioneers* run their own railways or tramway systems. The author travelled on such a train in Kharkov noting only one grown-up supervisor in the whole operation and he was not actually doing anything. 'They learn to work as a collective', he explained. 'They learn to trust each other and to co-ordinate their efforts, the important qualities they will need later in their adult lives.' Certainly the children were performing efficiently. They fulfilled their duties responsibly but with a marked degree of self-important bossiness. It was difficult to judge whether they were enjoying themselves but at least the trains were running on time and they were working together in true collective harmony.

Consolidation of the 'collective' approach to life seems to be the root of *Oktobrist* and *Pioneer* activities. Individualism is not stifled exactly but a high degree of conformity with peer group standards is encouraged at the expense of individuality. Kassoff sees four major purposes behind the youth organisations; to strengthen the control of the Communist Party over the people; to foster the kind of attitudes that will contribute to the economic and social modernisation of the country; to create the perfect citizen for tomorrow's society by influencing children in their formative years; and, through the formalisation of all youth institutions, to prevent dissident forces from emerging in any period of disruptive change. The writer's impression was that these aims were largely fulfilled. The *Pioneers* and *Oktobrists* are perhaps the least opaque window on Soviet youth. It is not easy to discover exactly what happens in the closed seminars of the universities, or in the lessons in school, or in discussions at KOMSOMOL meetings or the DOSAAF[25] club but it is not difficult at all to observe the *Pioneers* at their practical pursuits and to gauge their patent popularity.

There is no essential difference between an *Oktobrist* and a *Pioneer*, the younger group merely working at a less complex level. The ethos is the same, in fact the *Oktobrist* phase is little else than three years preparation for the solemn ceremony of induction into the *Pioneers*, the sign to the Soviet child that he has entered the ranks of the Communist Party. He takes the *Pioneer* Oath in the presence of his teachers, parents and relations pledging himself:

> Warmly to love my Soviet Homeland and to live, study and struggle as Lenin willed and the Communist Party teaches.[26]

He then promises to follow the 'Rules for *Pioneers*':[27]

> The *Pioneer* loves his homeland and the Communist Party of the Soviet Union. He prepares himself for membership of the KOMSOMOL.
>
> The *Pioneer* reveres the memory of those who have given their lives in the struggle for the freedom and the well-being of the Soviet homeland.
>
> The *Pioneer* is friendly with the children of all the countries of the world.
>
> The *Pioneer* studies diligently, is disciplined and courteous.
>
> The *Pioneer* loves to work and to conserve the national wealth.
>
> The *Pioneer* is a good comrade who is solicitous of younger children and who helps older people.
>
> The *Pioneer* grows up to be bold and does not fear difficulties.
>
> The *Pioneer* tells the truth and guards the honour of his detachment.
>
> The *Pioneer* strengthens himself and does physical exercises every day.
>
> The *Pioneer* is an example for all children.

The great oath-taking ceremony may take place in the Lenin Room at the *Pioneer* Palace but preferably a more prestigious building is selected, the city's 'House of Enlightenment' perhaps, or the local headquarters of the Party. As much dignity as possible is mustered. One of the large marble halls in Moscow's Museum of the Soviet Armed Forces is frequently used for these occasions.

The 'Rules' embrace most of the concerns of 'communist morality' in terms comprehensible to the *Pioneer* age group. With the implicit stress on love of homeland and a determination to defend it, on honour and a solicitude for the less fortunate, on a care for nature and a need for a healthy mind in a healthy body, this list is not very far removed from the codes of conduct advanced by certain Western youth organisations. The difference lies in the basis of the authority, in the fact that the Communist Party has set itself up as the arbiter of morality, as the Vatican of the New Soviet Man.

The *Pioneer* teachers do not seem to approach their task of inducing communist morality too academically. Like woodwork and cookery, morality is a practical thing for the under-fourteens, taught by the example of Lenin and the teachers. It is taken for granted that it is based on Marxist–Leninist principles – whatever that suggests to the young mind at this stage – that it is scientific and therefore, completing the syllogism, atheistic.

Atheism is taught positively, reinforcing the doctrine preached in the formal schools, but the philosophy is presented in visual, practical terms. To the Western eye the arguments are crude. Wall-posters, for example, show the dismal house of God, decrepit and demanding of money, contrasted with the *Pioneer* Palace offering all manner of self-development facilities and warm human comradeship. God is also depicted as living on a cloud, seriously incommoded by the large number of Soviet space-vehicles rushing past his ancient domain, disturbing his age-old peace. That the cosmonauts, themselves the product of Soviet education, have failed to discover any trace of God in the course of their space journeys, is adduced as proof to the *Pioneers* that he does not exist. And yet the children require an alternative. The *babushka* dies hard and leaves the awkward question, 'where do we come from?' It is not so easy to satisfy children with a scientific explanation based on frog spawn and DNA, they need a 'Creation' story – and one exists. A *Pioneer* Palace director told the author that the children learn that the initial cause which formed the cosmos is still unknown but that in due course it will be revealed by scientific research. In the meantime, and as far as the earth–planet is concerned, it is assumed that a life-force was engendered somehow during the cooling process and it is this, as yet only partially understood, life-force, which is responsible for the cyclic renewal of animal and vegetable matter. Nothing mystic in this explanation, but a few minutes later she opened the door on a drama group composed of ten-year-olds acting out the advent of the life-force on the barren surface of the earth's new crust.

Photosynthesis worked extremely rapidly with a lot of help from fairy-like creatures dressed in green who soon filled the empty scene with large primeval plants. At the same time these good creatures of the life-force had to contend with the bad fairies, the death-force bent on a policy of defoliation to return the planet to its barren state. The representatives of this death-force, symbolising evil and decay, were dressed very like Bourzhins. And, like Bourzhins, they were fated never to win.

If the Director was a little embarrassed by this incomplete Marxist–Leninist book of Genesis she recovered wonderfully when she came to speak of the part the *Pioneers* play in the nation's military training. Since 1967 two years of military instruction every week have been a compulsory feature of the timetable in formal schools. This has in practice meant little more than lectures from veterans or reservists, mainly about their own experience of military service in World War II or subsequently.

It is the *Pioneer* teachers who provide the practical side of the training. Every *Pioneer* Palace has at least one ex-service officer whose responsibility it is to school the children, male and female, in the basic crafts of the military profession – map-reading, reconnaissance, marksmanship, first-aid, etc. Field exercises are staged on an impressive scale in cooperation with other *Pioneer* Palaces, culminating in quite massive manoeuvres during the summer camp period. The whole year's training is a Union-wide 'military game' code-named *Zarnitsa* (Summer Lightning) and divided into various competitive sub-sections. Success in these 'socialist competitions' is eagerly sought and any child who wins an award is lionised in his own *Pioneer* Palace in the true Malchish Kibalchish tradition. *Zarnitsa* is a popular exercise, but how could it not be so? Playing soldiers on such a grand scale with such lavish equipment would be popular with children of any age or clime. *Zarnitsa* is hardly play though. *Tovarishch*, the official *Pioneer* handbook, is witness of the degree of military detail children are expected to absorb in their *Pioneer* years. It has a fat military section containing coloured drawings of Soviet Army equipment, tables of ranks and insignia of officers and soldiers and a very clear explanation of the basic roles and missions of the five Soviet military services. To a Western reader the blatant militarism of the handbook is astonishing and chillingly reminiscent of the Hitler Youth doctrine of the 1930s, but to the Soviet teacher it is quite in harmony with his education directive:

Every teacher must explain to students the policies of the Communist Party and the Soviet Government concerning the country's defence, the requirements for and importance of military service, and the need to develop the moral–political qualities required in future soldiers. Essentially, the work of every teacher and all educational activity is directed towards training pupils to fulfill their civil obligations, to labour selflessly on behalf of the homeland and to be able and ready to defend it with gun in hand.[28]

Slowly the *Pioneers* come to realise that they are the next generation upon whom the task of holding the gun to defend communist society and the Soviet Constitution will soon fall. Their teachers' aim is to continue the development of the 'Malchish' posterity identification, expressed typically in the *Pioneer* poem, 'They Who are on Duty Today':[29]

> On the frontiers of our land
> The sons of the Fatherland stand
> Peering eagerly into the darkness,
> They who are on duty today.
>
> The young ones meeting the dawn,
> Under a canopy of wings and rockets they
> Are protecting our Soviet airspace,
> They who are on duty today.
>
> In the hearts of our manly sons
> Is the valour of their forefathers
> And they glorify the red star symbol,
> They who are on duty today.
>
> Invincible these, our sons,
> Steeled with the armour of experience
> They are keeping the peace in all the world,
> They who are on duty today.

The KOMSOMOL

The child, now reaching adolescence, is thus prepared to enter into the KOMSOMOL organisation (Young Communist League) at the appropriate age. Here, under the direction of both professional instructors and older members, his civic and military education will be developed further. The average KOMSOMOL member's life span (14–28 years of age) covers the later period of formal school, his higher or technical education phase, his two years of military conscript service and still leaves him six or seven years of membership after he returns from the army before he reaches the upper age limit. Obviously therefore the activities of the KOMSOMOL are conducted on several levels. In the earlier pre-military service years the programme is an extension of *Pioneer* training with an annual all-Union military exercise of the *Zarnitsa* type, *Orlyonok* (Young Eagle), but on an even greater scale. It should perhaps be pointed out that both *Zarnitsa* and *Orlyonok* are frameworks for sporting pursuits as well as military, but the predominance of the latter cannot be doubted from the organisational structure of the very framework itself. The *Zarnitsa* basic unit is the 'battalion', led by a 'commander' with his own permanent staff of eight and with companies composed of *Pioneers*. In each company there is a *Pioneer* commanding officer, a *Pioneer Zampolit*, platoon commanders, signallers, riflemen, cooks and medical orderlies. There is also an editor for the battalion's combat journal.[30]

Sport in the true sense of the word is clearly incidental to the military aim of these 'exercise games'. The first *Orlyonok* exercise (1972) was commanded by one of the cosmonauts, Major General Beregovoi, who emphasised in this directive to games leaders that participants would be expected to pass the performance norms of the All-Union Physical Culture Complex of 'Ready for Labour and Defence Organisation of the USSR'.[31] Igor Ilinskiy expresses the attitude to sport in a nutshell:

Since 1945 when the Second World War ended there have been more than one hundred big and small wars waged on our planet. International imperialism has encircled the socialist world with military bases and neo-fascists rear their heads from time to time in one part of the world or another. And that is why the KOMSOMOL members must regard it as their sacred duty to strengthen the Soviet Armed Forces, to get military training, to be vigilant and to build up their physical strength by taking up sport.[32]

In passing it may be noted that hand-grenade throwing is a recognised sport in the Soviet Union.

Orlyonok does not involve the elderly, post-military service members of KOMSOMOL whose activities are not of direct concern in this context. According to the handbook it is:

> Intended for students – both boys and girls – in senior classes in formal schools, technical schools, and special secondary schools. It is also for working adolescents in the sixteen to eighteen year-old group. Competitions, marches, tactical exercises, games and meetings are all designed to prepare youth for military service and to contribute to the pre-military training programme. Both boys and girls study civil defence measures.[33]

Pesterev also recorded that seven million young people took part in *Orlyonok* in its first two years (1972 and 1973) and he explained how these 'military-sport games' help them to 'master the compulsory school programme of pre-military training'.[34]

Like the *Pioneers*, the KOMSOMOL is far from being a purely military training organisation. It is also very deeply engaged in teaching and exercising younger people in their civic responsibilities, guiding them through the philosophy of communist morality and preparing them in due course to take their place in the 'establishment', the Party–Government complex.

For many the KOMSOMOL is a training ground, a stepping stone to a career in the bureaucracy, either in the Party or in the Government. The KOMSOMOL structure and organisation mirrors that of the Party and experience of KOMSOMOL office is a prerequisite for membership of and preferment in the Party.[35] Kassoff argues that the encouragement of the KOMSOMOL was the Party's method of taking it over, stifling its historically democratic origins and making it totally subservient to the state, transforming it from a school for political leaders into a system for controlling the entire generation. The author's observations incline him to endorse this view although Ilinskiy, while admitting the 'class' orgins of the KOMSOMOL justifies this Party control:

Notions about 'youth leading the way' and slogans calling for total independence for the KOMSOMOL and for 'equality' with the Party, which the present-day revisionists and opportunists are still trying to propagate, are not only unsound but are also harmful, because they cloud the judgement of young people and distract them from the true revolutionary path.[36]

Wherever the truth may lie, KOMSOMOL members are manifestly active on the social scene, attending congresses, marching in parades, giving their spare time to voluntary projects and in general doing good. Enthusiasm is the key-word of the KOMSOMOL and while their heroic, self-sacrificial contributions to the heavy-industry building programmes of the 1920s and 1930s are no longer called for to the same extent, they nevertheless still do contribute a remarkable proportion of their time to domestically useful community projects. The very rules of the KOMSOMOL demand enthusiasm, insisting that the right to be a member must be lived up to in practical deeds, by active participation in the building of a communist society. At the same time the internal scene must not distract members attention from the wider world, from their 'communist world-outlook'.[37] Ilinskiy remarks that great and important as the domestic tasks and problems of the Soviet state are:

> KOMSOMOL members must not be concerned about them alone as long as imperialism exists and hundreds of millions of young people in various parts of the world are being exploited and oppressed by it. The problems of the working class youth fighting for their social and national liberation are of great concern to Soviet KOMSOMOL members. They are aware that the strength of the socialist community depends on how closely linked the youth organisations of the fraternal socialist countries are and on how well united the family of the peoples of the USSR will be. Therefore the KOMSOMOL members clearly understand the passages in the rules which point to the need for further strengthening the friendship of the peoples of the USSR and the fraternal ties of Soviet youth with the youth of the whole world . . . the KOMSOMOL has become a genuine school of internationalism and solidarity and has won great prestige and authority in the international youth movement.

So here once more are the 'communist world-outlook' and the championship of the world peace movement. The KOMSOMOL also concerns itself with communist morality and preaches communist humanism in counterpoint to its philosophy of atheism. KOMSOMOL literature stresses the need for kindness and compassion and discusses such concepts as good and evil, justice and injustice, honour and ignominy, honesty and dishonesty, etc. 'Marxist–Leninist ethics' has recently been introduced as a school curriculum subject in its own right and, although still an optional extra, it is expected that in future ethics will be taught with equal emphasis along with mathematics, biology and languages.[38] Bogat outlines current Soviet thinking on the basis of morality. He describes the present period in Soviet history as the 'ethic period', distinct from the earlier 'romantic–revolutionary' and the later 'heroic–military' and 'socio-economic' periods when the individual and his spiritual needs were subservient to the great collective need to establish the state. Now the individual soul of the 'New Soviet Man' is receiving attention, somewhat belatedly perhaps, and not in any close relation to the older religions but strictly according to Marxist–Leninist ethics. The starting point[39] seems to be an explanation of the deficiencies of the earlier periods:

It would be unfair to criticise Soviet society immediately following the Revolution for its lack of refinement or unimpressive exterior as do some speakers at public debates. Nevertheless, in the early days of its existence our country was guided by a desire to create many material things which would build a new socialist society. This desire was embodied in the literature of those years and even reflected in the titles of many books, such as *Cement* and *Hydrocentral*. The literary magazine *Our Achievements*, published by Maxim Gorky, concentrated less upon ethical achievements than on the building of industrial plants. Gorky wrote that, at a certain period of history, socialist society will inevitably become more introspective and will engage in deeper self-analysis.[40]

Evidently that time has come, and with an impressive casuistry the Stalin era with the horrors of the White Sea Canal project, the purges, the Gulags and collectivisation are all wiped away from the young Soviet conscience in one stroke. The spiritual, moral and cultural revolution has arrived, explaining not only the excesses and failures of the past but also the anomalies of the present. Why for instance have the Western nations been able to make their apparently immense material progress while the Soviet economy has only been able to crawl out of the slime? Bogat explained:

> The astounding achievements of the technological revolution in the West take paradoxical forms, often alienating people from reality. In Soviet socialist society, by contrast, they stimulate concentrated self-analysis. The achievements of scientific progress do not oppress the individual in the Soviet Union but, on the contrary, they stimulate the development of his inner world.[41]

The young person is not left alone to ponder the sour grapes content of this Marxist–Leninist philosophy. He is guided in his aims by many writers. Bogat writes typically:

> Besides objectives in space and time, such as finishing school, entering university, presenting and defending a doctoral dissertation and conquering the desert or outer space, etc., there are also other goals and other values, those pertaining to the inner world of man. What I am referring to is not the belief that man should abstain from the good things of life, for man has never refused anything that is good and useful. Man accepted Christianity but took the best that had been accumulated in pagan antiquity into that new spiritual state as well. Similarly, our communist morality has absorbed all the moral treasure accumulated through the ages. Man will reject neither cybernetic machines nor many other good things that do not think at all. The point is not that man should refuse what he needs and what he can put to good use, but that in all matters inner values should be most important.[42]

It smacks perhaps of Marcus Aurelius but it does neatly represent the sort of philosophy the young KOMSOMOL member discusses round the camp fire during *Orlyonok*. One wonders whether it entirely stifles the, 'Is there a supreme being?' type of discussion popular among Western youth.

Equipped thus, with a general education, an appreciation of

civic responsibilities, a carefully nurtured patriotism, an antagonism towards the non-communist world, and some notions of Marxist–Leninist ethics and communist morality, the young Soviet male at the age of eighteen to twenty-one presents himself to the recruiting officer or, more accurately, to the Office of the Military Commissariat in his home town or district.

The DOSAAF Organisation

Mention must be made of yet another youth organisation before attention is turned to the serviceman's political education within the ranks of the Soviet Armed Forces proper. This is DOSAAF, the Voluntary Society of Cooperation with the Army, Aviation and the Fleet. Formed in 1951 by the amalgamation of several earlier societies for cooperation with the military and military industries, DOSAAF[43] is described as 'a popular defence–patriotic organisation whose purpose is active cooperation for strengthening the military capability of the country and for preparing workers for the defence of their socialist homeland.[44] It is another mass organisation with a membership of '80 million workers and students over fourteen years of age'.[45] Although DOSAAF purports also to be a sporting organisation, its interests lie totally in the paramilitary sports, shooting, parachuting, flying, sailing, etc. There are DOSAAF centres in all Soviet cities, towns and even large villages DOSAAF units are established in all schools and schoolchildren on reaching fourteen years of age, teachers and technical staffs are expected to join.[46]

DOSAAF is responsible under the Law on Universal Military Obligation for the pre-call up training of specialists, signallers, drivers, radio mechanics, etc., ensuring thus that maximum military advantage will be gained from the two-year conscript period. Accurate details of the DOSAAF training system are difficult to come by but it is known that one in three of all conscripts and, probably, all officer candidates have received specialist training under DOSAAF auspices. *Ab initio* training of the Soviet Air Forces' pilots, for example, is carried out at DOSAAF airfields and DOSAAF staffs contain a large percentage of regular armed forces personnel. An enormous organisation, comprising more than 330 000 clubs or units, its importance can be gauged from the fact that its chief is a four-star officer, at present Admiral of the Fleet G. M. Yegorov, a member of the

Supreme Soviet and a Deputy Defence Minister having parity
with the heads of the five armed services and the head of the Civil
Defence Organisation.

DOSAAF is often considered to be the military training
executive serving the KOMSOMOL and *Pioneers*, the schools and
the factories, engaging exclusively in practical matters, drilling,
training and arranging exercises. Ideological matters, one would
have been forgiven for thinking, could be safely left to the others.
But this is not so. DOSAAF is just as heavily into ideology as are
the schools and youth organisations. Emphasis is slightly different
perhaps, with the 'steeling of the will' themes prominent and less
mention of ethics or communist morality but even so the content
of the journals of the DOSAAF press[47] tends to be more ideological
than technical, concentrating on morale rather than morality. If
the subordination and lateral liaisons of DOSAAF are somewhat
unclear to the outsider, its aims are stated without much
equivocation in its Programme of Action:[48]

Under the direction of the Communist Party the DOSAAF
Committees, in cooperation with the trades unions, the
KOMSOMOL and other social organisations have acquired a
rich experience in educating the masses in their patriotic and
international obligations, in preparing youth for service in the
Soviet Armed Forces and in developing the military-technical
aspects of sport. Drawing on this accrued experience DOSAAF
continues to intensify and expand its activities.

As always, the basic plan must maintain a concern for the
further refinement of ideological work among the membership
of DOSAAF. In essence this must be founded upon the
explanation of Soviet policies internal and external, the
teaching of Lenin's great testaments regarding the defence of
socialist society, the decisions of the Twenty-fifth Party
Congress, the Constitution of the USSR, the speeches of the
Party's General Secretary, L. I. Brezhnev, and other Party
documents.

Every member of DOSAAF is proud to belong to this
patriotic organisation and eager to express this pride with
practical actions aimed at increasing the defence capabilities of
the socialist homeland and the military might of its Armed
Forces. The DOSAAF Committees are charged with providing
assistance to all members in their efforts towards this end.

This general policy is reflected in all the books published in the 'DOSAAF Propagandist's Library' series, a seemingly never ending stream of tracts with titles such as, 'We are Raising Patriots', 'True to Lenin's Testaments', 'An Honourable Obligation',[49] etc. Nothing indicates more graphically that DOSAAF activity is not all flying and basketball than the content of the essays collected in a recent DOSAAF publication on the subject of training pre-call up youth.[50] It reminds a reader in Britain, where conscription was abolished a quarter of a century ago, of the disruptive nature of the call-up, the anticipation of which obsesses a young man in his last years of school or early years of trade training as the hurdle that must be surmounted before he can settle down to a career. As Kostikov points out, 'In front of all young men lies their period of military service, the time to fulfil their honourable constitutional obligation to defend the socialist homeland.'

The various essays are all ideological, even an essay on sport which suggests that Soviet youth has a constitutional obligation in this direction also; that socialist aesthetics are closely related to sport, since correctly controlled exercise is essential to the harmonious, proportional development of the body, that it produces grace of movement, skill and confident coordination of faculties. Physical culture parades are of great importance in that they produce feelings of physical well-being and of 'bodily beauty' which will help the young soldier to withstand the rigours of service, cold, heat, hunger, thirst, deprivation of sunlight, etc. Nowhere is it hinted that sport or any other physical activity might be indulged in by the young man for its own sake. It can be enjoyable only insofar as it helps 'steel his will' and prepare him to meet the enemy.

DOSAAF sends him off to the Armed Forces well-versed in military skills and with abundant reminders of the nature of his enemy. It is no longer simply the Bourzhins. His instructors will have conscientiously followed their directive[51] that:

All members of the DOSAAF are to be trained in a spirit of class-hatred for imperialism and schooled to a high state of vigilance. Notwithstanding the successes of our foreign policy we must not allow the level of our propaganda activity to fall. We must continue our efforts to expose the reactionary nature of imperialism and its aggressive designs.

POLITICAL EDUCATION IN MILITARY SERVICE

I, a citizen of the USSR, on entering the ranks of the Armed Forces take the oath and solemnly promise to be an honourable, brave, disciplined and vigilant soldier, to protect strictly our military and state secrets and to obey without question the orders and instructions of my commanders and superiors.

I swear to study my military profession conscientiously, to protect military and civilian property and to serve our people, our Soviet homeland, the Soviet Government until my last breath.

I shall be prepared always to defend my homeland – the USSR – and as a soldier of her Armed Forces to defend her skilfully with worthiness and honour, sparing neither my blood or my very life if necessary for the achievement of full victory over our enemies.

If I should break this my solemn oath, then let me suffer the severe penalties of Soviet law and the hatred and the complete contempt of all workers.[52]

The *Zampolit* and the Main Political Administration

Sooner or later after reaching his eighteenth birthday the average young male Soviet citizen will take this oath. Only 12 per cent[53] of his fellows will escape military service altogether, exempted for academic reasons, because of medical deficiencies or as a result of successful draft-dodging. Only the latter two categories give complete exemption, since academic exemption for graduate or post-graduate study is merely partial and the student will be required to serve his conscription period at a more convenient time before his twenty-seventh birthday or, if it is commuted, he will be obliged to undertake the training commitment of a reserve officer which, by and large, will give him a similar exposure to military–political affairs instruction.

If the bulk of the Soviet Armed Forces manpower is raised from eighteen year-old conscripts, then its officers are recruited even earlier – at seventeen. Every January, the military newspaper *Red Star* puts out a trawl for 50 000 suitable, educationally qualified officer candidates.[54] It catches them without difficulty as far as is known and they are each sent to a four-year course at one of 125 higher military training schools, specialised according to arm of service, e.g. artillery, tanks, air force, motorised-rifle, etc. On completion of the course, approximately at the age of twenty-one, the candidates are commissioned as second-lieutenants and assigned to units. The curricula at these officer schools is highly technical, one of the probable causes of the Soviet Armed Forces' officer-quality problems, e.g. low levels of initiative.

In either case, officer–candidate or conscripted soldier, the new recruit will soon meet the *Zampolit*, himself a graduate of a higher military school for specialist political officers, and his political education will begin, or more accurately, it will be continued along the lines already familiar from school, KOMSOMOL and DOSAAF days. It will certainly come as no shock, except perhaps insofar as the intensity of the instruction is concerned, with 30 per cent of his training time devoted to 'tempering' him ideologically and 'steeling his will' to fight and conquer his imperialist enemies.

The *Zampolit* function reaches back to 1918 when he was simply known as the 'Commissar for Political Affairs' or, a little later the *Politruk*.[55] Originally he was established to maintain political control over the older, specialist officers from the Tsar's army and to conduct political education among a mob of soldiers who as yet understood little of the Marxist–Leninist character of the cause they were serving. He was recruited (probably) from the corps of very active communist agitators who had done so much to subvert the Russian Army at the front in the 1916–17 period. The 'programme of public enlightenment' instituted by Lenin in the earliest days of the Bolshevik Revolution was spearheaded by the Red Army. Military trains staffed by young agitators, soldiers and civilians, were despatched to cover the whole railway network, whistle-stopping at every town and village, spreading the gospel of the October Revolution with speeches, cinema shows, brass-bands, poster cartoons and such like impedimenta of face-to-face propaganda. In the days before broadcast radio and television, except for the uncertain delivery of newspapers, this was the only practical way of reaching the people. And it was successful. The propaganda train was a powerful influence in rallying the Red cause, its effect on the outcome of the Civil War was probably decisive and, although the propaganda train has long since been at rest in the museum, the glory ascribed to the political commissar of those days has become the honoured tradition of the *Zampolit* of today.

The tradition is portrayed by the contemporary Soviet media as one of continuous development, forged in the heat of the Civil War, steadfast in World War II and still today, in the face of external aggressive forces, an essential element of the country's military shield. History has not, however, run quite so smoothly as this, the commissar, *politruk* or *Zampolit* having had a somewhat chequered career. At certain periods he has been very definitely 'in', at others just as positively 'out'. Nemzer traces his career up to 1950.[56] It has ebbed and flowed through the years as a reflection of fortunes in the protracted struggle between the Armed Forces and the Communist Party. Soviet writers use the euphemistic shorthand terms 'duality of control' and 'unity of control' when referring to this struggle. From the outset in 1918, Armed Forces commanders resented the interference of the political commissar who had the power to question and, if he so wished, to veto their orders; an unsatisfactory, debilitating arrangement which during the 1920s and 1930s they sought to change. The Political Directorate during all that time was a rather untidy civilian body viewed by the Armed Forces as a parasite on their backs, creating confusion and inefficiency. The Party on the other hand, treated the Armed Forces as though they were too much occupied with their strictly military duties at the expense of Party tasks. Possibly also they were seen as an elite body which could one day challenge the autonomy of the Party's rule. By 1937 the Armed Forces had succeeded in ridding themselves almost completely of 'duality of control' having satisfactorily demonstrated to the Party that they were a politically reliable instrument.

But the Stalin purges of that year proved the contrary, the officer corps was almost destroyed, certainly it was totally demoralised, and had to be replaced by emergency commissioning measures. Stalin was forced to re-impose 'duality of control' for a short period – until 1940 when he judged it prudent to return again to 'unity of control'. Then came the shattering defeats of 1941 and an immediate need to restore morale. The political officer was brought back in droves but this time it was declared policy to train him in military skills, thereby to increase his credibility with the real soldiers, something which had been lacking in the earlier years. He began also at this time to build his own legends. Nowadays, to the point of overkill, all sectors of the Soviet press run stories of the brave, World War II *Zampolit* who saved the day for his men and his country by his extraordinary heroism. It is often debated whether the Party's propaganda efforts did indeed hold the country together during World War II or was it just the Russian soul, as Tolstoy maintained it was in 1812? However, this is not a question that Soviet writers are allowed to examine. Accepted history now claims that it was the former and all praise for saving the nation goes to the Party and the wisdom of its leaders. This could scarcely have been otherwise in Brezhnev's time since Brezhnev himself was a humble *Zampolit* during the war. A Soviet joke current in his last years tells of Marshal Zhukov, then commander-in-chief, presenting his plan for a forthcoming offensive to Stalin. 'Admirable', approved Stalin, 'but have you cleared it yet with Colonel Brezhnev?' It has to be noted, however, that when Chernyenko succeeded the limelight has to be shared with the Border Guards. A military background has yet to be contrived for Gorbachev.

In 1955 it was Zhukov as Minister of Defence who made the last serious attack on the Main Political Administration and the *Zampolit*. Overnight he reduced the number of the latter by one-third and, according to rumour, intended to abolish dedicated political control altogether. The result is well-known – he was ousted by Khrushchev in 1957, for this and other cardinal sins, and the full establishment of the MPA was restored. Superficially at least the relationship between the Armed Forces and the Party seems stable at the present time and the claim that the 'Army and the People are One' could probably be sustained.

It would be rash however to predict that this stability will continue forever. Kolkowicz[57] warns us that the relationship is 'essentially conflict-prone and thus represents a perennial threat to the political stability of the Soviet state'. This might be so. The fact that already ten chiefs of the MPA have been removed either by assassination or execution indicates the heights of ferocity the conflict can reach. The current office-holder (appointed 1985) looks very secure at the moment, threatened only by death from natural causes and the MPA has evolved a *modus vivendi* at all levels both with teeth–arm colleagues and local Communist Party bodies. These days it is thus a confident *Zampolit* who greets the newly inducted officer-cadet or conscript. In any case and in spite of political vicissitudes it is probably a fact that the *Zampolit* cannot be done without. The author recalls a conversation with a *Zampolit* who described his duties as 'the physical welfare and spiritual care of the troops in his charge'. In other armies he would be called the padre! And like the padre he is an interpreter of scripts, a very necessary role in a country where the cryptic and obscure media statements make it almost impossible to understand government policy on particular issues without the help of an interpreter. A photograph in Nemzer's 1953 book shows a *Zampolit* briefing his troops on 'the lowering of prices'. Many briefings on similar mundane facets of policy still fall to his lot in 1986.

The *Zampolit*'s Terms of Reference and Tools

To the outside world the terms 'commissar' or '*Zampolit*' conjure up an image of an ogre, an instrument of terror, a handmaiden of the KGB. Above all else they symbolise the oppressive nature of the Soviet state. There is plenty of evidence that at least some members of the Soviet Armed Forces also view the *Zampolit* in this light.[58] The vast majority is however successfully encouraged to regard him differently – as the 'Father and Spirit of His Unit',[59] a kindly person, a wise and true communist ready to assist soldiers at all times of doubt and uncertainty. Malevolent or benevolent as may be, his duties are laid down with unambiguous simplicity in 'Instructions for *Zampolits*':[60]

1. To indoctrinate his unit with a spirit of high idealism, diligence and selfless devotion to the homeland.
2. To indoctrinate personnel with a hatred toward the nation's enemies.

To assist him in this dual task the MPA supplies him with a profusion of training materials in the form of books, journals, tracts, posters, films, etc. These he uses as a basis for lectures, seminars and other forms of discussion group. Obviously he must tailor his presentation to suit his audience, allowing for varying levels of age, rank, education and experience but the essence of his message will always follow the line of his directive, i.e. 'we are good and must be better. Our enemy is evil'. To the lowest levels of his flock he shows luridly drawn cartoons removing any uncertainty as to the identity of the nation's enemies, frighteningly grotesque military monsters adorned with USA emblems, predatory Wall Street financiers with dollar-signs for eyes, fat, leering directors of the US military–industrial complex, 'Cowboy' Reagan, etc. Nor are the jackals forgotten, Mrs Thatcher and John Bull and his Jackboot in Ulster, West German statesmen dressed as Hitler complete with swastikas; other members of NATO as occasion demands and, of course, President Pinochet of Chile. Spies of the CIA are also fancifully drawn as are the serpent-tongued announcers of Voice of America, the BBC and Deutsche Welle. These are the nation's enemies and the bizarre cartoon stereotypes no doubt give them palpable form in the eyes of at least the more simple-minded troops.

The journals range from *Communist of the Armed Forces*,[61] full of long tedious articles on communist duty and the nature of the enemy, down through various illustrated coloured journals full of shorter tedious articles on communist duty and the nature of the enemy. *Communist of the Armed Forces* sets the political line to be followed on any current issue. Lesser journals follow in their own style. A prominent feature of each issue is a section headed 'For Leaders of Political Study Groups'. Each month it treats a distinct theme and advises on the teaching of it. As an example, one typical theme was 'The Soviet Socialist State – the Main Instrument for the Building of Communism and Defending it from Imperialist Aggression'. The *Zampolit* is advised that:

> For teaching the given theme it is necessary to acquaint the people with the Leninist ideas of the socialist state as a new higher type of state, the main instrument for the building of socialism and communism, to describe the regular development of the state showing the leading role of the Communist Party in the Soviet system of government and to explain its role in increasing the defence capability of the state.
>
> It is suggested that the teaching of this theme requires eight hours, divided into two hours of lectures, two of individual study and four hours of seminar discussion.[62]

These themes from *Communist of the Armed Forces* are soon reflected in the other military journals, the exhortatory books published by the Military Publishing House giving a tedious homogeneity to language and message content over the whole range of publications at any particular period. Analysis of the author's collection of about 500 books suggests that they might have all been distilled into ten books or less without significant loss of content. The same point applies in large measure to the daily, *Red Star*, the Ministry of Defence's own newspaper and one of the *Zampolit*'s principal tools for the maintenance of the 'communist world-outlook in both officers and soldiers'. It is often said by the Russians themselves that a life subscription to *Red Star* is the best bargain in the world. It costs only two kopeks a copy, and one copy is all you need since the content repeats itself every day. There may be more than a grain of truth in this as far as its pure soporific properties are concerned but *Red Star* is vital reading for the Soviet soldier who wishes to follow the subtle periodic shifts of Soviet foreign policy.

The *Zampolit*'s Message

Conveniently for the reader, *Red Star* features at least one weekly article which, in compendium fashion, covers the whole gamut of current international relations issues as assessed or imagined by the Soviet Union. The article for 8 January 1982[63] has been selected as typical. A stock opening explains that the adventurist policy of the United States of America and her allies is creating a serious danger of war but, and the writer quotes from Mr Brezhnev's speech at Bonn in 1981, 'We need not yet say war is inevitable because, as a counter to this current explosion of imperialist aggression there exists the USSR and all the peace-loving peoples of the world'. Their threats, the article continues, appears at the present time to make war more imminent than ever before because of 'the further exacerbation of the deepening crisis of capitalism', with the third slump in ten years and inflation running at dangerously high levels. The number of 'deprived people' (i.e. unemployed) in the West has reached 28 million and there is an increasing social unrest manifesting itself with an ever-growing number of strikes as the class struggle intensifies. That is the internal position, and bad enough, but the West's external relations are in a worse state owing fundamentally to the imperialist scramble for raw materials and scarce resources. The once all-powerful United States is now under economic attack from Japan and Western Europe and, as a result of this pressure, has lost 20 per cent of the export trade she enjoyed in the 1970s. Migolatyev sees this crisis as having adversely affected US foreign policy and having led to 'the reckless reactionary adventurism

known as Reaganism' and that now the President is desperately
'playing the cards of the vital areas of American interest' for his
own selfish ends. At the same time the US ignores the growing
strength of socialism, 'the success of national-liberation
movements and the growth of freedom-loving, democratic forces
as a whole'. In its furious rush to put the brakes on 'the objective
process of the social renewal of the world', imperialist reaction is,
the article claims, determined on a policy of destroying the
balance of power and that hard-won degree of *détente* that the
Soviet Union has struggled over many years to achieve. To this
end all the various anti-Soviet and anti-communist forces and
agencies have been mobilised to foment an arms race. SALT II
was not ratified and severe economic measures have been taken
against the Soviet Union – the article omits an explanation of why
they were taken – and US officials and indeed the President
himself have uttered irresponsible threats implying the possibility
of a first-strike nuclear attack against the Soviet Union.

NATO is also brought well to the fore in Migolatyev's review,
ranged as it is against the new international concert of socialist
states. NATO only exists, he writes, because the imperialists fear
the solidarity, unity and friendship of the socialist states and for
this reason they seek to divide them, set them one against the
other, in the hope that they might weaken these fraternal
countries and their peoples. Hence their deep engagement in
subversive activities against individual socialist states, notably in
Poland, there they have striven hard to re-establish a bourgeois
capitalist order through the agency of the anti-socialist forces
there whom they have instructed in all forms of sabotage. All of
this, says Migolatyev, constitutes interference in the affairs of
other sovereign states and is therefore contrary to the Helsinki
Accords. President Reagan, in orchestrating this dangerous game
has lied and uttered threats to an unprecedented extent and his
crude meddling in Poland forced the Poles to adopt the temporary
expedient of military government while measures were taken to
create the conditions necessary for extricating their country from
the capitalist induced crisis, for upholding the law and restoring
social order.

Further afield, he continues, the imperialists are exerting their
utmost efforts to weaken the growing influence of the socialist
states now established in former colonial territories, falsely
accusing them of responsibility for international terrorism. They

are also cleverly manipulating the misguided government of China in their plot to set up a Washington–Tokyo–Pekin–EEC alliance, an anti-socialist and anti-democratic alliance. He notes that to support these main policy goals the US government is seeking yet more military bases around the world, particularly in the Middle East where it aims at nothing less than the occupation of those countries either by neo-colonialist penetration or by the use of military force to suppress national-liberation movements and steal their oil.

Migolatyev winds up his article by reminding his readers of the American determination to develop the neutron bomb, the Cruise missile and binary chemical weapons despite the strongest opposition from the working-class population in all the capitalist countries and ignoring the always-open Soviet offer to meet at the conference table to negotiate peace and an end to the arms race. He rounds off this *tour d'horizon* with the rhetorical question and answer, 'Where then is the so-called Soviet military threat? It does not exist.'

Typical of *Red Star*'s editorial policy though this article of Migolatyev is, it falls just short of being all-embracing because it lacks any reference to the human rights issue. The line on this as pursued in other articles of a similar kind is the denial of all the accusations the capitalist world makes against the Soviet Union alleging violations of the Helsinki Accords. It makes the counter-claim that those dissidents who, according to the capitalist media are merely seeking political freedom are, in reality, nothing more than catspaw agents of the West, criminals or lunatics and therefore the Soviet government for the protection of socialist society, is justified in putting them out of the way. In any case the West, in denying political freedom to negroes, Red Indians, Basques, Salvadoreans, Falkland Islanders, Ulstermen, French Canadians, railway workers and women, forfeits any moral right to criticise the Soviet Union for its firm policy towards those who violate its code of law and the constitution which guarantees personal rights of job security, education, housing, medical care and security in old age to an extent far exceeding the wildest hopes of the exploited workers who labour in the chains of capitalist society.

Any sign of thaw or climacteric in East–West relations does not alter the tenor of this media rhetoric. The January 1985, Gromyko–Schultz, Geneva agreement to resume arms talks must be considered such a climacteric yet it did not perceptibly deflect Colonel Mikhail Ponomarev from his customary anti-Western position expressed in his weekly political review article in *Red Star* (13 January 1985). In the light of undeniable fact he admitted that an agreement to re-open talks had been reached but he warned in Cassandra terms that this was only the beginning of what was sure to be a long haul. His military readers were informed with masterly innuendo that the Americans had been totally responsible for the 1983 break off of talks and only through Soviet patience and timely Soviet initiative had it been possible to bring the parties together again. Even so, based on the US record of intransigence and an anti-Soviet urge to rearm, the Colonel's prognosis is bleak. And he parades in support of his view a succession of 'star wars' references and cites a number of supposedly reactionary, ultra-conservative lobbies supporting military expansion. The Reagan–Gorbachev summit (1985) has produced no softening of media tone towards the West.

If these frequent articles are designed to inform Soviet military personnel of the antagonistic character of capitalist–imperialist foreign policy, reinforcing their earlier perceptions of the bourgeois enemy gained during their school days or KOMSOMOL period, then there are also other articles and books describing the nature of the beast opposing them, the capitalist–imperialist military forces and the actual bourgeois soldier himself.

The *Zampolit*'s official handbook[64] contains typical and quite graphic examples of the content of these publications. It is a pocket-book only, but it holds a wealth of information likely to be of immense use to the *Zampolit* in the preparation of lectures and equally of value to officer-candidates facing examinations in 'political affairs'. The foreword claims that:

It contains many facts and figures which reveal the aggressive policies of imperialism on the one hand and illustrate the growth of the communist working-class and the national-liberation movement on the other.

Chapter five of this *vademecum* is headed, 'The World Capitalist System' and it opens with a long quotation from Mr Brezhnev's Speech at the Twenty-fifth Party Congress in 1976. Two extracts merit inclusion here for comparison of line and consistency with the weekly definitive article from *Red Star* already quoted:

The capitalist world is infected with an economic crisis, the
depth and severity of which, as the bourgeois businessmen
themselves confess, can be compared only with the crisis of the
early 'thirties. It has spread simultaneously to all centres of
capitalist activity. . . . Capitalism has tried various expedients
– as the communists predicted – but has been unable to
eliminate the contradictions of capitalism. The sharp drop in
productivity and the rise in unemployment in the majority of
capitalist countries have been giving the capitalist economies a
series of severe shocks – the currency, energy and raw materials
crises, all exacerbated by the effects of inflation.

The speech goes on to describe the 'rat race' nature of the
inter-capitalist market system and observes that, far from creating
an affluent society for all, it is obviously failing altogether and a
bourgeois politico-ideological crisis is beginning to shake the
norms of accepted morality:

Corruption is becoming increasingly more apparent in the
highest reaches of capitalist governing circles. The slide in
moral values continues and crime flourishes. Communists do
not predict the 'automatic collapse of capitalism', it still
commands considerable reserves, but the events of recent years
indicate with a new emphasis that a capitalist society is a
society without a future.

Brezhnev, like his predecessor Khrushchev forebore to insist on
the inevitability of war with capitalism in its death throes but the
author of the handbook is not so inhibited, hinting that the final
clash between the two incompatible systems might not be delayed
much longer. Having delved into Lenin for less equivocal support
on the inevitability point he devotes a few pages to the profitable
business of the capitalist monopolies and the military–industrial
complexes of the anti-Soviet bloc countries, acquainting his
readers with the villainous constituents of the 'organisation',
listing such US firms as General Electric, United Aircraft, United
States Steel, General Motors, The British groupings of Imperial
Chemical Industries, British Leyland and (anachronistically)
Hawker-Siddeley. Listed also are the astronomic profits earned
by these corporations, accurate figures in all probability but
carefully selected from the fat years. These firms according to the

handbook, have worked together to create strong international conglomerates with a view to making even greater profits but there are dangerous strains in the system, fierce competition from the British for instance, who struggle for a survival share of the business. The West German arms manufacturers, so the *Zampolit* is instructed, are a greater challenge to American domination since they strive not only to achieve independence from America but also to wrest the lion's share of the world arms market from her.

The handbook concludes that militarisation has become the mainstay of the capitalist economy, greatly detrimental to the interests of working-class welfare and posing an imminent threat of catastrophic nuclear war.[65] The executive arms of these military–industrial complexes are the military blocs, principally NATO. The Soviet propagandist[66] has little difficulty in presenting NATO in monstrous terms but explanation of the motivation of the individual soldier serving in its massive armies is not quite so simple. The hordes of men cannot all be millionaire shareholders in the bourgeois military–industrial complex, some at least must be sons of the exploited working class. Conscription of course accounts for the bulk of the West European continental armies, the press-ganging of youths into service against their will, but there are many volunteers also, indeed the US, Canadian and British Armies are nowadays all-volunteers. It is unreasonable to imagine that there are sufficient traitors to their own working class who would join the capitalist armies for purely mercenary reasons. There must be other, sinister forms of coercion to produce the required numbers. The handbook suggests that there are several. It sees chronic, mass unemployment as the most effective recruiting sergeant, but there are others such as the denial of higher education to the majority of youth coupled with the dominance of a reactionary, military ideology in the primary schools. All these influences combine to ensure that the ranks of the bourgeois armies are always well filled.

Training in the NATO framework is aggressive. In addition to their anti-Soviet role, troops are trained to suppress workers' demonstrations and risings of national-liberation movements. The recruit is transformed by his bourgeois upper-class officers into a cruel, merciless soldier, ready to carry out any kind of 'bandit task'. The writer of the handbook quotes Western journalists when he notes that 'cold professionalism' is the hallmark of the imperialist armies. Marshal Grechko was more descriptive when he wrote about American soldiers:

> Unauthorised, barbaric methods of war-making are . . . characteristic of the US Army. We know for instance of the unseemly role performed by their 'Special Forces', the so-called 'Green Beret' detachments. The Pentagon attaches particularly great significance to the organisation of such detachments. Three basic requirements are placed on all candidates for such detachments . . . to have strong fists, a minimum of intellect and a faultless reputation from the viewpoint of the militarists. Sadism and cruelty are cultivated in the future saboteurs. The idea that they belong to a special elite of society, supermen, for whom no moral or other barriers exist is persistently instilled in them. The mission of these cut-throats also includes appropriate conditioning of other US troops to a similar level of expertise in inhuman actions.[67]

General Bruz informs Soviet anti-aircraft and anti-missile defence forces of the nature of their specific enemy, the United States Air Force, in a little more detail. He alleges that a special organisation exists for the purpose of 'brainwashing'[68] USAF personnel under the direction of the USAF Directorate of Public Affairs.[69] The organisation employs various methods of ideological influence and periodically issues instructions to its staffs in the field in the form of publications with titles, revealing its policy goal, such as *Democracy Versus Communism*, *Know Your Communist Enemy*, etc.[70] With his tongue clearly outside his cheek Bruz informs his readers that all USAF units have public affairs officers responsible for the 'brainwashing' programme who work in close association with ultra-right wing organisations, the 'John Birch Society', the 'Minutemen' etc. These bodies conduct militaristic, anti-communist propaganda on Air Force stations with the full consent of commanding officers, establishing 'schools of anti-communism' and arranging 'survival conferences', 'freedom forums' and 'hate seminars'.

Bruz's kettle calls pan black in an impressively big way when he mentions the US Corps of Chaplains and their rôle in the 'brainwashing' process. Religion was and still is, he writes, a faithful instrument for the ideological and psychological manipulation of servicemen. He claims that chaplains act, not only as reactionary propagandists but also as 'spies and spiritual overseers, specialists in detecting political non-conformity and unreliability'. But the main burden of the chaplain's sermon is anti-communist in sentiment, aimed at fostering a hatred of the USSR and its allies in the hearts of US servicemen.

Air Force chaplains in Bruz's interpretation:

> . . . instil in the pilot's conscience an obscurantist attitude concerning 'the inevitability of wars' and enkindle in them a spirit of bellicosity, self-confidence and aggressiveness. The large majority of aircrew officers are believers. They conscientiously observe the directives of their chaplains whom they look upon as their 'spiritual mentors' and as 'God's apostles' in the armed forces.

Chaplains are only one branch of the highly ramified 'brainwashing' machine which, with powerful technical resources and 'methods of social deception' combined with bribery and repressive measures succeeds, according to Bruz, in dominating the minds of all USAF personnel, ensuring that they remain trustworthy defenders of the capitalist order ready for the sake of their barbaric goals to kill people and destroy all that mankind has created:

> History bears this out. Hiroshima and Nagasaki are dramatic illustrations and, likewise, the dirty war in Vietnam, where the American aggressors sprayed chemicals to destroy crops and poison both the human and animal population. They also used napalm and fragmentation weapons specially designed to kill people.[71]

Bruz reserves his best invective for the crews of Strategic Air Command's bombers, 'the carriers of death' who, 'indoctrinated with misanthropic and chauvinistic views are ready on the word of command to drop bombs on the peaceful cities of the Soviet Union and other socialist countries'. In his conclusion he stresses the importance for Soviet commanders and political workers to bear in mind these facts about USAF personnel when planning the training and education of their defence personnel in order to:

> . . . instil in the defenders of our homeland's aerial borders a

heightened vigilance, a hatred for the imperialist aggressors and a willingness tirelessly to increase the combat readiness of units and sub-units.

Colonel Ivanov, writing in *Red Star*, draws a similar picture of the Federal German Republic's Armed Forces showing an ideological 'brainwashing' apparatus which, with 'a spurious objectivity', seeks to nurture young soldiers in the strongest spirit of anti-communism and anti-Sovietism. He sketches the structure of the apparatus based on political-affairs officers directing *Innerführung* training in close liaison with regular battalion officers.[72] *Innerführung*, he judges to be nothing more than simple instruction in anti-Sovietism on the lines recommended by the *Bundeswehr* High Command, i.e. slanders against socialism in proof of its aggressive, threatening nature. Peace is a theme also, but taught in accordance with the 'peace negotiated from a position of strength' policy of the US Administration. The real struggle for peace is presented as a danger to Western democracy.[73] At the same time a war psychosis is being developed by political officers of the *Bundeswehr* who encourage their troops as part of *Innerführung* training to read books such as, 'The Red Flag Over Bonn?', 'The Fundamental Importance of Germany in the Third World War', 'If the Russians Attack', etc.

The Federal German military chaplain is, in Ivanov's view, as potent a 'brainwashing' agent as his United States counterpart. Figures he quotes without reference to source put the ratios for active believers in the *Bundeswehr* as 80 per cent of private soldiers, 40 per cent of NCO's and 65 per cent of officers. With captive congregations of this size, the chaplain is of great assistance to the *Innerführung* directorate when he preaches sermons justifying the arms race and urging personnel to a crusade against the communist enemy.

A more sinister feature in the *Bundeswehr* than the padre is the renaissance of fascism. In the growing interest shown by young German soldiers in the heroic and impressive feats of arms performed by their Nazi predecessors, in their nostalgia for Nazi war relics and in their connections with neo-fascist organisations, Ivanov sees a great danger of resurgent Hitlerism. In the present age, however, this new Hitlerism would operate against the Soviet Union within the framework of the NATO Alliance. His parting message for the Soviet military reader encapsulates his warning that:

> With the assistance of a refined programme of ideological brainwashing, the soldier of the *Bundeswehr* is persuaded of the necessity to prepare for the possibility of war on behalf of imperialist interests. Analysis of the direction, content and scale of the *Innerführung* brainwashing organisation leads to the conclusion that the majority of *Bundeswehr* personnel support the pro-NATO policy of Federal German ruling circles. In the barracks of Western Germany a political climate, saturated with anti-communist and militaristic spirit, has been created.

There is little need of explicit calls for hatred in articles about Germany – hate for Germans is stamped on every Soviet mind. Fear is stamped there as well, just as indelibly, and the military propagandist has only to play upon the chord of fear if he wishes to fan the smouldering fires of anti-German hatred into bright flames. Hatred of Federal Germans, of course, because East Germans are excused, protected for many years now by the myth that they were all prisoners in Hitler's concentration camps.

Hatred for the British is different, no less intense, but of an intellectual or ideological quality in contrast to that felt for the Germans, which is simply an animal hatred born in World War II. First and foremost the British are never forgiven for the leading role they played in the Intervention as the original anti-Bolsheviks, arch-enemies who tried to suppress the new Soviet Union in its earliest days, who, by supporting the renegade White Guards, caused the Civil War to be so bloody and long. Polyakov leaves us in no doubt about how it was:

> The actual reason for the intervention is clear: it was prompted by class motives and expressed the striving of the leaders of the bourgeois states to crush the world's first workers' and peasants' state. Winston Churchill admitted on more than one occasion that his aim was to 'strangle it at birth'.[74]

Furthermore, and before Winston Churchill, it is the British who always turn up as the enemy of the old Russia in any Soviet version of history, the British who in the nineteenth century would have invaded Central Asia from India and marched on to Moscow had it not been for the Tsar's conscript armies standing in between. For this historical threat and for the old British Empire as a whole, the British have come to be regarded as the archetypal colonialists; Leopold II of Belgium is not even in the competition. Cartoons abound in both military and civil newspapers suggesting that the hook-nosed, pith-helmeted British colonialist in ridiculous shorts is still at work, horsewhip in hand, exploiting natives and stealing their gold. Notwithstanding the collapse of the Empire under pressure from national-liberation movements the British have not, it, would, seem, lost their dreams of global expansion but they pursue their aims now with greater guile than of old. The City of London and its neo-colonialist financial system backed by the military power of her NATO allies is Britain's contemporary weapon-system in her colonialist strategy. But Britain's actions are only possible for as long as she is content to remain the obedient servant of her puppet-master, the United States. It would not be otherwise in her state of post-imperial weakness. Soviet information media in unison gleefully 'proved' this Anglo-US neo-colonialist connection throughout the course of the 1982 Falkland Islands War:

> The true imperialist essence of the USA as a power which actively backs up the neo-colonialist aspirations of Great Britain has been exposed with amazing speed in a matter of weeks ... what has happened today in Argentina which has become the subject of the neo-colonialist action of Britain, supported by the USA and its NATO allies, could tomorrow become the fate of any country of Latin America.[75]

The paradox of the British soldier, the volunteer mercenary tool of capitalism, fighting the conscript army of the Argentinian right-wing military junta, poses a still unresolved doctrinal dilemma for the *Zampolit*, accustomed as he has become in recent years to presenting him in routine fashion as the scourge of the national-liberation movement in Ulster. Some idea of what the Soviet soldier learns about his British opposite number can be gleaned from 'What They Teach Tommy', an article supposedly about education in the British Army.[76] 'Tommy', it alleges, is constantly deluged with anti-communist propaganda to ensure that he will go off willingly to maintain the terrible tyranny his government has imposed on the freedom-loving people of Northern Ireland, prepared mercilessly and cold-bloodedly to murder his own compatriots there. The most evil media employed by the sinister Royal Army Education Corps in influencing 'Tommy' are cited as the *Daily Express*, *Sun* and, quaintly perhaps, *The Army Quarterly*.

The military forces of the United States, West Germany and Britain are the main objects of vilification in the Soviet military press and in the teaching of the *Zampolit* but other states are by no means immune. It depends upon who is doing politically what to whom at any given moment. The other NATO members, Japan and Communist China receive their full share of the barrage in season. Even the Swedes and the Swiss, who are not seen as neutral in Soviet eyes, are regular targets for sniping.

It is difficult in restricted space to present more than a sample of the main message the *Zampolit* conveys to his officers and soldiers with his seminars or his slogans and quite impossible to give any real impression of the enormous weight and constancy of his outpourings. The aim of it all is almost certainly to convince them of the undoubted existence of a real external enemy, probing, challenging and threatening at every point on the periphery of homeland. If young men can be brought to accept this either from conviction or from fear then it is reasonable to suppose that they will listen the more attentively to the other side of the *Zampolit*'s message, 'the steeling of the will', the need to prepare themselves spiritually and psychologically to meet these terrible foes.

The 'Steeling of the Will'

Mikhail Kalinin was closely associated with ideological work among the KOMSOMOL in the immediate years following the Revolution. He was already President of the Praesidium of the Supreme Soviet when in 1940, nine months before the German invasion, he addressed the Lenin Military–Political Academy. Among the usual Soviet banalities in his speech was the advice to his audience that:

. . . the first task that stands before you as political workers, is to develop in the men of the Red Army and Red Fleet the ideas of communism. Developing the ideas of communism means . . . to make comprehensible, close and dear to them everything that is being done in the Soviet state . . . The political worker has a tremendous quantity of facts from our really colourful life with which to strengthen in young hearts a patriotic pride for their entire subsequent life.

Comrades, to inculcate the ideas of Communism means to educate youth so that it loves the Soviet homeland with all its youthful fervour, loves it not only consciously but with all the five senses of man. . . . Quite often one hears from our commanders and warriors such declarations as, 'We are ready to die for the Soviet state, for our great homeland'. I regard this slogan as deeply patriotic. But I would make it more precise, more truthful, deeper. Of course, to die – this is a great act, an heroic act. But the question is – how to die? One must not die passively, without the most desperate struggle . . .

In educating the Red Army and Red Fleet in the spirit of communism you must not rush about seeking to turn all soldiers and sailors into formal Marxists or Communists. Try to develop in each man the consciousness that cowardice at his post, flight and treason are shameful things and that death is a thousand times better in any case.[77]

A Westerner asks why 'steeling the will' is considered necessary at all in the Soviet Armed Forces. Given those herculean efforts made in the whole range of Soviet schools and youth organisations from the nursery school upwards 'to educate youth so that it loves the Soviet homeland with all its youthful fervour' and to breed standards of communist morality proof against all such temptations as cowardice, flight and treason, why is there any need for the *Zampolit* to cover the ground all over again? The answer possibly lies in emphasis. When the young man gets into the Armed Forces he is no longer playing soldiers as he did in his Pioneer days. It is no longer *Zarnitsa* with its simple concern for socialist competition and high scores for shooting; no longer DOSAAF with the ultimate goal of a diploma to drive a truck. It is the army, the real thing. He is now taking his turn in defending the homeland 'with his very life if necessary'. The homeland is foreclosing on all those Pioneer and KOMSOMOL pledges of service and those high-minded communist ideals now take on a practical urgency. He might actually be called upon to spill his own blood, a point brought forcibly home to him in those gruelling weeks of weapon-training and live-firing exercises when his superiors strive to steel his body as well as his will. War is imminent, as his political studies prove, and he must be ready physically and psychologically to endure the unimaginable horrors of the modern battlefield and stand victorious at the end of the day. To make him thus ready, to create in him the required invincible morale is the *Zampolit*'s duty and, as with political studies, the Main Political Administration publishes a multitude of books and pamphlets to assist him.

The conscript is introduced first to the traditions of the Soviet forces. Novikov is currently the most popular text book in this area.[78] Essentially it is a continuation of the Pioneer book *A Soldier Walked Down the Street*, but this time, whilst it retains the pattern of generation to generation continuity, it is accurately historical in its stories of Soviet war heroes. But correct though its facts might be, the presentation is eulogistic, the pages liberally strewn with sombre poetry of remembrance. Contemplating the memorial statue to the defenders of Nyevskaya Dubrovka who were all decorated for 'unparalled heroism', a poet writes:

> Men of Nyevskaya Dubrovka,
> How you fought, how you bravely stood,
> I can see the long days and nights
> Mingled there on your stone brows.
> Under the museum roof, through your
> Party membership cards and your rifles
> I see you and I hear you,
> Men of Nyevskaya Dubrovka.

Visits to memorials and museums are a recognised and important feature of the recruit's training. Usually on a Sunday – there is no real day of rest either for the conscript soldier or for the officer-cadet – parties are taken by the *Zampolit* or members of his staff to pay homage to the local heroes. This author, when observing these parties always detected a quiet reverence in the young men as they examined the exhibits and listened to the *Zampolit*'s explanations of their significance. In many ways the outings are a close equivalent of the church-parades of bygone days in the West. The church-like atmosphere of these places of worship is perhaps conveyed by a notice-board in the Central Museum of the Soviet Army in Moscow:

Esteemed Comrades!

Displayed here are weapons and military equipment used in the battles for the freedom and independence of our homeland. Treat these sacred relics with great care and respect.

The *Zampolit*, with true atheistic consistency, tells us that memorials are for the living, not the dead, in order that the sacrifices of former generations will not be forgotten. The modern generation saw nothing of the Revolution or the wars and has no memory of the terrible conditions suffered by their predecessors. It is important therefore that they should be schooled in the traditions of those times. As Major General Smorigo[79] expresses it:

> This is necessary for a correct understanding of the heroic history of the Communist Party, of the Soviet state and of our Armed Forces. It is necessary also for the cultivation of a sense of socialist patriotism and proletarian internationalism and a class approach to the facts of life. In the teaching of these things, commanders, political organs, the Party and KOMSOMOL organisations in the Armed Forces are giving greater attention in their propaganda activities to the labour traditions of our Party and to the military traditions of the Soviet Armed Forces.

Another credible reason for the great concern in the Armed Forces for 'steeling the will' lies in a hint dropped by General Yepishev, former head of the MPA, that perhaps the schools and pre-service youth organisations are not as successful as they claim, notwithstanding the creditable zeal of their evangelism. 'We come across instances', said the General, 'of young men coming into the Army displaying elements of political naivete, of pacifism and indifference to the threat of war from our class enemies.'[80] He suspects that these attitudes have arisen because in some cities and towns the various authorities responsible for youth training have concentrated too heavily on the teaching of primary military skills at the expense of ideology. While he recognises the importance of rifle-shooting and grenade throwing, Epishev stresses that they are not everything. He suspects that teachers tend to muffle their explanations of the true class nature of patriotism. He points out that it is not simply a matter of a fondness for one's native land but a much wider and more significant concept. It must be Soviet patriotism that is taught – defined as a love for the socialist state, the Soviet Government and the Soviet ways of life. Yepishev insists that the inculcation of this love is the main purpose of the military–patriotic teaching effort.

It is perhaps not surprising that there should be some signs of pacifism among Soviet youth in view of their government's championship of world peace, *détente* and disarmament. The posession of large military forces and the frequent proclamation of a readiness to use them must to some seem inconsistent with a policy of peace. How could the Soviet Union ever come to embark upon war as a matter of policy? To the conscript, the *Zampolit*'s answer is simple. He brings out more cartoons of the ravenous capitalist enemy, explains the Soviet military policy is and always has been defensive, and points again to Winston Churchill's interventionists and Hitler's fascist hordes to prove it. He is not above pointing also to Napoleon although his defeat was not strictly in accordance with Yepishev's doctrine of Soviet patriotism.

To officer and officer-cadet audiences his answer is the same but presented in more convoluted form on the basis of the Marxist–Leninist classification of wars, just and unjust.[81] In summary, just wars are arbitrarily classified as:

1. War in the defence of socialist countries against imperialist aggressors.
2. Civil wars of the proletariat against the bourgeoisie.
3. National-liberation wars against colonialists.
4. Wars to liberate the people of bourgeois countries who have become victims of imperialist aggressors.

Materials available to the *Zampolit* justify the Soviet intervention of Afghanistan under '1' and the Provisional IRA campaign in Ulster under '4'.

Unjust wars are defined with more colour but less precision as the predatory and reactionary wars reflecting the policy of the imperialist bourgeoisie. By means of military violence the imperialists strive to enslave other countries, to establish neo-colonialism, to suppress the national-liberation struggles, to destroy the proletarian revolutionary movement, to weaken the socialist camp and strengthen the capitalist system led by the monopolists of the United States whose aim is to attain world supremacy by military means. One way or another, the *Zampolit* has to show that in spite of their desire for peace the Soviet Armed Forces are at any time likely to find themselves engaged in a war to preserve it. It has happened so before:

> Comrades. Do not for one moment forget . . . that peace is a priceless achievement of our people. The self-sacrificing heroism of many generations has won for us the right to call ourselves the soldiers of peace.

Soldiers of peace perhaps they may call themselves but they are not squeamish about the possibility of nuclear war. Their realistic training for the nuclear battlefield and the lurid illustrations in their civil defence instruction pamphlets are testimony of this. They have never shrunk from thinking the unthinkable and are under no illusions as to the likely nature and extent of a future war. Hence their obsessional concern for high morale. All Soviet military writers echo Marshal Grechko on this point, stressing that morale is 'the main thing', in a nuclear world war far more important than ever before. A high morale among the civil population must be maintained if the nation is to withstand the unimaginable horrors of such a war but victory will only come as a result of successful military operations. The morale of the armed forces on the actual battlefield is therefore crucial and the *Zampolit*'s task of 'steeling the will' is paramount. Colonel Skirdo in his book on military leadership and the relationship between the armed forces and the population in war foresees that:

> . . . a world nuclear missile war will be waged by armies many millions strong, and victory will depend to a considerable degree on troop morale. Only those whose morale is high will be able to endure all the trials and tribulations of modern combat with modern weapons. Victory will go to the army whose officers and soldiers, in their great numbers, believe strongly in their principles and in the righteousness of their cause, displaying valour, fortitude and the will to win.[82]

Skirdo's nuclear world war is a real possibility and the national will must be forged to win it but, meanwhile, there are smaller, capitalist-ignited wars in progress already, and that in

Afghanistan involves the Soviet Union to an appreciable degree. The US imperialists and the Peking hegemony-seekers with the consent of Egypt and Pakistan, hatched a plot to unseat the still weak Democratic People's republic of Afghanistan set up after the 1978 Revolution. Honouring their treaty of friendship with that country, the Soviet Union sent a limited contingent of troops to assist in the struggle against their enemies.[83] Morale is no less important in small campaigns than in large wars and the ephemeral military press underlines that by the encouragement it gives to the *Zampolits* serving with that contingent. They are reminded that such struggles as that in which they are engaged, although demanding of great effort and sacrifice, are of ultimate benefit to mankind. As the Officer's Handbook has told them, victory in the defence of socialist states or wars of national-liberation 'weakens the position of international imperialism, results in the defeat of reactionary regimes in the aggressor countries and contributes to the victory of democratic socialism in these countries over the world capitalist system'.[84]

The *Zampolit* is not a lonely figure. His assistants are the Communist Party and KOMSOMOL members at all rank levels who are strongly encouraged to continue their Party activities during their term of service. These are the people who are expected to lead discussion groups in unit 'Lenin Rooms', pursuing their own enlightenment and inspiring those of their fellows who are less enthusiastic about the Party and its works. In every Armed Forces' unit there is a Party Cell which by self-criticism or direct criticism of others monitors the efficiency of the unit and develops a close liaison with local government bodies, schools, factories, collective farms etc. Although it is the ambition of most regular officers to become members of the Communist Party proper, it is the KOMSOMOL that has the greater influence on account of age limits. All the conscript bulk of the Armed Forces is under twenty-eight years of age and therefore not eligible for full party membership. Only beyond this age and as officers or warrant officers are servicemen eligible for full Party membership. Marshal Grechko explained that:

The activities of the KOMSOMOL members in the Armed Forces are multi-faceted and fruitful and their achievements in combat and political training are significant. But KOMSOMOL members do not rest on their laurels. With the fighting spirit and enthusiasm characteristic of them, and under the leadership of communists, they firmly and confidently march on toward new successes in training and service.[85]

Soviet officers in discussion with the author disclosed that in practice KOMSOMOL activity does not reach Grechko's ideals. The existence of a Party cell, composed mainly of private soldier KOMSOMOL members who are theoretically empowered to criticise their superiors for performances not compatible with Communist traditions or not in the best interests of the unit's military efficiency, makes for an impossible command situation. Or it would do if not for a tendency for the cells to be less than energetic in their criticism. Members realise that fierce criticism of the superiors is unlikely to enhance their military careers. From time to time however they do lash out and, through the columns of *Red Star*, expose the sins of their officers or NCO's, usually putting paid to the careers of the unfortunate objects of criticism. Line Commanders cannot therefore ignore the party cells and are careful to frame their orders as compromises that the Party cells will accept without complaint. They admit this is to be an inhibiting arrangement, damaging to initiative, but they understand it. Some of them even praise it for the 'dialectical' contribution it makes to correct decision making. All seem confident that if war comes the Party will not be the cause of any sclerosis in the command and control system any more, they say cryptically, than it was in World War II.

The obvious need for liaison between the Party cells and the command structure gives the *Zampolit* an important operational function over and above his propagandist and educational duties. Frictions in the liaison appear to have become greatly reduced since the *Zampolit* began to receive full military training. The training has to some extent neutralised the criticism that he was not a real soldier and therefore did not understand real soldiers' problems. Now, in theory at least, he understands better and his standing in the military community has risen a little as a result, although he still fails to win the respect he would like to receive. For all the many press articles painting him as such, in the eyes of his audience he does not typify the 'New Soviet Man', that essential communist self-image about whom he preaches.

The 'New Soviet Man' will be a product of the 'New Soviet

Culture' and, among his other duties, the *Zampolit* is expected to instil this culture. For a Western mind it is difficult to acquire a satisfactory notion of what Soviet communist culture might be, since it cannot easily be distinguished from the programme of political 'enlightenment' already outlined. The dictionary does not help:[86]

> Communist culture is based on high levels of productive strength and communist social relations. The characteristic features of spiritual culture under socialism are democracy and the development of socialist internationalism based on a Marxist–Leninist world-outlook.

Whatever it might mean it is a military commitment. The *Zampolit* is reminded by such books as *The Army – a School of Culture*[87] that although the conscription period is relatively short, it has a lasting effect on young men. Not for nothing are the Armed Forces popularly called 'The University of Manhood'.[88] Ninety per cent of the nation's young men graduate from this 'university' and this entrusts commanders and military political staffs with a heavy responsibility for the harmonious development of the soldier's personality, the refinement of his cultural and moral qualities which transform him into a noble defender of the world's first socialist state. It appears more than probable that for the *Zampolit* there is no frontier between culture and political enlightenment, no question of art for art's sake. Certainly he must encourage the arts, with the proviso that pictures are socially realistic, songs are patriotic and literature reflects communist principles of morality, but his concerns are wider than this – all-embracing, in fact:

> The indoctrination of the defenders of the homeland is inseparable from the indoctrination of all workers and has the general aim of forming those qualities needed in builders of communist society. The Communist Party unswervingly follows the testaments of the great Lenin who directed that 'the education of contemporary youth must be based upon indoctrination in communist morality'. Within the meaning of this term are included not only political–ideological, military and moral indoctrination but also the cultural–aesthetic and physical development of the soldier.[89]

Anikovich leaves the *Zampolit* in no doubt of the need for high standards of instruction. He finds it hard to believe that, at the time of the October Revolution, 80 per cent of the country's adult population was illiterate, but now, after so comparatively short a time, that same percentage of service personnel, conscripts as well as officers, has had the advantage of at least a complete middle-school education. No longer therefore will the simple slogans of the propaganda-train days serve as political indoctrination; today's young men can accept a more complex approach, a 'cultural' approach. Units, for example, where films are shown merely for entertainment are strongly criticised for wasting propaganda resources. The cinema is an excellent indoctrination medium but the films must be carefully chosen and showings followed by critical discussions in groups led by Party political workers if the audience is to be intellectually satisfied.

But it is the lecture that is the most favoured medium, again of course followed by discussion (*Besyeda*) or individual essays. The recommended sources for lectures are, *The Collected Works of Lenin* and, at least until he died, Brezhnev's trilogy, *Malaya Zemlya*, *Re-birth* and *Virgin Lands*, all of which recount the history of Soviet Society. The *Zampolit* is however spared the tedium of original research into the actual volumes. He is expected to use those structured lessons on themes from these sources published in confetti quantity by the military publishers along with counterpoint pamphlets describing the nature of 'enemy' culture. *Bourgeois Culture in the Service of Reaction*,[90] sub-titled, *A Methodological Recommendation for the Conduct of Lectures and Discussions*, is perhaps the most widely distributed of these. Levin and Kamsyuk, with copious quotations from Lenin, present bourgeois Western culture as a set of totally negative attitudes developed in the masses by their manipulators, the reactionary ruling circles of capitalism. They claim its features amount to nothing less than 'anti-humanism', its cynical philosophers and artists holding no belief in the ideals of man nor in the creative power of the human mind. Such a culture depending as it must, solely on the titillation of emotions cannot enrich the life of man, it only dulls the senses and allows the privileged operators of the moribund and obsolescent bourgeois system to retain their control of society for a little longer.

An especially prominent characteristic of this 'anti-human' culture is the use it makes of all its branches to justify militarism and aggressive war. Its most formative writers include among others the best-selling, Allan Drury, Mickey Spillane, Robert Conquest, Ian Fleming and Andrew Sinclair. Their fictional heroes do not spare themselves in the struggle against communism, and their readers, by identification with these characters, themselves become imbued with a bitter anti-communism. Fleming's hero, James Bond, who customarily employs the most devilishly refined means to achieve his questionable ends in this struggle, is cited by the authors as the worst influence of them all.

The graphic artists are encouraged in a comparable way to 'dull the senses' of the masses with those elitist forms of escapist art which distort the reality of life – 'pop-art', 'op-art', 'body-art', 'mini-art', etc. Beyond this, bourgeois Western culture is only explained to the Soviet soldier in terms of its subservience to the interests of contemporary militarism. Quoting the New York *Daily Mail*, Levin and Kamsyuk report a sample week of television in that city when 197 cases of murder, 143 of attempted murder, 36 robberies with violence, 14 poisonings, 13 kidnappings and 14 escapes from prison were screened. They adduce this as proof that bourgeois media policy is to brutalise the public, to accustom it to violence as an acceptable societal norm. A public schooled in this way will also unquestioningly accept the anti-Soviet nature of its children's education and the need for the economic burden of the arms race.

A far cry from culture though this all is to Western understanding it does not seem out of place under that heading in Soviet writings. The clear-eyed objective nature of Soviet ideology shines with greater purity when contrasted with the decadent Western alternative, whose heroes like 'Superman', 'Clark Kent', 'Steve Canyon' and their ilk epitomise the ugliness of its nihilistic militarism. Choosing his texts from the abundance of 'educational' material available to him, our *Zampolit* tries to persuade his audiences that Soviet ideology offers a sounder foundation for human development than the hollow, rotten capitalist system however brightly it may gleam from afar. As Lenin put it, 'We must indefatigably resist any kind of bourgeois ideology in whatever fashionable guise or glittering uniform it might parade itself.'[91]

No review of a *Zampolit*'s duties would be complete without at least mentioning two other related areas of his responsibility.

First, the teaching of atheism. In the continuing struggle against the *babushka*, the Main Political Administration is once again generous with instructional aids. But the content of these anti-religious tracts reveals nothing of substance not already familiar to the soldier from his school days. Repetition is no crime however in Soviet pedagogic theory, the important thing is that no remanent virus from the superstitious past should be permitted to sully the communist world-outlook of military personnel.

As might be expected, Lenin supplied the *Zampolit*'s text when he explained 'that one needs to know *how* to fight religion, and that it is necessary to explain to the masses the origins of faith and religion in materialistic terms.[92] In the steps of this great teacher, the *Zampolit* will indeed explain that builders of communism must be convinced of the deep truth of Marxist–Leninist doctrine and the genuine nature of its scientific approach to the evolution of a communist society. He must also appreciate the enormous significance of the role of science in the task of exploiting the earth's resources to achieve maximum satisfaction of its population's material and spiritual demands. Old religious beliefs can play no part in this development. Dolgikh and Kurantov[93] leave the *Zampolit* very aware of where the battle lines are drawn:

An uncompromising war is waged in the ranks of the Armed Forces against anyone who attempts to preach religious sermons to young military men or in any way tries to propagate bourgeois religious views and morals among them. Commanders and political workers, the Party and the KOMSOMOL all work continuously to imbue in the personnel of our Soviet Armed Forces that atheistic world-outlook through which they learn to recognise all that is excellent and noble in communist morality.

Lastly, the *Zampolit* must defend his personnel, not only against angels but against men. He is responsible for security education or 'vigilance' as he cares to call it. Here again, the message is only a repetition but in much greater detail, of all those stories he read at school about the hordes of foreign spies who sit patiently on the frontiers waiting only the chance to penetrate when the Soviet guard is down. Even here the instruction is ideological. It is not simply a question of teaching good security practices, although the textbook by no means neglects these, but of relating the subject directly to the communist world-outlook and, as with culture, of weaving it into the broad fabric of political indoctrination. The dark powers of capitalist NATO and hegemonistic Peking prowl around the Soviet Union like the 'Troops of Midian'. The Soviet soldier is warned by Kalachnikov[94] that 5 million foreign tourists visit the Soviet Union each year, many of them having no other aims than to acquire Soviet military secrets or spread malicious anti-Soviet propaganda. Spies are everywhere, some of them masquerading as diplomats or business men and the soldier must resist their wiles. He must be aware also of the massive technical espionage effort the notorious CIA mounts against the USSR. Kalachnikov describes this in highly paranoiac terms, concluding with a rallying cry for eternal vigilance. The Communist Party, according to Kalachnikov, will not be deflected from its determination to build communism and, in holding to Lenin's foreign policy of peace, will strongly rebuff any aggression against this principle. Security is a vital element of the USSR's military capability and therefore, where ever he might be serving, the soldier must be a vigilant sentry, protecting the homeland's secrets in the cause of peace. An extract from a long, near-epic poem included in Kalachnikov's book will perhaps give an impression of that emotional pitch of security training evident in the abundance of slogans and posters which adorn barrack-room walls:

> Even though you die, you must preserve security,
> Military secrets are never disclosed
> He who would break security, breaks his sacred oath.
> Remember you are always on watch – a sentry
> In the front line itself.
> Remember that it is the gullible fool who opens
> The gate to the foe. Remember,
> The enemy is a wolf, not a sheep.
> Obey your homeland's order therefore.
> Be vigilant. Keep your eyes skinned!

To this point an attempt has been made to reveal a small cross-section of the influence brought to bear on all ranks of the Soviet Armed Forces whatever their length of service, either as short-term conscripts or as career officers. Value judgements of the content of the mound of books and pamphlets surveyed in the production of this cross-section have been avoided as far as possible but it was inevitable that a few would intrude. The discovery made in reading through this mound, that the fundamental pattern of political indoctrination has not changed since the early 1950s, was striking. It has probably not changed since the days of the October Revolution. Nemzer included few actual examples of indoctrination content in his study but his analysis established three main themes:

1. *Strength* – The might of the Soviet Armed Forces.
2. *Emotion* – The glorious success of the October Revolution and the inexorable progress towards a truly communist society for all the world's workers.
3. *Hatred* – Hatred for reactionary and capitalist enemies within or outside the Soviet homeland.

Nothing it seems has changed except that the indoctrination system has become more experienced and more confident as the memories of those older Soviet citizens who remember Stalin become dimmer and fewer.

2   Is the *Zampolit* Effective?

> In many respects Russia may be considered as still a closed
> country. I have therefore attempted to aid the interests of
> science and literature by giving in my notes and appendices
> much varied information, not easy to be procured, on account
> of the rigour of the press and the paucity of Russian
> publications. My own difficulty in obtaining materials has been
> sometimes immense but perseverance has enabled me to attain
> my end.
>
> J. H. Schnitzler, 1849[1]

Alex Inkeles writing one hundred years after Schnitzler admitted
the great frustration encountered in trying to erect any hypothesis
about Soviet public opinion is the near impossibility of testing it.[2]
Thirty years on from Inkeles the position is virtually unchanged.
The riddle is still wrapped in the enigma. Gathering information
to supply even partial validation for answers to the questions,
'Does political indoctrination work? 'Is the *Zampolit* effective?',
has proved no less 'an immense difficulty' than Schnitzler's. The
Soviet media provide no satisfactory answers and, for reasons of
that vigilance discussed in the preceding chapter, the military
world is even more difficult to observe than the rest of their
society. The author makes no apology therefore for putting
forward some of his own experience of life in the Soviet Union to
provide a little support for tentative answers to these questions.

Yepishev's article was uncharacteristically revealing.[3] Not only
does he complain of the inadequacy of political indoctrination in
the youth organisations but also of the poor physical condition of
conscripts in spite of the heavy emphasis on sport in KOMSOMOL
activities. Not without cause; large numbers of eighteen year-old
recruits observed at railway stations and airports at the time of the
bi-annual inductions look weak and skinny. Certainly they do not
terrify in the way that the opposite flow does, the bronzed, sinewy
twenty-year olds who have finished their service. If the Armed

Forces can temper bodies in this way, success in their attempts to temper minds and steel wills should perhaps not be underrated. On Sundays, in the television show, 'I Serve the Soviet Union',[4] young officers and soldiers talk of their military duties and involvement with Party activities in an impressively fluent and confident manner. It would be naive to imagine that these performances are unrehearsed but in many random conversations with such personnel the author noted a similar fluency of expression. He detected however a modular quality in their statements and answers. Trigger questions about their attitudes to such subjects as the USA, China or even Afghanistan would elicit reflex answers in the polemical style of *Red Star*, delivered as though reciting poetry. Soldiers 'interviewed' in places as far apart as Archangel and Tashkent couch their responses in exactly similar words and phrases. They do not, or cannot discuss a subject further when their stock of modular expressions is exhausted. If the substance of their standard statements is contested they merely repeat them and relapse into silence. Unaccustomed to hearing an opposing argument they are surprised and nonplussed. In one only of approximately 150 conversations did a soldier deviate from the *Zampolit* line to express a significant criticism of the Soviet system. At the very least it would appear therefore that political indoctrination can produce articulate human parrots whose rehearsed views on generalised matters of the moment will, on discharge, be disseminated nation-wide in factory and collective farm. Although the influence of succeeding generations of ex-servicemen on their predecessors cannot in the present circumstances be quantified, it probably contributes greatly to that homogeneity in public attitudes which many travellers with experience of life in the Soviet Union beyond the protective cordon of 'Inturist' have noticed. But do these almost Pavlovian reflexes indicate other than that the whole 'enlightenment' programme produces nothing more than widespread apathy in the whole population? There is some evidence that it might.

First, the defectors. Viktor Suvorov[5] was an officer in the Soviet Army. He writes of a savage, sadistic discipline, of corruption and inefficiency in all ranks. In describing political indoctrination classes in a military prison, the instructor's lessons followed the broad path traced in the preceding section. The 'students' look forward to these sessions but only because they offer a seat for a while and relief from punitive labours in the freezing cold. As for the message, they are totally apathetic. Likewise Myagkov,[6] a defector from the KGB who had earlier trained as a paratroop officer; he suggests that the training was a sham. So does Belyenko,[7] the Air Force pilot who escaped spectacularly in his Mig 25 to Japan in 1976. Referring to political indoctrination in a tank production plant where he once worked, he reported that workers irreverently mocked the promised future with obscene complaints about the real present; 'The slogans, exhortations, theories and promises of the Party were as irrelevant to their lives, to the daily, precarious struggle just to exist, as the baying of some forlorn wolf on the faraway steppes.'

These three men were defectors, brave men who saw through the pretensions of the Soviet Communist Party and decided to leave for the outside world. They write fully of their own disillusionment and imply that there are many more in the Soviet Union who share their feelings. All three were secret dissidents and came from parental backgrounds of dissidence, sceptical of the communist world-outlook and heretical towards Party principles. They do not, unfortunately, give any indication of the size or influence of the group of their like-minded colleagues. The incidence of real opposition or dissidence within the Armed Forces, potential or actual, cannot be measured. Extrapolating from the civil scene, it must be the minutest fraction. Except for a few well-known heroes, dissidents in the Soviet Union do not often raise their heads. Their total number is unknowable but their influence on Soviet society would at the present time seems to be insignificant.

Next, the social scientists. A bright meteor recently flashed across the sociometric sky but did not dispel much of the darkness. Gabriel tapped a new *émigré* source of witnesses – the Soviet-Jews allowed to leave the country after 1977.[8] To 1094 of these who had served at any time in the Soviet Armed Forces, in various ranks between the beginning of World War II and 1977, questionaires were sent out to establish what Gabriel has since sub-titled 'An Attitudinal Portrait of the Soviet Soldier'. However, only 113 of the addressees responded and since they belong to one oppressed ethnic minority group, the sample is weak, although Gabriel argues plausibly to the contrary. Without doubt the survey has added much to our knowledge of the Soviet soldier's attitudes to the more concrete factors of service life, pay, food, leave, discipline and welfare, but in the matter of political indoctrination it must remain suspect. The time-factor alone makes it so, the survey spanning as it does, 40 years. Gabriel finds that 77.2 per cent of his officer sample considered that ideological training was of 'very little importance' or even 'of no importance at all' in motivating soldiers to fight. The percentage figure for NCO's and soldiers corresponded remarkably closely at 81 per cent.[9] These are interesting findings, and disappointing, no doubt for the professional *Zampolit*, but they scarcely prove that those proportions of personnel do not believe or accept his ideology. Answers to further questions in the survey show interestingly that other motivating factors would be more important than ideology in determining the Soviet soldier's will to fight in a future war, e.g., the close ties of the small unit peer-group and a reluctance to appear cowardly in front of one's comrades.

Defector reports and sociological studies of the Soviet Armed Forces (however incomplete that data) cannot by any means be discounted but, so far, their evidence has been tantalisingly ambiguous. The defectors in particular have provided much support for the view widely held in the West of a captive nation groaning under its KGB yoke, waiting patiently for liberation – or liberalisation – and the dawn of political freedom. It does not appear like this to Westerners who have lived in the Soviet Union for any appreciable length of time. An unavoidable subjectivity is of course the weakness of their testimony but they do see a different picture, a population which, after 65 years of Party 'enlightenment', has come instinctively to believe in its destiny to reform the world. Soviet citizens are the first to admit that there are shortcomings but they are sure that these will disappear, indeed, would have disappeared long ago had it not been for the heavy financial burden resulting from their munificent aid to developing countries and the cost of an arms programme forced upon them by the military ambition of the West to crush them. They must and will contain this threat, confident that scientific Marxist–Leninism guarantees them ultimate victory in the ideological struggle with capitalism.

But not only are there political dissidents in Soviet society. There are criminals also, layabouts, and not a few intellectuals who have opted out. While this latter category outwardly conforms and is therefore hard to identify, in reality they have retreated into a private spiritual monasticism, with neither hope nor care for the future. Again, while these categories undoubtedly exist, their size relative to the total population is unquantifiable but there is scant evidence that they are large. Some authorities maintain that the great majority falls into the latter, opted-out, category, that the average citizen goes about his daily life oblivious of the wall-slogans and heedless of the boringly repetitive mass-media. They argue that the endless waves of self-adulation have created only widespread ennui and apathy. They adduce a sullenness of response directly proportionate to the stridency of the propaganda as proof of its ineffectiveness.[10]

The author would not easily be persuaded so. He would rather agree with Inkeles that education is the prime factor in the cultivation of public attitudes, in this age of far greater influence than the mass-media directly:

> The young generation does not depend for its inspiration solely on the system of mass communication but is trained under more favourable conditions in the schools. Here, Soviet youth acquires its predisposition to believe, and since this *predisposition* is the single most important element in securing belief itself in the audience of any medium of mass communication, the products of the Soviet schools provide the Soviet agitator, newspaper, radio and film with an ever renewed and susceptible audience.

Predisposition to believe is a concept too often neglected by students of Soviet media effect. In the same way that a Pioneer will be ready to approve of editorials in *Komsomolskaya Pravda* before he has even seen a copy for the first time, so also will the average recruit to the Armed Forces be predisposed to listen to and agree with the *Zampolit* as soon as he enters the barracks on his first day of service. Since the biggest school and probably the last they will ever attend, is the Armed Forces, young newly-adult men will finish their term with much sharpened perceptions of the nature of the capitalist enemy and of the party's tasks in striving for victory in the ideological struggle against this enemy. On discharge they will return to their native parts of the Union as mature Soviet citizens, whatever their ethnic origins, not as units of the mass to be indoctrinated but as indoctrinators themselves working for the greater glory of the Party, in conformity with its great aims and principles.

Conformity is another key to the understanding of Soviet political indoctrination. In many ways the Soviet Union today can be likened to Western European countries of a century or more ago when 99 per cent of the community were professed Christians irrespective of whether they went to church or understood the doctrine. It was good, respectable and economically advantageous to conform. It needed great courage to proclaim atheism or agnosticism and face life as a social outcast in consequence. The unbeliever usually lost his job, certainly his career was truncated and his family suffered. It is so now in the Soviet Union. All virtue and advantage rest on conforming to the Party's rules, all hope of advancement in one's profession or social position. This is the real bedrock of Soviet power – 'If you don't work, you don't eat'. The non-conformers are not allowed to work. It is a brave man therefore who is not prepared to pay even lip service to the Party. But the majority not only conforms, it believes. The West does not generally appreciate the extent to which the Soviet schools and propaganda organisations have succeeded in implanting a communist ethic in the Russian soul. The concerted indoctrination effort imposes a respect for communism on top of a deep and natural patriotism – on Mother Russia herself and all the old folk-heroes – and the synthesis is a natural love of communism. That this love exists cannot be satisfactorily proved but it can be strongly sensed in the pride and enthusiasm the ordinary citizen displays in Soviet achievements and the obviously genuine pleasure he takes in celebrating them, not only on the great festive days, 1 May and 7 November, but also at smaller gatherings, e.g. shop-floor and office parties to mark the fulfilling of a norm or the breaking of some other 'socialist competition' record.

And the citizen's pride in the Armed Forces is also manifestly genuine – whether he lives in Moscow or Uzbekistan – and he really does appear to believe that 'The People and the Armed Forces Are One.' It would be difficult to argue that many generations of *Zampolits* have not contributed enormously to the achievement of this national cohesion. Year by year for 65 years they have graduated more than a million men, imbued them with the best traditions of the period, the Winter Palace, Pskov and Stalingrad and despatched them home to 'build communism' in the four corners of the Union. Among the agents of Sovietisation in the non-Russian areas, they have probably been the most powerful.

The *Zampolit*'s immediate concern however must always be with the present generation, to ensure that its will is steeled sufficiently to face the test should war come during its term of service. Most of the evidence, in the author's opinion, suggests they are generally successful. If they were not they would have disappeared into history long before now. It must be assumed therefore that their students would fight fanatically in the defence of their homeland if called upon to do so. Soviet Forces have their weaknesses, but morale is probably not among them. The hate element of the *Zampolit*'s message would seem to be the paramount influence he exerts, consolidating the soldier's earlier indoctrination in school or KOMSOMOL with a top-dressing of astonishing virulence. There is no sign that the MPA has any intention of changing the curriculum. Over the years living standards in the Soviet Union have markedly improved but there has been no concomitant modification in attitudes. *Détente* has come – and possibly gone – scientific and cultural exchanges have promised some closer approach to the West, millions of Westerners have visited the USSR since Stalin died, but still there is no sign of compromise. The convergence theory has been repudiated with as much heat as capitalism itself and the nation continues to persuade itself that, much as war is to be avoided, it is ready to meet that final challenge from capitalism whenever it should come. In the light of this there is little hope for genuinely improved relations between East and West until some form of propaganda *détente* is arranged, until the MPA can order its *Zampolits* to throw away their distorting mirrors and present a world-outlook less poisonously biased in content. Sadly, even if a decision to do so were made by the MPA today, the hate accumulated through the years, so instinctive now in Soviet breasts of all ages, would probably take as long a period to dissipate as it did to generate. This is a point of profound significance largely unappreciated by those who direct Western affairs.

The subjective nature of this analysis must again be emphasised. More conclusive evidence is needed before the effects of political education on Soviet servicemen can be evaluated with confidence. It is hoped that sufficient information and argument have been presented in these pages at least to introduce the subject as an important area for further study. To ensure that the door is left wide open, the last word goes appropriately to one who would not agree with the interim assessment made here. An ordinary Soviet man watching a great military parade in Red Square, gesticulating towards the red, white and gold slogans, said:

> Of course its all meaningless. We could never beat the Americans and those old men up there know we couldn't. We ran away from the Germans in 1941 and we'd run away from the Americans now if they were to come. And the Americans wouldn't be as stupid as the Germans. They'd know how to treat us.[11]

With that sentiment corroding away in the Soviet folk-memory could it be perhaps, after all, that the *Zampolit* is only whistling in the dark?

3　Morale and Other Factors

Political indoctrination and its influence is only one factor of morale. There are others. Richard Gabriel highlights some of these and attempts to assess the influence on morale of such elements of military life as living conditions, the quality and adequacy of rations, the amount of free time allowed and how a soldier spends it, the effects of overcrowding in barracks, lack of privacy, ethnic problems, etc.[1] These and allied factors have been considered also by Goldhamer and other writers and their various assessments are reviewed collectively here.[2] They are also openly acknowledged as seriously adverse tendencies by authoritative Soviet sources.[3]

THE ETHNIC FACTOR

A convenient entry point to the discussion is the attitude of the conscript recruit to the imminent inevitability of military service. Immediately, the ethnic question springs to view. While the Russian-speaking Slav may as already implied be either sympathetic or apathetic to the prospect at least he is resigned to it. A good academic case or a highly-placed father, or a combination of both, may win him deferment from conscription but following a recent tightening of the regulations it is much less likely to give the complete exemption that it might have done some years ago. He accepts his lot therefore with little fuss although he tends to consider it rather a waste of his time. It is as natural to him to be conscripted as it was to start school. The non-Slavs, in particular the Central Asians, Georgians and Balts are not so acquiescent, indeed many are resentful and obstructive to authority. Very often they pretend not to speak any Russian – in spite of school or KOMSOMOL dossiers indicating that they do –

but with a progressive use of penalties and punishments the not-so-stupid authorities usually manage to bring down the gift of tongues upon these dissimulators. But coercion of a penal nature provides only half a solution. The inescapable truth is that the non-Slav recruit just does not want to serve in the Soviet Forces.[4]

The Soviet authorities are not strangers to their ethnic manpower problem and, having lived with it for many years, they are more than aware of it. They rely on strict discipline and intensive training to integrate the non-Slavs into the Armed Forces and make the best possible use of their conscript period.

A useful study of this ethnic factor conducted for the Rand Corporation was, like Gabriel's analysis, based on the responses of a panel of Jewish *émigrés* consisting, in this case, of 36 officers and 91 other ranks.[5] Again as with Gabriel it suffers from statistical difficulties but in the author's view no specific Jewish bias was encountered and the responses showed a broad general agreement over a wide range of national affiliation and service experience. One feels, however, that the evidence is doubtful in certain respects. Interviews covered issues such as recruitment, pre-induction training, in-service training, linguistic and ethnic matters.

The Rand study confirms much that has been observed or suspected earlier by other authorities and also exposes new facets of the ethnic question. The authors note for example that pre-conscription training takes place on a much reduced scale in the non-Slavic regions of the USSR. The level of *DOSAAF* membership is lower as its activities are more limited in scope than in the Slavic regions.[6] This accords closely with random but frequent glimpses afforded to Western travellers, especially in Central Asian areas where shooting ranges and other training facilities have a run-down, unkempt appearance almost as though lip-service only is paid to such training.

In-service technical training of an advanced nature appears to be available only to non-Russian recruits with a competence in the Russian language. This competence is unevenly spread, varies from service to service and, notwithstanding expedient dissimulation by the competent, many conscripts are genuinely unable to speak Russian. In the Ground Forces, for example, they need only be taught a dozen commands in Russian in order to play their cannon-fodder role. A much greater knowledge of the language is necessary among technical tradesmen. Ann Sheehy has examined this question and suggests that it is tending to become more rather than less of a problem as technology becomes increasingly more complex:

> The lack of knowledge of the Russian language among a number of the young Russians drafted into the Soviet Armed Forces to perform their compulsory military service has always constituted a problem. In recent years however it has been aggravated by the growing sophistication of military technology, the increasing proportion of Central Asians and Transcaucasians among draftees, and the enhanced national awareness of the non-Russian peoples of the USSR.[7]

It is more than obvious that the military has a vital interest in the teaching of Russian and has strongly backed the drive to make Russian the 'second mother tongue' of all non-Russian Soviet citizens. But although the campaign has extended even into the kindergartens the results have not reflected the scale of investment in language teaching. Sheehy suggests that Russian has become more widely known owing to the greater mobility of the population rather than as a result of formal teaching but that the undoubted increase in Russian language capability has been offset by the three factors she mentions. That of increasing technological sophistication is hardly surprising. It is the second factor that probably gives sleepless nights to the Defence Council. The low birth-rate among the Slav sector of the population is a trend that is not likely to be reversed in any medium-term forecast. At the same time a 'demographic explosion' among the Central Asian and Transcaucasian peoples is rapidly increasing the proportion of non-Russians in the annual conscript intake. The 1970 census forecast that by the mid-1980s non-Russians would constitute 15.3 per cent of the total, i.e. approximately one in six conscripts will be Central Asian compared with one in fifteen for the mid-1960s. The results of the 1979 census showed a continuing and commensurate upward trend.

The Rand responses indicating how language and its related problems affected individual soldiers were mixed. Three-quarters of the total sample[8] argued that an inadequate command of Russian leads to poor military performance. The remainder of the sample on the other hand maintained that minorities who do not speak adequate Russian on induction usually learn enough after about one year to enable them to perform adequately in their allotted tasks. This group of respondents conceded however that these tasks would be of a routine and repetitive nature, minorities with little or no command of the Russian language being assigned as a rule to simple labouring jobs:

> The minorities did not have difficulties fulfilling their duties because of their poor knowledge of Russian. They had been instructed so many times that they finally understood what they should be doing. Commanders would tell them over and over.[9]

In spite of their manifest difficulties the authorities nevertheless insist on a 'Russian Only' rule throughout training. But this cannot be enforced outside instruction periods, with the result that ethnic groups form within units, communicating in their own native tongues.[10] Paradoxically therefore and contrary to the Government's Sovietisation aims, conscripts tend to leave military service with a greater sense of their own ethnic origins and a knowledge that they are set apart from the mainstream of Soviet society. Living in their own environment before call-up they are not so aware of these differences and during their service period it is not surprising that they lead to enhanced fears of Russian domination. It is noted in the study that in spite of the propaganda claims, the Soviet Armed Forces thus fail to foster a 'spirit of brotherhood among the diverse peoples of the USSR'. Nor does there seem to be consistency in the official approach to the problem. Although training media by decree are in Russian, none of the Rand sample mentioned Russian instruction for non-Russian speakers. Western observers are, on the other hand, convinced that language classes for minorities are conducted but on how widespread or effective a scale cannot be determined. It has been observed however that a majority sample of non-Russian conscripts at about the mid-point of their service seem able to understand directions, engage in simple conversations and make themselves understood in everyday-life situations. They are thus able to carry out basic orders but again it is not known how much of this ability is the result of study at school or of instruction during service. In any case the authorities appear to pay little attention to their own 'school of the nation' dicta and are content to consign the bulk of their minority conscript intake to construction units where little or no true military training is given and consequently a knowledge of Russian is not so important.[11]

Diversity of language thus constitutes an influence that could adversely affect the cohesion of military formations and be consequently damaging to morale, not least for the marked racist tendencies it exacerbates. The Rand sample revealed that racism continues to be a dominant feature of the relationship between 'Slav and non-white, non-Slavs, especially Central Asians and other Turkic-Moslem peoples'. More than half of the subjects interviewed had participated in, witnessed, or knew of someone who had participated in violence stemming from ethnic conflict. Such racist violence is most prevalent in combat units of the Ground Forces where small numbers of non-Slavs fall victim to persecution by the large Slav majorities. In contrast, there appears to be less racial tension or violence in the construction battalions where the ratio of non-Slavs to Slavs is high. The evidence also suggests that non-Russians have fewer nationality inspired conflicts laterally among themselves than do Slavs against non-Slavs although witnesses had observed some conflict between Balts and Central Asians and between various of the Turkic-Moslem groups. Traditional animosity between Georgians and Armenians was also reported.

It should be noted that 'racial violence' in the Soviet Armed Forces is no mild or trivial affair of horseplay. It really is violent. Rand documents many extremely vicious cases. Examples are quoted here to convey some impression of scale:

A Young Uzbek soldier whom everyone picked on because he was racially and culturally different finally had enough. One day when he was supposed to be on guard duty, he took a machine-gun from the rack and ambushed the entire guard detail, killing several and wounding many of the rest. He should have killed them all, but he was a terrible shot.

This Vikhreshku (a Moldavian) was bright and talented, a musician and a poet. One day another Moldavian was badly beaten by a Russian lieutenant. Several of his ribs were broken and he was sent to a medical unit. Vikhreshku caught up with the lieutenant and killed him with a machine gun. After that, he set fire to the headquarters and shot himself.

There was constant tension between the Latvians in our unit

and the Central Asians. After a particularly vicious and insulting verbal attack on the Central Asians, the Latvians were attacked with knives and a slaughter ensued. This conflict went on for many months before it could be brought to a stop and many people were injured.[12]

Confirmation of official concern for ethnic minority difficulties can be obtained from almost any issue of *Red Star*, along with remedial advice. One proposal which seems to have been widely implemented is to encourage 'military friendships'. An ethnic Russian is paired with a non-ethnic for the whole conscription period. The Russian will act as guide and counsellor to the other for two years, in the official hope that the non-ethnic will absorb more of the Russian language and become therefore a better trained soldier into the bargain. The extent of this practice is not known but individual soldiers have explained that the paired non-Slav, never becomes more than an assistant to the Slav soldier. Full military value from non-Slav soldiers is unlikely to be extracted from this system but the authorities probably considers that the longer-term goals of reduced tension, improved racial understanding and a wider spread of the Russian *lingua franca* outweigh the short term advantage of maximum operational efficiency.

Brave though such attempts at eliminating racial and language differences might be, real results will only come in the very remote long-term. Although the Rand sample presents some evidence of Russification[13] – or Sovietisation – other factors are aggravating the problem. National stereotypes, for instance, die hard. Russians are irritated by the Balts because of their Germanic qualities of order and precision. Balts on the other hand hate the Russians for having annexed their countries. They still consider themselves independent and despise the Russians as inferiors. The gulf between Russians and the Baltic States populations, according to the evidence of Western travellers is becoming wider with the years rather than narrower. It would be a rash Soviet commander who put any great degree of trust in Baltic soldiers.

Likewise, the Caucasians, especially the Georgians and Daghestanis are never slow to display their independence. On their part, the Russians consider them violent, undisciplined and, above all, anti-Russian. The greatest cleavage however is between the Central Asians and all the other Soviet peoples. The

'Muslims' were all indiscriminately lumped together by the Rand witnesses as lazy, stupid, primitive and unreliable:

> Of course, everyone treated the Chuckmeks [Central Asians] with contempt. Normally, these Asians are very bad soldiers. . . . People treated them with contempt because chuckmeks are something like a lower race to Russians and Ukrainians. They are not strong physically; they are very stupid. They couldn't handle equipment . . .

> There were two Kazakh Tatars in our squadron of the air defence brigade. The other soldiers did not like them and jeered at them. They knew the Tatars did not eat pork, so one Russian would put a pig's ear in a Tatars soup. Or they would put a foot-cloth on his head while he was sleeping. They would make the Tatar do all the work, like clean toilets, and so forth, just because he was a Tatar.[14]

These graphic examples illustrate the existence of a problem but it remains difficult to quantify the racial factor as an influence on cohesion in the Soviet Armed Forces, or on morale in general. The testimony from all sources suggests however that it is of some magnitude. Its reduction no doubt demands the current level of 'Sovietising' propaganda and *Zampolit* agitation. But there is some evidence also that perhaps racial harmony – especially among the non-Slav groupings themselves – is not necessarily a goal of Soviet authority. Indeed, on the divide and rule principle it has been suspected by a number of foreign observers that the official aim is quite the opposite, that racial tensions are tolerated if not encouraged. As one Rand witness, a former lieutenant went on record:[15]

> The tendency is such that in order to improve control over soldiers, conflicts among them must be encouraged in every possible way. The most important goal is to avoid any feelings of solidarity by soldiers of different nationalities. There are no instructions or directions to this effect, or at least I received none. But one knows that it must be done this way.

Another witness, also a former lieutenant, was more positive in his claim that it is official policy to exacerbate these differences:

Authorities encourage these inter-ethnic hostilities because it is easier for them to control a multi-national society in which people of different nationalities do not understand one another. They wouldn't be secure if, for example, Georgians, Armenians and Azerbaizhanis lived in harmony. Some officers receive political instruction in this policy; it is sufficient if only a few officers in a regiment know about it.

If such a tendency were prevalent even to a small degree it would detract seriously from the credibility of the propaganda claim that the Soviet Armed Forces are 'a school of brotherhood and internationalism'. From Soviet writing it is difficult to divine with truth either way, but it is probably safe to infer from the weight of 'harmony' propaganda in their military press that, first, there is a problem and, second, that at least in the golden future the authorities would prefer to see it eliminated by complete Sovietisation (which in effect means Russification). Control by the conforming consent of the minorities is doubtless the ultimate aim rather than control by racial division but it is not improbable that some current use of the latter means is justified in the interest of the long-term ends. One of the basic faults of the Soviet system is that they have failed, or perhaps not even tried, to create a true Soviet nationality. Instead they appear to demand support from ethnic minorities for what is effectively a Russian state.

A divide and rule motive might also be discerned in the general Soviet policy of ensuring that conscripts do not serve in or near their own home locality. 'If you're an Uzbek, you go to Russia. If you're a Balt, you serve in Uzbekistan.'[16]

From the evidence of a variety of sources it would seem that the underlying reason for this logistically expensive principle is connected with the Soviet Army's traditional role in defence, not only of the frontiers from external threat, but also from a possible internal threat to the Communist Party. Exceptions to the principle are made from time to time, on compassionate grounds or as a result of successful bribery, but never with Ministry of the Interior troops (MVD) whose prime function is internal policing. Similarly, frontier guards do not serve on or near their own native frontiers. Far-Eastern frontiers for example are usually manned by Ukrainians or Byelorussians, western frontiers by Siberians. These considerations apart, to remove conscripts from their native areas allows the *Zampolit* to conduct his indoctrination programme unhindered by possibly competing home influences.

Apart from natural 'fed up and far from home' considerations there is no apparent reason to suppose that this posting policy is of itself damaging to morale. Insofar however as it can and does give rise to friction with local inhabitants it could noticeably affect morale. The Rand study highlighted several neuralgic areas. Central Asians serving in Russian cities complained of strong antagonism on the part of the Russian citizenry, Latvians resent it when Russians in central parts of Russian profess not even to have heard of Latvia while, on the other hand, Russians serving in Central Asia or the Caucasus are not allowed into the towns for leave or recreation. Several Rand witnesses spoke of having been stationed within 15 miles of Tashkent without even once having been permitted to visit that city. Others testified similarly about the Western Ukraine, recalling that:

> the locals hated all the people in the army. Whenever there was interaction with the locals it always ended up in a fight. "They despised the Russians and the Russians hated them." Western Ukrainians are described by many respondents as "fierce nationalists" who refuse to speak Russian with soldiers for any reason. Young officers who had served in this area reported never having left their barracks and the avoiding of all contact with the local population.[17]

Travellers touring the Western Ukraine confirm this report in essence but cannot support the claim that young officers, or soldiers for that matter, never leave their barracks. Observation of unmistakably Russian military personnel of all ranks wandering freely about Ukrainian garrison towns proves the contrary although it can be conceded that sightings of individuals on their own are extremely rare. Usually they are seen in groups or, at least, in pairs. The same is also true in the Baltic States where relations between the military and the civilian population are at their most strained. Virtual confinement to barracks is however a feature of conscript life in forces stationed outside the Soviet Union. In the Group of Soviet Forces, Germany, (GSFG) as the prime example, the conscript has virtually no contact with the East German population at any level of intimacy.

Troops sent to GSFG or to the other Eastern European garrisons appear to be predominately Slavs. The reason usually advanced for this preference is that the non-Soviet Warsaw Pact populations are reassured that their defence is in trustworthy hands and they are not being 'occupied' by Mongol hordes. There is doubtless some truth in this although the isolation policy renders it of small importance. Rand evidence suggests another reason:

> There are many Russian peasants from Kalinin, Yaroslav and Tula regions who are sent to serve in Eastern Europe. They are sent there because they are sufficiently civilized to know what a toilet is and how to behave themselves more or less in a civilized manner. At the same time, these peasants are less educated, less informed, easier to indoctrinate and less likely to ask questions.[18]

Western observers have not been able to distinguish this close-to-Moscow, uninformed, yet house-trained peasant dolt from the rest of his Russian compatriots in other regions and, again in the light of the near-total isolation of troops from the local populations, the point seems insignificant. It provides an illustration however of the more trivial evidence which demands assessment in any study of morale and motivation.

The true or main reason for ensuring that the great majority of troops stationed outside the USSR are Slavs, particularly in the non-Soviet Warsaw Pact countries, is almost certainly one of pure military prudence. These men would inevitably bear the immediate brunt of a war with NATO. The crucial early days would determine victory or defeat. Given that ethnic differences could depress morale both within the army and between it and civil populations, why then have them around in the vital area at the vital time? A policy of not posting them there in any significant numbers ensures that no major problem will arise.

OFFICERS AND THE ETHNIC FACTOR

So far, ethnic differences have been considered almost exclusively in relation to conscript soldiers. Do they have similar effects in the officer corps? Similar in many ways perhaps, but in overall significance they are less pronounced. Education is perhaps the most important attenuating influence. Any breed of Soviet citizen can apply for officer training and be accepted if he passes the selection boards. If his education standards are satisfactory this presupposes that his degree of Sovietisation is also satisfactory, i.e. he is a vigorous supporter of the regime, his KOMSOMOL record is whiter than the whiteman's and he has fluency in Russian. These hurdles are very high. Few are called and even fewer chosen but there are some success stories and reports that these 'sophisticated' minority-group officers have serious integration difficulties with their Slav colleagues are not very numerous. Their impeccable KOMSOMOL/Party background and their entry to the commissioned *élite* will have made them true members of the 'establishment' and jealous of the privileges it bestows. They will tend to be more Soviet than the Slavs and unlikely to rock the ethnic boat. Rifts between such officers and their fellow-national, ungroomed, conscript soldiers do occur however but they are minimised by arranging as far as possible that they never serve together. Not that this is the complete answer since reliable evidence proves that Slav conscripts do not take kindly to serving under 'black' officers.

The officer corps will not remain immune to demographic trends and the erstwhile Defence Minister, Marshal Ustinov shortly before he died expressed this rising concern over the nationality question when he publicly declared the need to combat ethnic prejudice in the armed forces. General Yepishev's First Deputy Chief of the MPA also raised the issue recently in an uncharacteristically frank article.[19] He wrote of the continuing existence of radical antagonisms in the armed forces with an implied warning that the problem might become more acute, an undoubted reference to the steadily increasing proportion of Central Asians in the conscript cohort. A sign that authorities see the solution in bending to the wind, another writer almost simultaneously noted the Party's concern that all nationalities be represented not only in the hitherto overwhelmingly Russian officer corps but also on the directing staffs of the officer-training institutes.

The effect of these trends in the longer-term future is not easy to predict. Despite some obstruction in implementing it, official hopes are still staked on the plan for eventual all-Union Sovietisation, a state in which ethnic origins would have only vestigial significance. Until that distant day dawns, radical differences will continue to have a degrading and divisive effect on Soviet military cohesion, efficiency and morale.

Important though the ethnic factor is as a morale and motivational influence it is possibly exaggerated beyond its true proportion by both West and East. Traditional Soviet confidence in their understanding of the problem and their ability to contain it in the face of the trends has been shaken probably to the same unwarranted extent that Western hopes that increasing racial tensions will destroy the fabric of the Soviet Armed Forces have been raised. The longer-term future cannot be foretold and it is not beyond the bounds of possibility that these will prove ultimately disruptive but, in the meantime, other factors of Soviet service life in aggregate will have more immediate influence on corporate morale.

STATUS OF THE ARMED FORCES

Another factor is status. Is service in the Armed Forces popular with Soviet young people or is it merely a prison sentence? Already it has been suggested that for Slav entrants it is a penance to be borne with resignation. For those of other nationality groups it is something to be avoided at almost any cost. This is diametrically at odds with the media picture of the Armed Forces as the noblest of all professions, the bulwark of socialist society. It is clear that despite substantial propaganda efforts the regime has not been able to develop support for conscription. Gabriel[20] concludes from his sociological sample that Soviet youth feels that it has very little to gain from military service and adduces sufficient evidence to suggest that conscription itself may be contributing independently to the formation of negative feelings, both towards the notion of service and, implicitly, towards the regime.

Conscripts among the sample were asked if they had gained anything at all from their service. Only 27.4 per cent felt that they had. In contrast, 69 per cent claimed that they had obtained nothing from it and, to the summarising question, 'Was conscription a waste of your time?' a massive 83 per cent answered that it was. This negative attitude and another of Gabriel's conclusions that conscripts' families are indifferent to the idea of their sons' period of military service suggest a poor reward for the

long-sustained propaganda campaigns both of the MPA within
the armed services and the national political enlightenment effort
as a whole. The belief that the 'People and the Armed Forces Are
One' does not therefore appear to have been inculcated as
strongly as the jingoistic media output would imply. The sample
indicated that less than one per cent (0.9 per cent) of families were
'proud that I was serving my country'. In contrast 6.2 per cent
replied that their families were 'generally not happy about my
going into military service', but fully 76.1 per cent indicated that
their families 'felt resigned because military service could not be
avoided'.[21]

The apparent absence of family support for the idea of conscript
service is mirrored in Gabriel's findings by similar attitudes in the
conscript peer group. 'Did your friends think that going into the
military was a good thing, something to be proud of, or just
something that could not be avoided?' Only 4.4 per cent of the
respondents to this imprecisely worded question[22] felt that going
into the military was 'a good thing'.

Gabriel's survey creates an impression above all else of a
resigned acceptance of military service with some resentment that
it seriously interferes with civilian career plans. And, since the
experience is common to the majority of Soviet youth, service
offers no compensating cachet of distinction or glory, neither
personally nor in reputation among family or peers. Essentially
this is a genuine impression despite Gabriel's methodological
weaknesses, although a convincing weight of subjective evidence
does not in any way suggest a force resigned to a moronic level.
Soviet soldiers, particularly those in their second year, can look
healthy and happy. Observers also report less negatively about
civilian support for conscription and the armed forces than
Gabriel's respondents indicate. Many parents are proud of their
conscript sons. Their attitude is not unlike that of British
ex-National Service conscripts who claim to have hated every
minute of their time in uniform but in retrospect would not have
missed it and now recommend it as a necessary, formative
experience for all succeeding generations.

One cause of low status is of course low pay, about £7 per month
for the newly joined conscript, scarcely enough to provide
toothpaste. A 0.75 litre bottle of vodka would absorb a whole
month's pay. It is thus unrealistic for a conscript to consider
saving money towards his release; a negative, or at least a neutral,

influence on morale. Probably more dispiriting than the absolute low level of pay is the knowledge that the most junior officer receives approximately 20 times the private soldier rate. Officers are seen as rich beyond the dreams of avarice; one of the contributory factors to the great gulf in the relationship between commissioned and non-commissioned ranks, a gulf as wide today as ever it was in the old army of the Tsar.

An officer's pay is also good in comparison with salaries received by civilians in posts with relative responsibility though perhaps not as good as in earlier years. His status in society is commensurately high although the military profession is not as universally respected as the idealised self-images of the military press would appear to assume. Status and pay at their present levels are not likely to have any adverse effect on officer morale. Although commissioned service in the Armed Forces is considered by many provincial young men as a direct method of escape from the dreary provinces into 'high society', to a position with a status probably far beyond that which they might reasonably expect otherwise to reach, it is not nearly so highly regarded by the more worldly-wise, metropolitan youth of Moscow and Leningrad. But even so, status and pay are not likely to have other than a positive influence on officer morale.

THE TRAINING PROGRAMME

Of far greater concern to the bulk of the recruit entry than status and pay are the stories they have heard from generations of predecessors about the rigorous nature of conscript training mentioned by Christopher Donnelly in Chapter 4. They know they must expect hard physical conditions, realistic battlefield exercises and a demanding training programme allowing no rest or respite. Suvorov's testimony[23] regarding the corruption and brutality of senior soldiers and NCOs is attested by a wealth of old soldiers' tales and, bizarre though it seems in Western eyes, it does not seem to be exaggerated. Many conscripts as a result approach their period of service with some trepidation.

It is difficult to create a useful impression of these negative aspects of Soviet military discipline without some narrative. First, and probably the most copiously supported by the evidence, is the unofficial power of command wielded by senior conscripts over the junior first-year entrants. The life of the latter is made miserable to the threshold of endurance by the senior men with the assistance and connivance of their NCOs. A recent defector describes the system as he experienced it during his service aboard a minesweeper of the Black Sea Fleet.[24] His story is broadly consistent with those of soldiers from the Group of Soviet Forces, Germany and from military districts within the Soviet Union. The only significant difference is that the ordeal of conscription lasts an extra year in the Navy.

An intensive introductory discipline and drill course is followed by an easier period of technical training before appointment for sea duty of a very harsh nature. Aleksandr P. was posted to an anti-submarine surface ship based on Sebastopol. His first year was torture pure and simple. After a long day's work it was the practice of the bosun not to dismiss the watch to its quarters but to allocate further duties of an arduous, dirty and demeaning character, duties which occupied the whole of the off-watch period. The unfortunate sailors would then be allowed 15 minutes to wash and change before the start at their next watch. And this cycle was repeated for several nights until individuals became totally exhausted and hallucinated by lack of sleep. A few days of less pressure then followed, then another spell of exhausting round-the-clock working, this forming the pattern followed throughout the first year. Officially officers are unaware of this persecution, the conscripts having quickly learned not to complain:

> If during the day the commander, enquires why you are so listless, you explain that it is difficult to get a good sleep aboard ship until one gets accustomed to the routine. If you were to complain that they make you work all night long you would be beaten up by the NCOs and senior sailors. Doing the work is preferable to this.

Under such conditions the conscript sailor learns little about his profession. According to Aleksandr P., nothing at all in his first year; only in his second year are his nautical skills allowed to develop. The third year again is virtually non-productive since this is the year of privilege when the, now senior, conscripts are allowed to be idle except for their role as persecutors of the new men. One of the privileges of this lotus-eating class is to have personal servants allocated from the first-year men whose duty it becomes to wait on their lords and masters at table and make their beds. The slightest imperfection on the part of the servant in this curious 'fag' relationship invokes instant punishment, often corporal punishment. These privileges notwithstanding, there is plentiful evidence that service bores the third-year conscripts and they long for release.

The exercise of such power and privilege doubtless softens the retrospect of the conscript as he returns to civil life but it is unlikely to foster good corporate morale across the whole span of the Armed Forces. Sadistic practices might establish an immediately responsive discipline but it will be a wooden discipline of fear, detrimental to efficiency. Certainly in Aleksandr P.'s ship there was no cohesive discipline. As his tormentors chased him mindlessly through filthy and nugatory tasks they cried, 'You aren't the first and you won't be the last.' We all went through it. It's a matter of tradition. But this was little comfort to the victim. 'They claimed they were humane', he said, 'and at the same time they treated us like beasts.'

The effect of this iron discipline must however be assessed with caution. Aleksandr P. was broken by it. He seized the opportunity of a ship's visit to Tartus in Syria to escape. He slipped over the side during the night into a dangerous sea while at anchor in the roads. After many hours in the water, and barely alive he was very lucky to have been spotted and picked up by a foreign vessel. A sensitive soul, he had elected to take this sort of risk rather than serve any longer in that unhappy ship.

This story is typical of many of those who do flee to the West, motivated to escape from a harsh discipline rather than by the imagined attractions of the world outside the Soviet Union. There is also abundant evidence that an opportunity to cross the frontier is not an essential prerequisite for desertion. The desertion rate is high, with soldiers – and even officers – taking off from units in the Soviet interior, without any rational hope of ultimate escape. Of course not all desertions arise directly from the harsh nature of the discipline and the figure for those who do cannot be estimated with any degree of accuracy. It is however clear that it is a tiny fraction only of the total personnel.

CRIME AND MORALE

No peacetime military organisation can be free of crime and the Soviet Armed Forces are no exception. Unlike Western forces where morale is fostered by sport, entertainment, leave and variety of experience, with the result that the crime-rate stemming from boredom is low, the Soviets seem to prefer restriction of freedom as their crime prophylactic. Gabriel's witnesses speak of the isolation of many out-stations, the fully-programmed training day from reveille to lights-out, leave almost non-existent and all leisure time closely supervised by the *Zampolit*. The troops have minimal contact with the civilian world – this is especially so for units based outside the Soviet Union – and altogether their conditions are akin to imprisonment. Living quarters are crowded and uncomfortable by Western standards and although Soviet toleration thresholds in this regard are almost certainly higher than ours, the filtered complaints in *Red Star* indicate that the troops are far from happy with their lot. It is not surprising that such a depressing environment gives rise to a high rate of desertion or absence without leave, attempted suicide, and the acts of violence associated with drunkenness. These crimes persist despite authority's corralling policy and despite, for non-commissioned personnel, a total ban on drinking in barracks or in garrison towns. Drink nevertheless is on occasion illicitly obtainable with inevitable results. Vehicles are stolen and crashed, superiors are attacked, comrades are murdered and men hang themselves in fits of acute alcohol-induced depression. Copious defector evidence confirms this state of affairs with narratives that have created an impression in the West of serious alcoholism in the Soviet Armed Forces. It is far from the truth [25]

Alcoholism may be a national disease in the USSR, its continuing growth menaces longer-term Soviet progress and is the reason behind Gorbachev's order for 'the Intensification of the Struggle against Drunkenness'. But it would be a mistake to over-emphasise its effects on the Armed Forces. One credible *émigré*, Mikhail Tsypkin,[26] who held a reserve commission in the Soviet Army before he emigrated to the United States in 1977, reminds us that young Soviet soldiers drink often for the same reasons that young Western soldiers drink – out of bravado perhaps, or simply as a relaxation, a relief from the training routine. Such drinking will produce serious crimes but only unusually will it lead to alcoholism among fit 18 to 20 year-old men. Furthermore their drinking takes place off duty – it could not be otherwise given the tightly controlled working day – and cannot therefore seriously affect combat readiness. The penalties are stiff and comparatively effective. Those found guilty of simple drunkenness are thereafter deprived of Sunday rest-days and all further opportunity to visit the garrison town. They are also severely punished with up to 15 days confinement in the guardhouse in harsh conditions.

There is little doubt that such a penal code is a deterrent to would-be drinkers. This and the difficulty of obtaining drink in normal circumstances combine to keep the problem reasonably in check. Things get out of hand when the troops go for do-it-yourself solutions, concocting drinks from alcohol-based toilet preparations, boot-polish or aero-engine coolant. The results are often spectacular and have given the Soviet conscripts a reputation for alcoholism that is probably undeserved. Certainly a grim picture is painted by *émigrés* who describe the lengths that soldiers go to in their quest for alcohol, offering their equipment, motor-fuel or tyres on the black market in exchange for vodka or schnapps. It is highly likely that this evidence too is over-drawn since opportunities for such barter transactions only occur in the greater freedom of field exercises when, in some circumstances, close contact with the civil population is possible. These charges are well founded but notwithstanding the resultant rise in crime statistics there is little to suggest that they have much effect on the conduct of exercises. In garrison towns open to Western observers drunken soldiers are rarely, if ever, seen. This is not because the conscripts are motivated by any old-fashioned Rechabite principles but because they cannot afford to buy vodka out of their almost non-existent pay, because strict barrack-gate controls prevent them having much to barter with local citizens and because the towns are heavily patrolled by military police. The Soviet serviceman is under compulsion to remain sober and, although it is not doubted that alcohol causes frequent and serious breaches of discipline, he must be wryly amused at the great weight of anti-alcohol propaganda exhorting him to abstinence. The very weight of this propaganda demands that the problem be not lightly dismissed but it is almost surely the case that lack of alcohol is itself depressing to his morale rather than the universal state of chronic alcoholism often, and erroneously, depicted.

The same cannot quite be said for officers. Myagkov,[27] Belyenko[28] and others have reported a heavy dependence on alcohol among officers of all ranks, alleging that this seriously saps efficiency. Drunken officers are frequently seen in Soviet towns, relaxing on trains or in aircraft, often in a state of stupor. But again this is not necessarily alcoholism and unlikely to have a very marked effect on efficiency Service-wide. Drunkenness in both officers and other ranks is well contained by a strict disciplinary code which imposes draconian penalties for desertion, absence and unfitness for duty, the types of crime typically caused by drink. Comparative studies on alcoholism in the armed services and civilian sectors have not been published, even if they have ever been undertaken, but it would be expected that the civilian record would be several shades darker than the military.

Corruption is probably a more powerful threat to discipline and efficiency than vodka. Soviet society is oiled by corruption. Without it the economy, creaking though it may be, would not function at all. It is for this reason unlikely that Gorbachev's current anti-corruption drive will succeed. Nor is expected that he will push it too hard. The need for patronage and bribery are understood by all Soviet citizens; favouritism and nepotism have no pejorative connotations. The recruit is not surprised to find that the Armed Forces are similarly lubricated. *Per se*, corruption is not therefore seen as a threat to morale. As noted above he will on his first day of service become a victim of persecution by his NCOs and the 'old-hand' conscripts from last year's crop. His newly-issued uniform will be forcibly exchanged for an old one, he will be obliged to perform degrading tasks and to endure the arbitrary punishments imposed by his persecutors along the lines of those suffered by Aleksandr P. above. He will soon discover that an easier life can be bought, that by handing over his miserable pittance of pay to an NCO he will be granted a measure of immunity and that likewise, cleaning an 'old-hand's' boots might spare him some penalty later. The demands of the extortioners are not satisfied for long however and the immunity to persecution soon lapses unless more money is forthcoming or more boots are cleaned.

There is ample evidence that these practices are widespread. Recruits who receive money from their parents pass through the ordeal of their first year of service without great strain, the less fortunate adapt if they are naturally resilient – the great majority –

or, if made of more delicate clay, they go to the wall, driven to desertion or even suicide.

Not only the non-commissioned ranks suffer from corruption. Officers also are not above it. Once again the endemic presence of corruption in society makes it less a matter of concern to Soviet officers than it would be to the morals and conscience of Western counterparts. Place-seeking and favour-currying are common to both systems along with preference and nepotism but there would seem to be an uglier face to corruption on the Soviet side. Suvorov[29] sketches the type of domestic privileges acquired by officers, especially the more senior ones, over and above the sizeable 'perks' of the job. Wives are not it seems above selling on the black market goods bought in the special shops to which they have access, not in any small way but in big-business volume. Officers themselves sell awards, recommendations and assignments for actual cash or other considerations. Corruption at all levels of rank has been quietly practised through the years without much discernible damage to morale except perhaps to the more idealistic of communist souls but since the late General Secretary Andropov spoke out on the subject of corruption at the 1983 Plenum of the Central Committee of the CPSU, about the need to protect public property and prevent the abuse of office for personal gain, there has been a deal of media exposure of common malpractice.

The military sphere has not been allowed to go unscourged. *Red Star* of 14 June 1983 tells the cautionary tale of General Turkin and his inspection of an army unit in the Siberian Military District. The commanding officer went to extraordinary and illegal lengths to arrange sumptuous hospitality for the general, amongst other preparations he sent one of his sergeants home to his native Armenia to procure a supply of the finest Armenian brandy. On his arrival at the unit the general was soon asking for more, rare books for instance which could not be obtained in Moscow and, with even greater avarice, an imported Japanese tape recorder. It is not recorded how, but the commanding officer managed to find these precious items and the general went away satisfied, presumably having awarded the coveted grading of 'excellent' to the unit. Paying for these solicited gifts was not nearly so easy as obtaining them and it seems that the funds had to be 'borrowed' from the money the unit had received for 'seasonal labour', in other words for work on the harvest or other civilian sector projects. Somehow during the accountancy the story came out. The general was as a result dismissed from the Army and the Party. Commensurate justice was meted out to the commanding officer and the affair was closed. *Red Star* concluded with a homily reminding readers that a thin, invisible line separates right from wrong in such matters but to those who hold to high moral standards the line is as obvious as the frontier between two states and as unbending as a granite wall.

Red Star has published several similar stories in recent months, with variations which imply that the writers are exposing the tip of an iceberg. It can be safely inferred from this that our General Turkin and the commanding officer were only acting in accordance with established custom and that such relationships of bribery and blackmail are quite normal between the inspectors and the inspected. Turkin and his subordinate were just unfortunate in getting caught. Soviet officers will readily own up to corruption among their ranks, but claim nevertheless that it is very small in scale compared with the civil sectors of society.

With such reportage, *Red Star* is crusading against corruption at all rank levels. It sees the elimination of all moral deficiencies, crime and corruption, as the prime task of the Communist Party, in particular of its cells within all military formations and units. The crusade did not die with Andropov although the earlier fury has abated.

DISCIPLINE AND THE PARTY

Fighting crime and corruption is nominally the duty of all Soviet officers but they are greatly aided in the task by the *Zampolit* preaching communist morality and by the KGB officer who is able to coerce when persuasion fails. It seems however that line officers are generally content to leave the enforcement of regulations to political officers, a practice inimical to good discipline and unit morale. A third influence is the Party itself which, through the medium of cells established at unit level throughout the Armed Forces, closely monitors the performance of the collective unit and the conduct of its individual members from the commanding officer downwards. These cells have a positive function in the maintenance of discipline since they represent the discipline and legitimacy of the communist state and all ranks, commissioned and non-commissioned, are the subjects of their control. Their work is directed by the *Zampolit* and covers all unit concerns from the teaching of Marxist–Leninism to simple welfare cases.

For an understanding of Soviet military discipline the concept of its nature as a part of state discipline is central. Snezhko provides a Soviet expression of this concept:

> Military discipline is a component part of state discipline and every instance of lack of personal discipline is viewed by us not only as a violation of the law and the regulations but also as a deviation from the standards of communist morality, as an act that is incompatible with the honour and dignity of the Soviet fighting man and citizen.[30]

Soviet military discipline is thus seen as a rigorous self-discipline, every infringement treated as a personal lapse of Marxist–Leninist morality which cannot under any circumstances be condoned but must be punished according to the law and the regulations. The law is reflected in the oath taken ceremonially by recruits at the end of their initial training (see page 38 for text).

This oath leaves the young soldier in no doubt about his duty and what happens should he fail to do it. It expresses clearly the nature of Soviet military discipline, a discipline based on fear, with the promise of certain punishment if the code is broken. In practice punishment is not awarded as automatically as the oath and the regulations imply but the fear that official action will reflect adversely on the commanding officer and his *Zampolit* is known to be a major cause of informal, often violent, punishment. On the other hand there is reliable evidence that counselling of offenders is common, usually by the *Zampolit* rather than the offender's immediate military superior, or by their colleagues during meetings of the Party cell. Open confessions here and the subsequent 'self-criticism' sessions are probably greater torment than the statutory punishment and a powerful deterrent to further lapses. In any case, as Goldhammer[31] observes, there is no correlation between morale and discipline because the close and constant supervision of troops restricts opportunities for real crime (cf. drinking) but at the same time does not prevent the adverse effect on morale of other factors. Probably the most depressing of these are the arbitrary and mindless punishments meted out by seniors, as described by Suvorov and others, mostly without legal authority and for acts which could not be construed as crimes even according to the all-embracing terms of the Soviet oath.

On the other hand, it could be argued that an extraordinary current emphasis on discipline is an indicator of morale and that recent revisions to regulations and the tone of articles on discipline in the Soviet military press indicate that the state of morale throughout the Soviet Armed Forces is at a very low point. In the past the remedy for all shortcomings in discipline or operational efficiency has been a call for more intensified ideological training. Under this system of state discipline breaches are seen as personal failures which in older religions would have been called sins. They are the responsibility of the individual sinner but, to an extent, also of the pastor, the *Zampolit* in the Soviet case. And more ideological learning and teaching is the *via dolorosa* to redemption. Or so it exclusively was until the mid-1970s.

Now despite a continued emphasis on the paramount importance of ideology it seems that a more secular view is being taken, encouraging a practical, human approach from superiors towards subordinates with an appeal for officers to show concern for the welfare of soldiers and greater sympathy for their problems. At the same time it is also evident from the writings that attempts are being made to enhance the independent authority of commanders and supervisors, to give them the greater flexibility required in combat situations. They are exhorted to look constantly for methods for improving the control of their unit or ship but not, it would seem, at the expense of discipline, in the maintenance of which they must still display 'an exacting attitude with adherence to principle and an uncompromising attitude towards infractions'.[32] It is clear from such texts that junior officers do not really understand this, an approach foreign to all their past experience and training.

As for the latest revisions to the regulations themselves, most of which pre-date the invasion of Afghanistan, there is a marked emphasis on security especially the security of firearms weapons stores. Stricter regulations concerning guard-mounting have also been introduced. Taken together it is these new security measures that give credibility to *émigré* reports that violence and desertion are prevalent crimes. Belyenko[33] supplies an illustrative account of such incidents:

> Conditions at Chuguyevka were not typical of those throughout the Far East. Reports of desertions, disease and rampant alcoholism were said to be flooding into Moscow from bases all over. In late June, Shevsov convened the officers in an absolutely secret meeting to convey grave news. At an Army base only thirty-five miles to the southwest, two soldiers had killed two other soldiers and an officer, confiscated machine-guns, taken provisions and struck out through the forest toward the coast intending to steal a boat and sail to Japan. They dodged and fought pursuing patrols for several days until they were killed. On their bodies were found diaries containing vile slanders [sic] of the Soviet Army and the gravest misrepresentations of the life of a soldier. These diaries atop all the reports of trouble had caused such concern in Moscow that the Minister of Defence himself was coming to the Far East and to Chuguyevka.

This report if true – there is no reason to suppose that it is not – encapsulates most of the besetting problems of morale in the Soviet Armed Forces. Drink, theft and desertion, in spite of the near certainty of recapture, all arising because of depressing living conditions or ethnic tensions. This juncture, with uncertainties having been raised by so many authorities, is where the reader might welcome background sketches of Soviet servicemen themselves in the context of the particular branches in which they serve.

Part II
The Three Services

4 The Soviet Soldier

C. N. DONNELLY

Twice a year, in spring and autumn, announcements in the Soviet military press instruct every young Soviet male in his eighteenth year to register his liability for conscript service in the Military Commissariat in his local town. The Military Commissariats (*Voyenkomat* in Russian) are the local organs of administration within the military district. Theirs is the task in the Soviet military system of administering the conscription process, recalling reservists for post-service training, supervising examinations for candidates for officer schools, and administering the military pensions and housing schemes for the retired, disabled or widowed. In time of war they administer the mobilisation process.

THE CONSCRIPTION PROCESS

Every six months, Soviet military and naval units make an estimate of their manpower requirements for the following year. The unit staff compile a list detailing the number of conscripts that they will need to replace those whose term of service is to expire, and the required educational level and specialist training skills that they would like. The list is submitted to their Military District headquarters or, in the case of units serving outside the Soviet Union, to the Soviet Military District which has been appointed to supply them with conscripts. It is the duty of the Military Commissariats to assemble details on those individuals who are liable for conscription during the following year, basing their information on school, KOMSOMOL and DOSAAF reports. They identify the conscript's nationality or ethnic group, the best academic performers, the best sportsmen, those who are good Russian speakers and those who are not, those with any

103

special technical competence and, of course, the individual's level of ideological reliability. It is then the task to the Military Commissariat system to allocate future conscripts for drafting into units which require people with their particular qualifications. The most important consideration is always that of security. The most ideologically committed go to the MVD and KGB units. High calibre men with a good level of education and ideological soundness go to the Strategic Rocket Forces, the fittest and the most daring may well be chosen for the Airborne Forces. The army conscript will usually be sent to serve far away from his own home area, and it is very rare for conscripts of German or Jewish origin to be sent to serve in Eastern Europe. Those who profess a religious belief or those whose political reliability is suspect, and also many of those whose little or no knowledge of the Russian language, quite often get sent to serve in the Construction Troops. The Tank Troops have traditionally been sent conscripts of less than average height, which in the current decade means quite a high percentage of non-European Soviet citizens.

Having registered for conscription, the young Soviet citizen will be given a date and time to report to a collection point from where he will be despatched to a military district basic training centre. At this centre he will be outfitted and taught basic military drill and, at the end of a very short training course, will swear the military oath as part of an impressive ceremony. One in six of the conscripts, normally the best educated and those who show the greatest competence and interest in military affairs, will be sent for their first six months service to a special NCO training unit where they will be taught the basic drills which it will be their responsibility to instruct and supervise. From here they will graduate, either as sergeants or junior sergeants, many still only eighteen-years-old, and will be sent to combat units to serve a further eighteen months. Those who go to, say, a motor rifle regiment will get positions as section or platoon sergeants or in some administrative or minor technical function. Conscripts not selected for NCO training are sent straight to their appointed unit for the whole of their two years' service. There are no regimental training depots such as exist in the British Army, nor are there special arms training schools, and the regimental system as the British Army knows it simply does not exist in the Soviet Army. There are no units consisting uniquely of one nationality nor are there units recruited on a territorial basis: all units will contain a mixture of different nationalities. The mixture of nationalities will not however be random, because of the system by which units bid for conscripts to certain specific military districts and because of the limitations of the conscript system. The national mixture will therefore be limited. The bulk of the sub-unit will normally be about two-thirds Slav, mainly Russian, and the remaining one-third will usually come from about two or three different ethnic groupings. The more *élite* a unit is, the more this will be the case, so that whilst a company of the Airborne Forces may include only two or three non-Slav nationalities, a company of Construction Troops or Rear Service Troops may have twelve or thirteen different nationalities in a single platoon. Sapper and Rear Service sub-units are sometimes formed almost entirely of Asiatic nationalities and conscripts with a very limited knowledge of Russian, but in these sub-units great care is always taken to avoid a preponderence of any one non-Russian nationality. The only official language of command is Russian, and it is estimated that some 30 per cent of conscripts to the army speak insufficient Russian for all but the most basic purposes on conscription. About a third of those can be expected to have little or no Russian at all. However, during their military career they will be expected to learn at least the words of command. It must be borne in mind that the Soviet military system is specifically tailored to take account of this linguistic problem. Furthermore, the Soviet Army today is, and the Russian Army of the nineteenth century was, one of the main ways for the central authority to promote the russification of non-Russian young men. One of the interesting developments of recent years is the extent to which growing great Russian chauvinism has increased the alienation existing between Slav and non-Slav conscripts in the Soviet Army. However it must not be thought that nationality alone is a bar to promotion and advancement. Those non-Russians whose command of Russian is good, and who strive to adopt Russian manners and customs (in other words those who generally accept and welcome russification) will find their nationality no bar to promotion.

The conscription system is centrally controlled and operates in the following manner: the General Staff will instruct, say, Odessa to provide a thousand soldiers for the Central Group of Forces, having a variety of specialisations. If the Military Commissariat organisation in Odessa finds that there is a shortfall and it cannot fulfil this norm, it will report this fact back. In the Belorussian

Military District, meanwhile, the Military Commissariat in Minsk, may have reported that it has on its books more conscripts than it has been asked for, in which case it will be directed to fill the shortfall to the Central Group of Forces.

Each combat unit in the Soviet Army is therefore at the same time a training unit, comprising on average 75–80 per cent conscripts, 5 per cent regular NCOs and in between 15–20 per cent regular officers. In *élite* units of, say, the Strategic Rocket Forces the percentage of conscripts would be somewhat lower, in less *élite* units such as the Conscription Troops it may well be higher. The standard of readiness of army units and formations varies. Units are maintained either at or near full strength, at or around half strength, and at 25–30 per cent strength or less. These last are called cadre formations. The half strength or cadre formations will be reinforced in times of crisis or war to bring them up to approximately full strength. In this instance rapid reinforcement will draw on reservists from the local military district and may well contain a much higher proportion of ethnic nationalities than is generally considered desirable, or than would be the case in a unit maintained at full strength in peacetime. It is for this reason, for example, that cadre units mobilised from 25 per cent strength or less to almost full strength for the invasion of Afghanistan in 1979 contained quite a high percentage of non-Slav Asiatic nationalities from Islamic areas of the South central USSR. That this policy represents a potential vulnerability is recognised. The experience of 1941, when many non-Russian nationalities in the Western USSR demonstrated their contempt for the Russian Communist *régime* by welcoming the invading German forces, has made the Soviet General Staff very sensitive indeed to nationalities problems within the Soviet Armed Forces. However at the same time it is possible to exaggerate this vulnerability and construe it as a weakness. It will only be a weakness if the potential enemy has the will and the means to exploit this vulnerability, and if the Soviet Army finds itself losing rather than winning the battles in which it engages.

Because of the conscription cycle, the conscript's two-year term of service in the Soviet Army breaks down naturally into four six-month periods. By all available accounts, the first six-month period is an extremely unpleasant one. The conscript undergoes very hard physical training, he is deprived all creature comforts and is very often subject to vicious bullying by his seniors.

Although this is clearly not a pleasant time by any standards, it is possible, here again, to mis-assess the affects of this very difficult first term. A harsh and even degrading first six months of national service was very typical of most Western conscript armies during the 1950s and, except on extreme occasions, this harshness did not lead to a drop in morale when the unit went into action. However, living standards and social conditions have risen in the Soviet Union over the last 20 years just as they have in Western Europe, and there can be no doubt that the harsh treatment which the Soviet conscript receives today is more resented than it was, and is not conducive to the conscript learning his military duties. The realisation by the Soviet High Command that this excessively rough treatment was proving counter-productive (because it destroyed the conscripts' enthusiasm and will to learn), resulted in the late 1970s in the introduction of measures to improve the conscripts' living standards, to reduce bullying, and generally to relax the very harsh disciplinary code. However, it remains true that, compared to his Western counterparts, the Soviet conscript soldier has a very rough time indeed.

During the first six months of his conscript period, the Soviet soldier will be taught basic military skills and will be allotted a task within his section. In a Soviet motor rifle or tank division at full strength there are between 10 000 and 12 000 men but also over 3000 vehicles. In other words, one conscript in every three or four has to be taught to drive. This is the biggest problem that the basic training system has to overcome and consequently, during the last few years, formation and garrison areas have established central driver training schools for greater efficiency in teaching conscripts to drive armoured or soft skin vehicles. During his first year a conscript is expected to master a special skill and also nowadays a related skill. In other words, he is expected to acquire at least some ability to perform the functions of another member of his team, be it of an engineer bridging crew or a self-propelled gun crew. During his last six months of training, the Soviet conscript is expected to pass on his skills to a junior conscript who will replace him within the sub-unit.

The life of the Soviet soldier like that of the Soviet citizen, is hedged around by restrictions. During his conscript service he is not allowed to wear civilian clothes at all, even when on leave. Those conscripts serving in foreign countries, such as in the Group of Soviet Forces Germany, are not allowed out of barracks unescorted. As an exception to this latter rule, those conscripts who at the end of their first twelve months of service volunteer for extended service, or those who are promoted or who have achieved junior NCO rank, are allowed the privilege of leaving barracks, although leave passes are very scarce. The conscript is indeed entitled to little or even no leave at all during his two years' national service, and will receive during his two-year term of service the equivalent in roubles to only about £7 per month pocket money.

The British soldier today would be appalled at the quantity and standard of food that the Soviet soldier is expected to live on. But the British national serviceman of thirty years ago would not be so surprised, except perhaps by the lack of variety and by the style of some of the dishes. Just like the Soviet convict, the Soviet conscript has his head shaven on induction into the army and expects, or at least hopes, to have his food rations supplemented by parcels from home.

Above all it must always be borne in mind that the conscript today in the Soviet Army has on the whole an easier time than he did in the past although it may not appear so to him because of the greater gap existing today between civilian living standards and conscript living standards. However the harsh lot of a Russian conscript is a tradition which goes back to the time of the Tsars and it is a tradition which only the conscripts themselves, with the possible addition of their mothers, would actually like to see altered. A sentiment oft expressed by the elderly or middle-aged Russian that 'it will do the young man good' is not a sentiment which is unique to the Russians. It is also worth bearing in mind General Suvorov's famous resume of his philosophy for training the eighteenth-century Russian Army, 'Hard in training easy in battle.'

As well as restrictions on what the Soviet soldier is allowed to do, there are also considerable restrictions on what he is expected to be able to do on the battlefield. He is expected to be obedient and hardy, and he is exhorted to be brave. He is also expected either to learn basic tactical drills or to operate a piece of machinery, but apart from that not a great many military demands are made of him. His prime function is to operate as a cog in a machine, to fulfil movements which he has learnt by rote and by drill. The average Soviet soldier, as opposed to those belonging to special formations, are not expected to acquire the degree of fieldcraft, of expertise in patrolling skills and the like, which the British infantryman expects to have to learn. The qualities of bravery, of obedience and of toughness are important qualities in any soldier, and it can be said without fear of contradiction that Soviet soldiers in the past have demonstrated all these qualities in good measure. However Soviet generals do recognise that the demands of the future battlefield may pose too many demands on the soldier and that, under stress, he may find it difficult or impossible to fulfil his military duties. This is particularly true if these duties include the operation of complex technical equipment or if the command and control or disciplinary structure, on which he so much depends, breaks down.

The Soviet soldier is no more and no less intelligent than the British soldier, but because of the limitations of the conscript system, because of the nationalities problem (and the associated linguistic problems) and also because of the thrift imposed upon the Soviet Army, the demands made on the Soviet soldier are not the same as those made on the British soldier either in barracks or on the battlefield, and this is especially true in the case of the NCO and junior officer. The soldier fills a different role in the structure of the military system as a whole and, therefore, his performance must be judged not in comparison to what a British regular soldier might be expected to achieve, but in terms purely of his ability to fulfil what will be demanded of him on the battlefield. The Soviet military system requires the conscript to perform simple battlefield tasks which have been learnt by constantly repeated drill, but to be able to perform them in any battlefield conditions. It is Soviet experience that reasoned thought is the first victim of battlefield stress and the Soviet military system does not therefore expect initiative or imaginative and constructive actions from its soldiers: it only expects reaction and drill movement. The very concept of initiative (in as much as it is ever asked of NCOs and junior officers) is taken to be no more than the initiation of the correct drill appropriate to the given circumstances.

Once he has completed his initial basic training the Soviet soldier is tested regularly on all the skills which he is expected to acquire. In training and on exercise, every action which the soldier or NCO and officer does is measured against an average standard or norm. The ability of each soldier and officer to fulfil this personal norm is measured regularly by his superiors. In turn the activities of each sub-unit and unit are also measured as a whole against a standard, and the ability of a unit or sub-unit to fulfil its norm is used as a means of assessing commanders for promotion. For as the responsibility for all training falls upon the commander, he will shoulder the blame or take the praise for the ability or lack of ability of his men. The conscript NCOs in the Soviet system are only assistants to the officers; junior drill managers. Of the same age as the conscripts who are subordinate to them, they are not the competent and experienced men which young officers in the British Army expect to have as their platoon sergeants, to rely on and to learn from when taking command of their platoon for the first time.

As the training tests are done against a standard or norm, at the end of each month the progress of the soldier's training can be assessed with reasonable accuracy. When sub-unit training is commenced, sub-units are tested as a group, and their ability to fulfil group tasks is thus assessed by senior staff officers. Competition is engendered between individuals within sub-units and between sub-units within a unit, as the best means of creating some enthusiasm for training. The best soldiers are rewarded by prizes, by the posting of their photograph on the unit board of honour, by the reporting of their achievement in their local paper back home or, occasionally, by financial awards and extra leave passes. Poor performers on the other hand are subjected to organised harassment by their comrades, under pressure from the unit political staff. Whilst these methods may not appeal to the British mentality they have proved quite effective in the Soviet Army as means of achieving what is quite a reasonable degree of efficiency for a mass conscript army. There is a regular inspecting organisation within the Soviet Army which by spot checks attempts to ensure honesty in the assessing of norms and the marking of examinations. Whatever its limitations, this regular system of inspection coupled with the running of the army on a fairly rigid training cycle, does mean that the commanding general of any formation will know at any moment what the level of training within his command is. Moreover, the scale of assessment he uses will be objective and measureable.

In every Soviet unit and sub-unit a daily training programme is established. This must be approved by the unit commander and implemented by the sub-unit commanders and their assistants. It is a rigid timetable which leaves very little freetime to the conscript. A typical daily training is as follows.

Soviet Army Daily Training Programme

1. Reveille	0600–0605	5 mins
2. Exercise & Accommodation Cleaning	0610–0630	20 mins
3. Washing and Bed-Making	0630–0650	20 mins
4. Political Interpretation of Latest News and Inspection	0650–0720	30 mins
5. Breakfast	0725–0755	30 mins
6. Six Training Periods of 50 mins each	0800–1350	5 hrs
7. Dinner	1400–1440	40 mins
8. Rest Period	1440–1510	30 mins
9. Cleaning Own Weapon and Kit	1510–1530	20 mins
(a) Political Education (Mon. and Thur.)		
(b) Equipment Maintenance (Tue. and Fri.)	1530–1830	3 hrs
(c) Group Sport		
10. Individual Tuition	1830–1940	1 hr 10 mins
11. Supper	1940–2010	30 mins
12. Free Time	2010–2140	1 hr 30 mins
13. Evening Exercise	2140–2155	15 mins
14. Lights Out	2200	

During the training year the scale of training builds up from individual training, through sub-unit (platoon, company and battalion) training ultimately to unit training, sometimes with an annual unit exercise. The training cycle may be interrupted by or may culminate in a large formation exercise. A great deal of basic training these days is done on training machines and simulators, for several reasons. These save time (in getting to and from training areas), they save money (in terms of track mileage and ammunition), and they permit a higher level of training on technical equipment to be achieved. These training machines vary from very primitive simulators to complex electronic equipment. When the trainee has mastered his skill on the simulator he will be allowed only a very limited time of hands-on experience on the weapon he is to serve. Many units and sub-units particularly in areas such as East Germany do very little training on their own equipment. A tank unit for example, will keep its tanks extremely well maintained and run on a regular basis, however for sub-unit and unit training the personnel of the unit are likely to be bussed to a local training area, where they will train on tanks or other AFVs specially kept for training purposes. This allows for great economy in training and as tank crews usually serve together for the whole of their conscript training period quite a high degree of efficiency can be achieved.

It is true that, taken as an individual, the Soviet soldier is not as versatile as his British counterpart. This does not necessarily mean, however, that he is therefore a poorer soldier, because the system to which he belongs does not require versatility or initiative of him. Indeed in many respects these qualities would be considered counter-productive when displayed on the battlefield by a conscript soldier. The Soviet soldier is well drilled and has proved extremely resourceful and well able to look after himself in all conditions. Concern is being expressed, however, in the Soviet Army, because the face of battle is changing; the increasing speed and dynamism of the battlefield and the increasing mechanisation of armies serve to increase the relative importance of technology. The ability of an enemy to inflict a large number of casualties in a very short space of time threatens the viability of the system if the casualties cannot be replaced. Sudden and rapid tactical changes may on the future battlefield make initiative and versatility more desirable than was the case in the Soviet Army in the 1941–45 war. Reconciling the possible demands of a future battle with the traditional Soviet system is a problem with which the Soviet Army is at present trying to cope.

Soviet military equipment has always been simple and robust but, while simplicity is still a characteristic attribute of Soviet military equipment, it is getting more complex. If the stresses and strains on the individual soldier and on the system are intensified by the use of chemical and nuclear weapons on the future battlefield, then the problems encountered will be immeasureably greater. To these military problems are added the traditional social problems which affect the Soviet Union, such as drunkenness. It may well be that the consumption of alcohol in the Soviet Army is not significantly increasing. It can also be argued that, as was often demonstrated in World Wars I and II, an inebriated machine gunner is not only still a good machine gunner but may be an even better machine gunner than one stone cold sober. However, it is equally undeniable that on the future battlefield, if the same drunken soldier has to operate an anti-aircraft missile his performance will not be similarly

1 Briefing for missile troops

2   Siberian Military District: motorised-rifle officers

3 Tank troops: Carpathian Military District

4　Border guards

5 Motor-rifle troops attack: Carpathian Military District

6 Airborne troops: military parade, Red Square

7 Political instructio– class, Soviet Navy

8   Summer combat training: Siberian Military District

9   Higher Military Academy: Terrain surveillance exercise

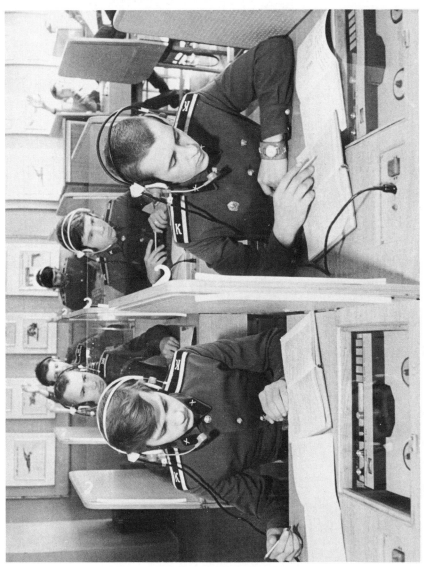

10 Higher Military Institute: language tuition

11 Field training: Siberian Military District

12 Baltic Military District: Sergeant Povaren, anti-aircraft squad

13 Winter training: Siberia

14 Odessa Military District: practice alert

15 Fighter bomber pilots

unaffected. In other words, it is not just alcohol abuse *per se* which is a growing problem for the Soviet Army, rather it is the growing vulnerability of the military system to drunkenness which is so important.

An important element that must never be omitted when assessing the abilities of the Soviet soldier is the traditional Russian attitude to discipline. This is itself a product of the Russian environment and of Russian history. Nine hundred years of almost unbroken rule by dictatorship has left its mark. The Russian has come to accept force as a valid method of rule. More than that he has come to expect it and to respect it, and to respect a ruler who rules by force. This is not to say that a Russian likes to be subjected to a strict rule, simply that he accepts and responds to it more positively than would his Western counterpart. This attitude is nowhere more evident than in the military disciplinary system. In wartime Soviet military discipline is draconian. Execution of a soldier is considered a matter of company punishment. Between 1941–45 upwards of 230 general officers or admirals were executed or were reduced to the ranks in penal battalions for breaches of discipline, failure to carry out orders, incompetence and the like.

On the one hand, this rigid discipline has enabled the Soviet Army to force through an attack or to maintain the structure of a defensive position, despite horrendous casualties, because it has overcome fear amongst the soldiers by an even greater fear of execution at the hands of their own superiors. As such, it has traditionally enabled the Soviet Army to compensate for a great many minor tactical deficiencies. However at the same time, this concept of culpability is the prime reason why senior officers or commanders at any level are loathe to allow initiative to juniors and insist on a rigid adherence to orders. This in turn tends to create stereotype and prevent the development of any low level flexibility, however much the new textbooks might call for this. If future concepts of operations and tactical developments in the Soviet Army do come to demand a significant degree of initiative, the overcoming of this traditional attitude to authority will be one of the greatest problems the Soviet General Staff will have to face if they are to achieve their goal.

THE JUNIOR NCO

Most Soviet NCOs are conscripts – junior sergeants, sergeants or senior sergeants – who have been selected on conscripton and sent for the first six months of their two-year national service to a NCO training unit. From here they take up sub-unit appointments for the remaining eighteen months. As they are, therefore, in the main only eighteen or nineteen years of age, they have no advantage of age or experience over their conscript colleagues. Consequently, the status of sergeant in the Soviet Army is not as high as it is in the British Army. Furthermore, because the sergeant carries no natural authority he has been invested with authority artificially, and his position is therefore somewhat difficult – rather like that of a corporal or lance corporal national serviceman in the British Army of the 1950s. He cannot in terms of ability or responsibility be in any way equated to a British regular NCO of today. He is above all a junior drill manager and an instructor of basic training rather than a junior leader. In a long war, of course, qualities of leadership would emerge irrespective of lack of differential in age. However the Soviet military clearly prefer that if a war in Europe is to be fought at all, it should be finished quickly. Consequently, they can afford to place no reliance on the development of such qualities in so short a time.

During his eighteen-months regimental service an enthusiastic and effective NCO can expect to rise from junior sergeant, through sergeant to senior sergeant. In barracks his task would be to supervise the practising of the basic training drills or of the section platoon drills and to supervise the overall conduct of the men. On the field of battle his task is to direct the sub-unit drills on the orders of his commander. The Soviet conscript NCO cannot be expected to relieve the junior officer who commands the platoon or company of the tedium of running the sub-unit or instructing in basic training in the way that NCOs do for the junior officer in a British Army unit.

Whatever the theory and whatever the limitations of ability, personality or time, experience has demonstrated to the Soviet Army that the platoon and section sergeants play a most important role in welding together the men under their control as an efficient fighting team, so that in the stress of battle they will fight on out of loyalty to each other as well as out of loyalty to the motherland. Whilst group loyalties and factions are feared by the

Soviet system and are suppressed, and only loyalty to the Party and to the motherland is officially condoned, Soviet military sociological research does recognise that small team loyalty is the strongest motivator at the lowest level on the battlefield. Consequently it is encouraged under the title of comradeship. However it is not easy to reconcile this with the system of informers, the organised harassment of defaulters, and the regular political instruction. It is an inherent contradiction in the Soviet system which might well fail in the stress of battle.

A simple conscript who during his two years service proves to be particularly competent may be promoted to lance corporal (*yefreitor*). As such he can be given duties equating to those of a section commander, such as being put in charge of a tank or vehicle. When he has completed the first year of his training, the conscript soldier or NCO can if he wishes apply for regular NCO service or apply to take the examination for entry into an officer training college. If he passes the examination for entry into an officer training college he will leave his conscript service to join the college at the beginning of the next academic year. If accepted for regular NCO service he must complete his two years' conscript service before this commences, but during his second year as a conscript he will begin to receive privileges for the remainder of that year. As a regular sergeant his status will be only slightly higher than that of a conscript sergeant, but his pay and allowances will increase dramatically from what was merely pocket money for the conscript, to a sum approaching the national average wage plus thirty days leave a year for the extended serviceman. He will ultimately become eligible for married quarters and will be allowed to use military shops. These are subsidised and very often better stocked than civilian shops.

Service, as a regular in the army remains one of the few ways in which a young man from the countryside can acquire both an internal passport, the right to work in a town, and a marketable skill. As a consequence, a high proportion of those applying for regular NCO service come from rural backgrounds. This means that they often lack the sophisticated and technical education that the modern Soviet Army would like to see in their junior NCO, and which a city dweller is more likely to have acquired. Complex military equipment in the British Army is both maintained and operated by regular NCOs, and the officer's task is mainly that of a manager and an organiser of resources. Because of the lack of experience and of technical qualifications of Soviet NCOs this is not possible, and the NCO is at best an operator of simplified weapons systems. In the Soviet Army complex equipment is maintained and repaired by officers. However, the ability of the Soviet conscript NCO must not be underestimated. Because his training concentrates on teaching him one or two specific skills, not only can those skills be broadly based but, by applying natural resourcefulness and persistence, the Soviet conscript or NCO can achieve a commendable level of skill in performing his specific function. For example, the driver of a vehicle – be it a tank or truck – will be expected to know not only how to drive the vehicle but also how to do the basic maintenance and servicing of the vehicle. If the vehicle breaks down he will be expected to try and repair it to the limit of his ability, and experience shows that he will indeed do so. He might therefore be more capable than a British corporal in keeping his vehicle moving under similar circumstances, particularly in view of the greater simplicity of many Soviet pieces of equipment. On the other hand, whereas a British corporal in the REME might be a competent electronic engineer, the Soviet junior sergeant in charge of a tank will be forbidden on pain of severe punishment to touch the electronic equipment in that tank; that task is reserved for the specialist technical officer within the unit.

ENSIGNS – THE SENIOR NCO

For several reasons, the officer's career became ever less popular in the Soviet Union during the 1970s and consequently the Soviet Army began to suffer a shortage of trained officers. One reason was that standards of living in Soviet civilian society had risen considerably during the 1960s, so that the young officer was no longer in a privileged position in relation to his civilian counterpart. Furthermore, while senior officers enjoy high prestige and a great many perks in their job, junior officers work hard with very long hours and very little free time, because the responsibility for basic training and technical repair all falls upon the sub-unit officer's shoulders. This was one of the reasons for the creation in 1972 of the rank of *praporshchik*, usually translated as ensign. The ensign rank (or *michman* as an ensign is known in the Navy) was an attempt by the Soviet Army to recreate a regular

NCO class with the same status and capable of filling the same role in the military machine as the British senior NCO.

The ensign rank is not so much at the top of the NCO ladder but rather a separate rank bridging the gap between NCO and regular officer. The term is sometimes translated as warrant officer particularly in US translations, but an ensign who may be in his early twenties, having completed a short course after his national service, will not equate in status to the British warrant officer. Rather he will be similar to the warrant officer in the US Army – very often a technically qualified person, who also occasionally commands platoons in cadre units. Junior NCOs who are sufficiently well qualified in academic or technical subjects, or who are sufficiently intelligent and well motivated to obtain qualifications through the army education system, can apply for extended regular service as an ensign. They enrol for terms of five years and those best qualified and experienced can ultimately become senior ensigns. Ensigns have uniforms cut on the officers' pattern, district rank badges and a much improved status over the NCO, with leave and allowances equating to those of an officer rather than those of a regular NCO.

Ensigns perform two major tasks within the Soviet military system. Firstly, they act as *starshina*, or company sergeant majors, or as deputy commanders of sub-units and, particularly in sub-units belonging to half-strength or cadre formations, as platoon commanders. Secondly, ensigns fulfil posts as technical deputies, taking responsibility for basic maintenance of equipment within a battalion. They are also often found in headquarters doing administrative tasks. Considering that it has only been in existence for twelve years, a very short time in the history of any military system, the ensign rank has been comparatively successful in providing the Soviet Army with a reserve of reasonably competent and well motivated NCOs.

SOVIET ARMY OFFICERS

One of the most interesting trends in the Soviet Union over the last two decades has been the development in the Soviet Armed Forces of an officer corps which is not just an *élite* but is also proud of being a hereditary *élite*. Furthermore, the Soviet officer of today is increasingly being drawn from the 'upper strata of a one-class society'. The adjacent diagram shows the career patterns available to Soviet officers. There are at least 150 military institutes of higher education, equivalent to the British Sandhurst, Dartmouth and Cranwell Colleges and a further 23 military academies requiring a higher degree for entry, equivalent of the British Army, RAF and Naval Staff Colleges and the Royal College of Defence Studies. This compares with just over 800 Soviet civilian institutions of higher education, universities, polytechnics, teacher training colleges and the like, and 52 universities in the USSR offering postgraduate degrees. It can be seen therefore that a significant proportion of institutions of higher education in the USSR are military schools, colleges and academies. It is true, of course, that most major military educational establishments are a lot smaller than their civilian counterparts, averaging between 400–1200 students compared to the 2500–3000 in the average civilian college, but they do nevertheless receive a disproportionately high financial and material slice of the nation's educational cake.

It is not generally appreciated in the West that the USSR has a two-tier educational system. Those children who are especially gifted or who are fortunate enough to have parents in influential and well-placed jobs, will instead of attending a normal comprehensive secondary school, often apply for admission to a special school. These are state controlled, fee paying and often boarding schools which offer a much higher standard of education than a normal school, and often specialise in specific subjects. Entry, of course, is limited. The original special schools concept was to provide better training and education to those capable of benefiting from it, but this widespread system is fast becoming the preserve of the privileged *élite* in the USSR, and attendance at such a school is the best springboard for a career in the government, Party or the army. For the army the nine Suvorov Military Colleges fulfil the function of special schools with a military specialisation.

The Suvorov schools were originally established during World War II for the sons of men killed in action. They take young men between the age of thirteen to eighteen and give a high quality of education with a fair slice of military training. Officer cadets wear a uniform almost identical to that of pre-revolutionary Tsarist cadets. Nowadays entry is restricted mainly to the sons of officers or senior officials, and officers of field rank get allowances which

Officer Education

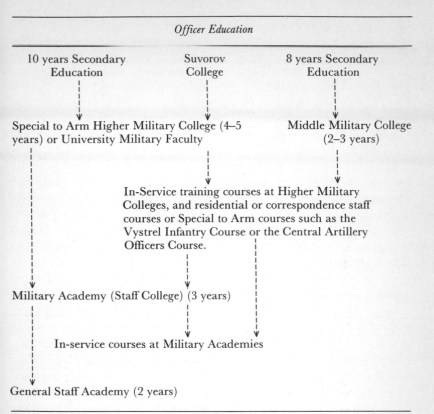

10 years Secondary Education → Special to Arm Higher Military College (4–5 years) or University Military Faculty

Suvorov College → Special to Arm Higher Military College (4–5 years) or University Military Faculty

8 years Secondary Education → Middle Military College (2–3 years)

In-Service training courses at Higher Military Colleges, and residential or correspondence staff courses or Special to Arm courses such as the Vystrel Infantry Course or the Central Artillery Officers Course.

Military Academy (Staff College) (3 years)

In-service courses at Military Academies

General Staff Academy (2 years)

help cover the cost of Suvorov or special schools boarding fees. Although these schools provide only about 5 per cent of officer candidates, they provide the best springboard for life as an officer. Graduates gain automatic admission to higher military colleges at the age of eighteen or nineteen.

There are two types of colleges which grant commissions in the Soviet Army, these are the middle and the higher colleges. The former takes students straight from school at the age of seventeen to eighteen, for two- or three-year courses. The latter accepts students at eighteen or nineteen years of age, from school, from Suvorov schools, from middle military colleges or institutes of higher education, and commission them after four or five years of training. Those completing the higher military colleges graduate with the equivalent of a university degree. Each year the pages of *Red Star*, the Soviet Army's daily paper, are filled with advertisments for the military colleges. Entry to these colleges is by competitive written and oral examination which the prospective candidates sit in their local Military Commissariats. In the Soviet system there is no objective test of leadership potential, such as the British Army's Regular Commissions Board, and standards vary enormously on entry, both between the colleges and the intakes. The long period of training, however, allows the misfits to be weeded out and allows officer cadets time to mature and develop their qualities.

Colleges are either all-arms colleges (sometimes translated as 'combined-arms') which, like Sandhurst, give basic infantry training, or alternatively they are special-to-arm, such as aviation, artillery, tank, naval, signals, the MVD and the KGB. The most prestigious and exclusive of the colleges are entitled 'command' colleges. Just as with civilian universities, the standard required for entry to the various colleges varies enormously and there is a similar variance in the quality of graduates produced. At all colleges, courses run are a balance between theory and practice, with a high level of general technical instruction. The Soviet officer undergoes a much higher level of theoretical and technical instruction than does his British counterpart and his approach to the organisation of war is very much more structured. The Soviets deride the British reliance upon initiative as 'an unwise reliance upon native wit'. The Soviet concept of a military doctrine incorporates a large fund of military expertise and experience on the basis of which the young Soviet officer is instructed and much of which, in the forms of norms and drills, he is expected to learn, memorise, and apply on the battlefield.

This was well expressed by M. I. Kalinin, writing in the Soviet Army Paper *Red Star* on the 7 June 1946.

It is the man who is well versed in military art who, at critical moments of the battle, can find the necessary resources to use against the enemy. It is deep knowledge of military art which makes creative military action on the battlefield possible. He who thinks he can get himself out of a hole by dint of native wit or by simple common sense, in place of knowledge and the study of military skill, will come to a sticky end on the battlefield in wartime.

Although conscription is universal in the Soviet Union, a small proportion of young men between the ages of seventeen and twenty-three escape conscription, not just on the normal medical grounds, but on the grounds that they have acquired places at universities and institutes of higher education. Exemption from conscription is normally dependent upon the student undergoing a reserve officer training course while at university. Those who complete this course are commissioned as junior lieutenants of the reserve. It is not a totally foolproof system of avoiding conscription, for it is not uncommon nowadays for young men to be posted to the army as their first job on completing a university or higher educational course for a period of between one and three years as, in effect, short service technical officers. The Soviet military system has a rapidly increasing requirement for highly qualified technical officers, in view of the fact that it is officers who service and maintain all the complex military equipment and do the tasks done in the British Army very often by corporals and sergeants. About half the Soviet officer corps are qualified as technicians and do mainly technical tasks. There is as a result a high overall ratio of officers to men, about one to five in all. This dependence upon highly qualified officers for technical maintenance does, however, make it possible to achieve a very high level of equipment and vehicle reliability and availability.

It should be clear, therefore, from the foregoing that, just as the Soviet and British Armies demand very different things from their soldiers, so also they demand very different things from their junior officers. A Soviet young officer is either a straightforward technician with NCOs to assist him or else he is a sub-unit commander whose task is basically the running of a repetitive basic training course and controlling a situation for which the drill and the norms are specified and in which no leeway is allowed. As all his conscripts are unmarried and in effect confined to barracks, there is little requirement for him to take a personal interest in their development as people. Consequently the qualities required of him are in many areas very different from those required of his British counterpart.

A typical posting in the Soviet Army is for up to five years, as compared to two years in the British Army, and promotion is often within the same unit, so that the young Soviet officer obtains a high degree of technical expertise but not necessarily a broad breadth of knowledge. Furthermore, he has traditionally been allowed very little opportunity to demonstrate initiative and independence. The demands of modern battle are forcing the Soviet Army inexorably towards a more flexible strategy and tactics, in which the value of initiative is more and more recognised by senior Soviet officers. Soviet young people today are showing an increasing degree of sophistication and a greater awareness of the West, and there can be no doubt that the modern Soviet officer is far more capable of showing initiative in the Western sense than would his predecessor a generation ago. But there is also evidence that despite the calls for, and the considerable lip service given to, the requirement for initiative, most young Soviet officers today are still given little scope to exercise it.

The long courses at the middle and higher military colleges equip the young Soviet officer to do jobs in his chosen arm of service up to and including battalion commander. However, officers, particularly those who have only completed the middle colleges and who are not therefore qualified to attend a staff academy, can and do attend a variety of residential, correspondence or part time courses in preparation for staff or command jobs. These are the equivalent of combat team, battery or battlegroup commanders' courses, or the Junior Division of Staff College courses in the British Army. The Soviet Army military academies equivalent to the British Army Staff College or the Joint Services Defence College, take the best qualified and most experienced officers for courses of two or three years duration. There is considerable flexibility as to the time in an officer's career when he can attend these courses, and captains and lieutenant colonels may well find themselves on the same course. Once again these academies are special to arm or all-arms, the most influential being the Frunze All Arms Academy followed closely by the Malinovskiy Tank Academy. There is considerable evidence that a selective general staff stream exists and that potential high flyers, identified during regimental duty as senior lieutenants or captains, are selected for the Frunze Military Academy and subsequently go on to hold demanding but influential appointments which will give them the best chance of developing their talents.

Unlike the British service staff colleges, Soviet military academies and colleges are centres of military research and learning as well as places of instruction. Senior officers, on the instructing staff or as research fellows, are encouraged to produce original research, often by analysis of operational experience. Many of these colleges can confer degrees of master or doctor of military science. It is they who produce a great deal of the operational analysis, technical experimentation, and tactical ideas on which the Soviet Armed Forces rely for their continued development. Several of these Soviet academies run special courses for officers from the Warsaw Pact or Third World armies.

The senior Soviet military academy is the Voroshilov General Staff Academy. This graduates between a hundred and a hundred and fifty Soviet and Warsaw Pact colonels or generals each year after a two year course. In contrast to the studies done at the Royal College of Defence Studies in the UK, Soviet senior officers study operational art and strategy and the handling of higher formations. They also undertake advanced operational research.

Although on the surface the Soviet military system may appear monolithic, there is actually a wide diversity of views, a considerable degree of debate, and distinctly identifiable camps of opinion in the overall structure. As within any element of Soviet society, because of the despotic nature of the system an individual can come to wield great influence within his own particular sphere of expertise. It is very easy to underestimate the importance of this in the Soviet military system. Whilst an officer may hesitate to display independence of thought or initiative whilst he is very junior or is acting as someone's immediate deputy, that same person will be able to exercise a great degree of control over his subordinates when he obtains a high position of command, or when he is given a relatively high degree of independence. It is therefore dangerous to assume that because, say, a battalion commander is allowed to show no initiative when his battalion is operating as an element of the regimental main body (and is thus under close control of the regimental commander) he will therefore be incapable of displaying initiative if his battalion is given a mission to operate detached from the main forces. On the contrary, in such circumstances a Russian's nature will render him very capable of taking decisions, and the only limit to his effectiveness will be his professional competence.

In the army, as in any other sphere of Soviet professional life, as the senior personnel rise to important appointments, they identify those of their subordinates whose ability and style they admire, and who have chosen to support them. The military academies act each as a focus for trends of thought and the development of themes and opinions within the disciplined framework of Soviet military doctrine. As the need for changes in the doctrine are perceived by groups of like-minded individuals, opinions as to the direction the change should take coalesce around individuals and around establishments, which engage in formal and informal debate at conferences, in the press, and on exercises. When a consensus is reached within one of these groups, and particularly when a convinced individual is posted into a position of power from which he can control the course of events, those subordinates who have been his supporters, and whom he has identified as high flyers, will find themselves posted into units or formations under his command or into positions of authority at military academies where they in turn can influence teachings and course of research along the lines of their particular opinion. Thus the traditional Russian system of nepotism and favouritism are applied to the benefit of doctrinal change and development.

WOMEN IN THE SOVIET ARMY

There are far fewer women in uniform in the Soviet Union than is often thought as, in the peacetime Soviet Army, women play quite a small role. There were women's battalions in the Tsarist and anti-Bolshevik forces before and during the revolution in 1917, and the Red Army employed women in special regiments of snipers and pilots in the 1941–45 war. However, despite the publicity given to these few examples women were not generally seen in combat in the Red Army except where they got into the battle as medics, medical officers, nurses, traffic controllers, drivers or as secretaries in headquarters staffs. The same is still true today. There may be as few as 12 000 women in uniform, a much smaller percentage of total strength than is the case in the British Armed Forces. Today they appear to be employed mainly in signals, secretarial, intelligence work and as medical staff. They are all volunteers with a limited rank system and they enjoy comparative freedom from the restrictive disciplinary system that their menfolk are subject to. Serious breaches of discipline are punished by dismissal. They receive a standard rate of regular NCO and officer pay, allowances and leave, and are allocated accommodation as necessary. A great many live at home in their garrison area or are married to servicemen, in which case they are guaranteed postings with their husbands.

5   The Soviet Airman

Westerners travelling in the USSR are allowed to see very little of the Soviet Air Forces. The majority of their first-line bases are located securely away from the tourist's eye in areas normally closed to foreigners. Not all however are so secluded. Those who travel on 'Inturist' package tours from Leningrad to Moscow will catch glimpses of bomber, fighter, helicopter and transport bases during the course of their 435 mile long, straight and flat journey by bus. The intrepid ones who take their own cars will see more airfields as they progress southwards through the rolling Ukraine to the Crimean or sub-tropical Caucasian resorts and if the weather is reasonably good they will doubtless observe flying activity. Likewise those who travel across the great plain from the Polish frontier on the Trans-Siberian Express to Nakhodka in the Far East will not fail to see something of the Soviet Air Forces on each of the nine days it takes to cover the 4350 kilometres.

Not that these travellers will be able to see much. They will observe usually from a distance of at least 1 or 2 miles and then only for a matter of seconds through gaps between building or trees where the airfields are inadequately screened from outside view. It is not surprising therefore that the sum of our knowledge of the Soviet Air Forces gleaned from Western travellers' tales is small. It is also ambiguous. The trappings of military airpower are manifestly there to see; hardened aircraft shelters, surveillance and precision radars, purposeful modern aircraft flown with apparent confidence contrasted with overgrown approaches, inadequate broken-down chestnut-paling perimeter fences, carelessly strewn stores, ancient motor transport, earth roads and domestic buildings well advanced towards total decrepitude. It does not add up. It is not the Western way – and yet it works, to the extent that the West is forced to regard the Soviet Air Forces as a potential foe of formidable dimensions.

The traveller will see little more if any of the human element of Soviet air power, the pilots, engineers and ground crew who

126

operate and service these enigmatic air forces. They can be seen strolling off-duty in towns and cities near to air bases or perhaps as fellow travellers at airports or on trains, travelling on leave to their, usually very distant, homes. One can talk with the conscript soldiers in the humble dining halls of any Soviet town or in railway buffet cars and very often at greater length, with officers in the more expensive hotel restaurants. But taken all together direct Western contacts with Soviet airmen are few and far between and would scarcely provide the basis for a sociological study of breadth or value. There are however other sources with which these fleeting contacts can be compared to provide a picture of the Soviet airman and his way of life which would not be unrecognisable to the airman himself.

First there are the defectors or *émigrés*. For a few years recently many ex-servicemen from all the various branches of the Soviet Armed Forces were allowed to leave the USSR following Brezhnev's more relaxed policy on Jewish emigration (1977). They have provided much information on conditions of service and attitudes of mind. Information of a technically more specific quality on the strengths and weaknesses of the human element of Soviet air power has also been forthcoming from other defectors, most notably from Lieutenant Belyenko who made a spectacular escape in a MiG-25 (NATO codenamed *Foxbat*) from his Far Eastern base in 1976, landing in Japan. Not only did Belyenko delight Western intelligence with his present of the *Foxbat*, his testimony concerning the way of life and the motivation of Soviet airmen such as himself and his colleagues was a unique contribution to our knowledge of the potential enemy. Like defector evidence in general much of what Belyenko writes is not exactly congruent with reports from others and has therefore to be taken with a good pinch of Siberian salt.

Another rich source of information on the Soviet airman are the aviation journals, *Aviation and Cosmonautics*, *Journal of the Air Defence Forces*, *Wings of the Homeland* and, to a lesser but not insignificant extent, *Civil Aviation*, the house magazine of the Civil Air Fleet. Frequently also in the bookshops of Moscow there appear books about the Soviet Air Forces. They are mainly historical or biographical but nevertheless they often afford interesting insights to the Soviet airman's psyche. The disadvantages of using such publications have already been admitted but they are written by airmen for airmen and however totalitarian the environment their content must broadly mirror the goals, standards and morals of their readership. In drawing inferences from this source the greatest danger lies in over-estimating Soviet aviators, in accepting as fact the idealised, invincible self-image projected in the pages of their journals. Clearly discernible between the lines however is the ordinary human, crew-room airman with the average balance of strengths and weaknesses as found in the personnel of Western air forces. The researcher is not fooled for long. It is not difficult to go beyond the bravado and the political cant to reap a satisfying harvest of technical, social and psychological information from these pages. To Soviet eyes a comparable study of the Royal Air Force based solely on the *RAF News* would surely lead to the initial impression that its members spend much of their lives presenting trophies to each other and shaking hands. It would not be long however before a more comprehensive picture of the RAF's activities emerged.

In sum this does not amount to an abundance of material from which to assess the Soviet airman in all aspects but from it a working sketch can be drawn. Is such a sketch necessary? Soldiers study their potential enemies down to the last shirt-button against the day they might meet them in face-to-face combat when this most intimate intelligence would be valuable. Unlike armies, the human elements of air forces rarely meet in this direct way, success in air warfare depending as it does primarily on order-of-battle and technical capability. NATO staffs are therefore right to regard the study of these factors as paramount and at first glance it appears superfluous to know very much about the human qualities of Soviet airmen and ground crews. The classical war-winning factor of morale is thus neglected since it is looked upon as a natural product of the prime factors. Numerical and technical superiority, or the right correlation of both, will guarantee good morale and vice-versa. This facile assumption could be dangerous. In a close-run balance or correlation of forces the quality of the human element might well be the determinant of the result should those forces engage. Would Soviet pilots fly as ordered in any war between the Warsaw Pact and NATO? Would they continue to do so in the face of heavy losses or would their morale and enthusiasm wither away in proportion to the attrition sustained?

This chapter cannot pretend to give unequivocal answers to these questions but they will expose some facets of NATO's potential opponents in the air not often included in the usual run of 'threat' presentations. These latter are invariably macro-views of the Soviet air armoury. In contrast, a micro-view is presented here; an attempt to assess the individual airman, his service training, his strengths, weaknesses and motivations. Some brief historical notes with an outline of the structure and development of the Soviet Air Forces are offered as a setting.

AVIATION AND THE REVOLUTION

The USSR is without doubt the most air-minded nation in the world. At least that is the opinion held by the Soviet citizen himself or the intuitive feeling he has towards aviation. Over the years since 1917 the aeroplane has come to be regarded as the child of the Revolution. That without the Revolution there would have been no significant development of aircraft for the benefit of the people. As steam related to capitalism so now are aviation and revolution popularly associated as the twin foundations of Soviet communism's influential Superpower position in contrast with Russia's decayed state under the last of the Tsars. Nor does the citizen doubt that the aeroplane was a Russian invention in spite of a certain vagueness of proof. He firmly believes that A. F. Mozhaiski succeeded in getting airborne in a steam-powered monoplane sometime in 1881. Unfortunately for posterity nobody photographed the event and, strangely enough there are no eyewitnesses' accounts. Tiresome though this has been for Soviet aviation historians, there are now in existence a sufficient number of paintings and prints of the alleged flight to provide a wonderful authenticity for the Mozhaiski claim giving the lie to the reactionary view held in some quarters that the honour belongs to the American brothers Wright for their short hop off the ground at Kittyhawk twenty-two years later. Curiously there was no development of Mozhaiski's triumph but this omission is explained as a crime of the Tsar and his government. Afraid that this new flexible vehicle, the aeroplane, would inexorably unite the Russians, release them from their bondage to the land and threaten the very roots of the old autocracy, these 'criminals' did their best to kill off aviation at birth. Their method was to impede its progress in every way possible, especially financially, strangulating the efforts of the brilliant native pioneers among whom were Mozhaiski himself and the highly venerated aerodynamicist Zhukovski.

Against this version of events there are the undeniable facts of Russian eminence – even pre-eminence – in military aviation before 1914 and an honourable fighting record in World War I, but these suggest no serious inconsistencies for the Soviet historian. They are explained away simply as the fruits of a regrettable dependence on foreign expertise and foreign capital. Time and the Revolution swept the Tsar away. The foreigners were swept away at the same time and the notion began to grow of a mystical nexus between aviation and the Revolution. Aviation was the long-sought tool that would annihilate distance. The remote villages and towns across the span of the Tsar's erstwhile empire – places the railway had not reached nor could ever reach – were now to be brought close together. The aeroplane was to perform a miracle. Its task was to weld the infant Communist society together and develop it economically to provide standards of life beyond the imagination of a nation shattered by war, civil war and exhausted from long centuries of oppression. Almost seventy years on and, judging from the density and frequency of Aeroflot passenger services, the apparently classless nature of the passenger lists and the other remarkable contributions to society made by the large air transport fleet, it must be conceded that the miracle has happened.

The military role of the aeroplane was perceived by the founding fathers of the Soviet state in a connected way. It had arrived on the stage of history on exactly the right dialectic cue. Lenin recognised that his new power needed defending. Surrounded by enemies on all sides, domestic and foreign, he could not recognise otherwise although armies were anathema to Marxists and in the longer term could not be tolerated. But the Revolution of 1917 was only the start of the process of communising the whole world and whatever the theories might hold the plain truth demanded that the foothold gained in Russia would have to be protected by military force until the transformation of society was complete world-wide. And here the new rulers looked to air power to rid them of their dilemma. Armies were the brutal expression of the forces oppressing the proletariat in the pre-Revolutionary era and could only be considered anachronistic in the new society. Air forces were perhaps something different. A powerful air force acting as a deterrent, threatening massive retaliation to any remaining capitalist forces foolish enough to attack the Soviet Union, would reduce and eventually eliminate the need for old-fashioned field armies. Under this concept, long before the nuclear age and formalised strategies of deterrence, Soviet aviation came to be regarded as the popular guardian of the Revolution with a 'world air police' function in prospect somewhat along the lines predicted by H. G. Wells in his *Shape of Things to Come*. The Red Air Force thus became, or by skilful propaganda was presented as, the first of the new Soviet armed services to proclaim itself a weapon of peace rather than war, supposedly ready to intervene in any struggle anywhere on the earth where a proletarian revolution was under attack from reactionary capitalism. The ideological dilemma had disappeared – and the Red Army was tacitly allowed to remain in existence and expand, the Marxist theoreticians and international communists quieted by this novel 'peace force' compromise.

There was yet another distinct aspect of this relation between the aeroplane and the Revolution. Aviation was the newest and most technical branch of industry. Upon its shoulders rested the responsibility of justifying all the claims of Marxist philosophy made in the previous three-quarters of a century. This was the supreme test by which the experiment of a Marxist state would stand or fall. Practical proof was demanded by the world at large of Marxist claims that the proletariat, given equality of opportunity, is the intellectual equal of his capitalist oppressor. If the proletariat could make aeroplanes work, they could make anything work. Providing demonstrable proof of this proposition became the Soviet Government's goal as soon as they were able to settle down in comparative peace after the end of the Civil War (1922).

BETWEEN THE WARS

During the Civil War a revolutionary air effort was possible only with the help of those elements of the old Russian Imperial Air Service willing to join the Bolsheviks. The former Tsarist officers had always been suspect because of their bourgeois background and so, in the 1920s they were eliminated as rapidly as expediency would allow. They were retained just long enough to train – after the Treaty of Rapallo with considerable help from the Germans – a first generation of peasant, truly proletarian pilots. Recruits for this training were accepted only from worker origins. The taint of bourgeois parentage or the slightest suggestions of bourgeois sympathies barred an applicant totally. But at that time the young men of the old bourgeois stock were not in the main willing to join anyway. A Red Air Force recruit members going home on leave during pilot training in the late 1920s and his ex-bourgeois friends asking him ruefully, 'Why have you joined the Bolsheviks?' [1]

But the new *régime* managed despite everything. Echoes from the period abound in the many memoirs written by senior Soviet Air Force officers. Their call to a flying career seems to have come to most of them while they were helping their poor exploited peasant grandfathers till the unyielding soil. They looked up to see great flying machines passing overhead and dreamed of becoming pilots. Along came the Great October Revolution and made their dream come true. Now in their dotage they are respected as the pure, proletarian pilot-sons of the Revolution and dedicated as ever before to its defence. What they do not seem to have noticed is that the passage of time along the way transformed them all by degrees into highly respected members of the upper levels of the new Soviet class structure, every bit as bourgeois as their pre-Revolutionary predecessors. And since, as the social scientists point out, hierarchies tend to maintain and reproduce themselves by recruiting in their own image it is from among the sons of this urbanised and privileged sector that the Soviet Air Forces now recruit a good proportion of their officer entrants.

The 1930s saw a tremendous expansion of all aspects of Soviet aviation. The national enthusiasm for the aeroplane was harnessed through a great variety of flying clubs, gliding clubs and design circles. The extent to which the government encouraged this activity at a time when it was still unable to feed the population and while Stalin was still engaged in his bloody purges demonstrates clearly the Soviet conviction that the nation's destiny lay with aviation. Inoshevskiy recalls as a young boy running with a glider tow-rope, oblivious to his shoeless feet and the freezing ground, his hands blue with cold, conscious only that it would soon be his turn to have a few seconds at the controls.

Not only did the clubs train an endless stream of pilots for both the Red Air Force and civil aviation they also produced navigators, engineers, wireless technicians in similar numbers and indirectly designers, from human stock which under the Tsar would have been known as the peasant/worker class. The controlling body for the clubs was known as OSOAVIAKHIM (Society of the Aviation and Chemical Industries for Co-operation in Defence). The Soviet Military Encyclopaedia describes this odd combination as a mass, voluntary society of military patriots. The chemical connection appears to have come from an earlier society, the *VNO* (Military–Scientific Society), formed in 1920 under the patronage of such famous Soviet military figures as Commissar-for-War Frunze, Marshal Voroshilov and Marshal Tukhachevskiy. OSOAVIAKHIM the organisation remained until in 1948 it became the DOSAAF mentioned in earlier chapters. Aviation in these years was emphasised as a sport and in 1935 the Central Flying Club was established in Moscow at the Tushino airfield. The club's function was to expand the aviation sports, flying, gliding and parachuting; to organise competitive events and, in the manner of the Royal Aero Club in Great Britain, to adjudicate and keep records. It all worked. The Soviet Union did indeed emerge as a first-class aviation power in an incredibly short time. The government's call to 'Fly higher, faster and further than anyone else' has become a classic slogan, still to be seen in the propaganda displays for aviation days.

By the time the second Five Year Plan (1933–37) was introduced the Soviet Union was well to the forefront in aerodynamic science, had established a large aviation industrial base and, with designs from the later famous Tupolev and Polikarpov, was able to say that Revolutionary air power had been achieved. Civil designs were connecting the population centres as planned and the Red Air Force had become a power to be reckoned with. In 1935 the outside world awoke to the fact of Soviet air strength when films of military exercises that year were released showing swarms of heavy transport aircraft disgorging large numbers of paratroops, the first the world had ever seen.

Enthusiasm alone could not have produced this miracle of corporate construction. Money was also needed. In a straitened economy faced at every turn with demands from a war-torn populace and driven by its own grandiose plans for the construction of a communist society, all requiring massive capital investment, the government would have found difficulty in financing their aviation programme had it not been for ODVF, the

'Society of the Friends of the Air Fleet'. According to Colonel Pinchyuk this society was formed in response to Lenin's own heroic efforts to establish Soviet aviation.[2] The Party issued the slogan 'Working people! Build an Air Fleet!' and on 8 March 1923 ODVF was created. Its aim was to build the air fleets, military and civil, as quickly as possible in face of the perceived external threat. ODVF's charter expressed this as:

> Imperialism urgently seeks to dominate the skies in order to strengthen its rapacious power over the earth. The danger from air attack is growing. Only a powerful air fleet will preserve our homeland from this danger. It must be clearly understood that without victory in the air we shall not be able to consolidate our victory on land.[3]

Lenin set an example by contributing to the fund from his own and his wife's savings and two million ODVF members then went about collecting money wherever they could, from anyone who would emulate the leader. Many thousands of workers over the whole Union were cajoled or coerced into regularly surrendering some of their pay in return for the honour of having an aeroplane or even a squadron named after their factory or province. In this way the air fleets were built with less strain on the economy and the drive for funds associated the proletariat even more closely with aviation.

What did they buy with the money? Like other European nations they developed World War I aircraft for civil and military purposes and through many mutations of design they passed from wood and canvas construction to the all-metal aircraft. In the late 1930s there was a final shift from the biplane to the monoplane, from wooden to variable-pitch metal propellors, to closed cockpits, streamlining and the retractable undercarriage. Mass-production techniques were introduced as far as feasible both in engine and airframe plants.

A large number of fighters were built, the moderately successful Polikarpov design the I-16 being typical of the many designs produced and flown. A single-seat fighter, a low-wing monoplane with a big radial engine it was reminiscent of United States fighters of the period and was heavily inspired, if not actually copied, from the barrel-shaped Curtiss designs of the day. It went into series production in 1934 and saw active service against the Japanese in 1939 and, in 1941, against the Germans.

In spite of the volume of fighter production and other similar-sized variants for the reconnaissance and fighter-bomber roles, it was into heavy aircraft that the money went. The 1920s and 1930s saw a progression of designs from the Tupolev bureau starting with the TB-1, a twin-engined, long-range reconnaissance aircraft. In 1929 a TB-1 made a record-breaking flight eastwards from Moscow through Khabarovsk to Seattle, San Francisco and New York. The Soviet airman was introduced officially to the outside world. As Soviet wings strengthened, such spectacular flights became almost a commonplace. Probably the most famous of these heavy aircraft was the giant ANT-20, the *Maxim Gorkiy*. With eight engines, passenger capacity of eighty, maximum speed of 140 mph and a range of 1250 miles, in 1934 it was years ahead of its era. Unfortunately it crashed during trials and the project was abandoned.

By no means were all those heavy aircraft failures. Tupolev's ANT-25 developed at the same time as the *Maxim Gorkiy* was a reliable success and gained world-wide notice when in 1937 one flew from Moscow across the North Pole to Vancouver, a non-stop flight of 63 hours over a distance of 5300 miles. Chkalov, the pilot, was lionised in America and even more so when he returned to the USSR. He became the epitome of the Soviet airman, the pilot's pilot and proof to the world that boilermakers' sons can fly as well as the next man. Chkalov died in 1938 within a year of his epoch-making flight, but notwithstanding World War II and the many heroes it spawned his memory remains the embodiment of all the aeronautical virtues, the model for all young Soviet aspirant pilots. Streets, parks and aviation institutes are dedicated to Chkalov, Pioneers deck his many memorials with flowers and his name is revered above all later heroes in the Communist pantheon of the air.

In August of that same year, 1938, General Loktionov, then Head of the Red Air Force was able to claim, certainly with the justification of numbers, that the Soviet Union had 'the mightiest air fleet in the world'. On the same occasion, Molokoff, Chief of Civil Aviation announced that in 1937, Soviet aircraft had carried 211 000 passengers, 36 000 tons of freight and 9000 tons of mail! Beyond all doubt revolutionary air power had arrived.

THE RED AIR FORCE IN WORLD WAR II

It is sometimes forgotten that the Red Air Force gained considerable experience of air operations in campaigns beyond its own frontiers in the inter-war years before the 1941 invasion. Many of its pilots saw action and gained 'ace' reputations supporting China in the war against Japan, but of greatest significance was the intervention in the Spanish Civil War of 1936–39 where the Soviet Union supplied virtually the whole of the Loyalist air effort opposing Franco's German and Italian-backed air force. The Germans openly declared this war to be a testing ground for their own new weapons and it soon became clear, considerable initial success notwithstanding, that the snub-nosed, Soviet I-16 fighters and the *Katyusha* light bombers were no match for the later marks of *Messerschmitt* 109 introduced in the middle and later stages of the war.

Although Soviet aircraft and pilots remained in Spain in strength until the war ended they never regained the initiative and the world judged them to be as inferior as they appeared. But Spain was no less a testing ground for the communists than it was for the fascists. They learned much about the wielding of air power and the patent inadequacies of their 1930s aircraft spurred on Stalin and his designers to produce a new generation of improved fighters, light bombers and reconnaissance aircraft.[4] Then as now based on technology bought or stolen from wherever it was obtainable, these new models appearing progressively from 1940 onwards ultimately gave the Soviet Union air superiority over the Germans in World War II. This is not to say that the Soviet types were necessarily of themselves superior to their German opponents – in no case was this true – it was simply that the Soviet factories, located in remote areas away from the battle zone and organised for mass production in accordance with the pre-war Five-Year Plans, were able to out-produce and therefore in the end to out-fight a Luftwaffe diluted by the demands of several encircling fronts.

There was, however, another war in which the Red Air Force was involved before the German invasion – the Fenno-Soviet War of 1939–40, the 'Winter War'. Throughout the four months it lasted, aircraft gave constant support to Soviet ground forces, on some days mounting between 200 and 400 sorties against Finnish fortifications, seaports, communications and populated areas.[5]

Opposition was more difficult to suppress than expected but overall the 150 aircraft of the Finnish Air Force could do little. The disparity in numerical strengths soon told. In effect, the Red Air Force was supreme from the first days. Early in the new year Soviet Forces launched the ground/air offensive which they sustained in spite of enormous losses until the Finns accepted peace terms on 12 March 1940. The swift victory to a great extent masked the same general inadequacies that were revealed in Spain. Not only were the aircraft themselves lacking in speed and effective armament, they were badly maintained and their pilots could not achieve the bombing accuracy required to destroy military objectives or undermine the morale of the Finnish Army.[6] Red Air Force losses were vastly disproportionate to the scale of the campaign. Kilmarx notes that several hundred aircraft on bombing missions were forced to land in the Baltic states – at that time still unoccupied – and over 60 landed on the ice in the Gulf of Finland. Even more were shot down by AA fire, Finnish anti-aircraft guns accounting for approximately 300 Soviet aircraft. Total Soviet losses over the four-month period rose to approximately 900 aircraft, more than half of them bombers.

One of the reasons adduced for the miserable showing of the Red Air Force in the 'Winter War' is the Soviet claim that its best elements were never employed. They were being conserved for the expected Nazi onslaught. Probably there is a sound basis for this claim. According to Kilmarx[7] the Russians employed mostly obsolete aircraft and at that time their older bomber units were without much doubt the most expendable component of their air force. Whatever the truth they were still not prepared for the Nazi invasion when it eventually came on 22 June 1941. In spite of its mystique as the embodiment of Revolutionary virtue and the champion of socialism, the Red Air Force made a disastrously clumsy start in World War II. After barely four months they announced a loss of more than 5000 aircraft, a figure which will never now be confirmed, but it does give some validity to the German claim to have destroyed 4000 in the first week. Whatever the exact figures, it is historical fact that the Germans caught many aircraft on the ground and chopped many others out of the sky, making the Soviet road to air superiority long and hard. But they got there. With an unimaginable effort in their factories in the Ural cities and beyond, the Soviet aviation industry and the Red Air Force wrought a joint miracle. In less than two years they not only rebuilt their air strength, they also wrested air superiority from the Germans, achieving a three-to-one ratio by late 1943. They received considerable assistance from the Western Allies toward this end – some 14 000 fighters and light-bombers – but their own output figures remain astonishing. They achieved a peak production rate of 35 000 aircraft a year.

With concentration first upon defensive fighter production and light bombers, in particular, the *Ilyushin-2, Shturmovik*, one of the most successful aircraft of the war, the Red Air Force was rebuilt in the form of a very large tactical air force devoted to the protection of rear areas and close support of the ground forces. As they moved westward and the German withdrawals turned into full retreat, the scope of Soviet air operations widened to a full range of battlefield interdiction tasks and deep raids into the German rear. The result was that by 1945 the Soviet airmen were the darlings of the nation but not quite in the same way as envisaged by the founding fathers of Soviet air power. Somewhere along the way the Douhet-Trenchard strategic vision of deterrent air power, capable if called upon to win wars on its own, had got lost. It had not worked out like that. Sorties were mounted regularly throughout the war by the Long-Range Bomber Force (*Aviatsiya Dal'nyevo Dyeistva*), which by 1944 comprised approximately 1500 aircraft, but targets were normally selected for their immediate relevance to the land battle.[8] Attacks further afield against economic targets and population were few and had little effect – except perhaps insofar as they boosted morale and had propaganda value.

Several factors had brought about the change of doctrine, among them the experience in Spain, the lack of efficient bomber designs and Stalin's distrust of the strategic bombardment concept, but most compelling of all was the priority to produce the aircraft needed to stem the tide of the German advance – the fighter-ground attack aircraft and the dive-bombers.

THE POST-1945 PERIOD

For the Soviet Air Forces the legacy of World War II was a large number of piston-engined aircraft designed for close-support tasks, rapidly obsolescent in the new jet and nuclear age. Stalin announced that the atom bomb was just another weapon, useful perhaps for scaring people with weak nerves but by no means had it outmoded large field armies. Ground forces he said, still decide the day, although it was as obvious to him as to anyone that the atom bomb had radically altered things. Behind the scenes he prepared to meet its challenge. As he captured sectors of German industry, German scientists and technicians, he harnessed them to assist the development of new Soviet aircraft and missile systems. Soviet defence policy in the immediate post-war years was to protect the country from the possibility of aircraft-delivered nuclear weapons from the United States – or even from Britain. Against the threat from the high-altitude bomber they produced a myriad MiG-15 and MiG-17 fighters and an early-warning system.

At the same time they developed their own nuclear capability for a 'deterrence by denial' posture based on the manned bomber and later on the inter-continental ballistic missile. These two developments and their wartime experience determined the shape of the Soviet Air Forces for the next thirty years, a shape which except for some recent and significant command and control reorganisation remains fundamentally the same today. The Red Air Force passed into history about 1948. Thereafter it became customary to refer in the plural to the Soviet Air Forces – functional groupings of aircraft according to role; a tactical air force for the direct support of field armies, a strategic bomber force, air defence fighters subordinated to the national air-defence system and a large force of transport aircraft. The MiG-15 generation gave way to the MiG-21s, the famous *Fishbed*, the TU-4 bomber, *Bull* made way for the *Badger* and the *Blinder*. The early piston-engined transports were superseded by the turbo-prop *Antonov Cub*, and the jet IL 76, *Candid*. The front line is at present held by the *Fencer* strike/attack bomber, the *Backfire* bomber, *Foxbat* and *Flagon* fighters, *Flogger* fighter ground-attack aircraft and a variety of transport, assault and attack helicopters. A new generation is already discernible, several types, either having entered service already or in an advanced stage of development. Amongst other types are three new fighters, the bomber *Blackjack*, very similar in appearance to the US *Rockwell* B-1, a huge *Galaxy*-sized transport NATO codenamed *Condor* and at least one new helicopter. All these aircraft will be designed and equipped to standards little, if any, lower than their latest Western counterparts. Thus the margin of technological advantage hitherto enjoyed by the West is becoming very narrow. What now of the men who fly and service these Soviet aircraft?

THE SOVIET AIRMAN – RECRUITMENT AND TRAINING

The young Soviet man who wishes to fly will in common with all his compatriots have received political education along the lines described in Part I. He will be a member of KOMSOMOL and well-instructed in the nature of the capitalist enemy. He will be aquainted with the evil forces of capitalism and the nature of the threat they pose to his homeland. All his enemies, the war-mongering United States, the former colonialists of Europe, the revanchist, fascist Germans and the Western military–industrial complex will have been subsumed in NATO as a credible and palpable enemy. He will hate and fear NATO. This background and an eagerness to fly and fight in the air are essential requirements for entry into the Soviet Air Forces. But air-mindedness and hate for his country's enemies are not quite enough. A career in aviation also demands academic standards, an ability in mathematics and physics.

In theory, opportunities for education in the Soviet Union are equal for everybody in what is described in Britain as a comprehensive system. Unlike British schools there is no official attempt made to 'stream' or in any way divide the class or modify the curriculum to allow the brighter pupil to develop faster. Except for scholars in special schools, e.g. for the physically handicapped, orphans, ballet students and those of extraordinary high IQ, children all proceed at the same pace and follow the same course. The more able are directed to assist and encourage the backward with the result that educational standards show a remarkable homogeneity across broad bands of the population. This system may not develop the finest intellects but it does establish that notion of the 'collective', so close to communist hearts. By eroding individual sensitivities it aims to accustom the pupil to criticising others and himself to the ready acceptance of criticism uninhibited by any considerations of *amour propre*. In practice it produces only that high degree of conformity already mentioned and a reluctance on the part of the individual to express original thought. One disadvantage of the system is the near impossibility of assessing progress without resort to truly competitive examinations. Whole classes tend to pass or fail collectively if their studies have been collective. Failure demands that the year's work must be repeated. It also implies criticism of teaching standards. Teachers are therefore understandably reluctant to declare failure and tend to leniency in their marking. In this way many Soviet pupils are credited with standards they have not achieved.

But not all the nation's potential intellect is born to wither on the altar of communist equality. Much of it is saved by unofficial malpractice. Schools in the Soviet Union differ for the same reasons as they do in Britain of anywhere else. Some are housed in new buildings in the more attractive districts; others occupy dark basements in crumbling apartment houses. Some have energetic principals and staff; others do not. In short, some schools are better than others. The combined string-pulling of the energetic principals and influential professional parents serves to gather the brighter children into the better schools. The State, in spite of its own attempts at levelling, is thus assured of a continuing supply of the high quality intellect needed for its direction and management. Equally the authorities have reason to be grateful to the poor schools. These collect the dull-heads and bad-hats who then drift away – often before the minimum leaving age – into those coarse manual jobs, essential to the community but not demanding of the brain. These assertions of inequality of opportunity would be firmly denied by Soviet educationalists but those Westerners who have been able to look at all closely at Soviet schools agree that they are largely true and careful reading between the lines of Soviet newspapers, particularly in references to juvenile crime and hooliganism, gives further proof that they have substance.

The Soviet Air Forces in recruiting from the educationally privileged sector of society ensure for themselves a supply for adequate entrants. Officer-candidates must have completed the full eleven years of secondary education. Soviet reticence makes it difficult with certainty to equate their classification of schools and qualifications with the British or American systems. The progression appears to be little different from our own and the end-product would suggest comparable skills, e.g. in mathematics, but to what extent the long ideological indoctrination affects the development of objectivity and reasoning power is far from clear. Terminal examinations offer some comparisons and from them observers have concluded that Soviet standards are more akin to those of the USA, i.e. that secondary education and first degree examinations are less demanding than the British but their post-graduate standards are higher.

But the majority of air force entrants are not higher education graduates although, depending on their age, they have had some polytechnic or trade-school training. The aspiring candidate applies between his seventeenth and twenty-first birthdays for admission to a Higher Military-Aviation Engineer Institute or a Military-Aviation Technical School. He does this either through the Regional Military Commissariat in his local area or direct to the particular institute of his choice. Twenty-four of these officer-producing establishments are listed in *Red Star* in January or February each year in the annual announcement calling for volunteers. They are spread across the whole USSR from Kaliningrad in the west to Irkutsk in Eastern Siberia. There are five different types of institute and school: eleven Higher Military-Aviation Institutes for pilots, two for navigators, seven Higher Military-Aviation Institutes, including one for signals officers. There are also four Military-Aviation Technical Schools. The Soviet authorities have always been uncharacteristically informative about the location of these schools and on quite a number of occasions they have invited groups of Westerners to inspect their facilities.

Candidates are summoned to the institutes and schools in July to sit entrance examinations based on the secondary education syllabus in Russian language and literature, mathematics and physics. These are probably to confirm scholastic claims, a wise precaution in view of the variable and doubtful standards of the national schools. For incentives the candidate is offered the 'opportunity to work selflessly to strengthen the military power of the Soviet Armed Forces ... and to serve the State in an honourable, responsible and, at the same time interesting and romantic post'.[9] On successful completion of the three or four-year course he is promised the rank of lieutenant with the title of 'Pilot-Engineer', 'Navigator-Engineer', 'Pilot-Technician' or 'Lieutenant of the Technical Service' as appropriate. Leave entitlement during training is generous – two weeks for New Year and a whole month in the summer. In view of the distances which might be involved it must comfort the candidate greatly also to receive the assurance that travelling and subsistence for this preliminary call-up will be free. No other financial inducements are offered publicly. Pay is perhaps not so important a consideration in the Soviet Union as it nowadays is in the West, but privilege is, and prospective candidates are well aware that officers of the Armed Forces are highly privileged members of the community who receive much better rates of pay than many of the civilian professions, e.g. medicine.

Other than direct entrance to the officer-training institutes, courses are also open to suitably qualified NCOs and conscripted privates. Exceptionally they are admitted with lower educational qualifications provided they have finished at least eight years of full-time school. Those candidates who are granted this dispensation are nevertheless burdened with an extra element of general education in the early stage of their course in order to bring them to the required standard.

Like the Soviet Army and Navy, the Air Forces also recruit in the military pre-schools. Innocuously called 'Special Technical Schools', the Suvorov and Nakhimov Schools were established in the mid-1930s originally for orphans of the Red Army and Red Fleet. Not unnaturally their number was vastly expanded during and after World War II although they have since declined again in number. They are basically 'eleven-year-olds schools' following the national curriculum but the pupils wear a military or naval uniform and the syllabus is expanded to include purely military subjects, e.g. drill and weapon-training. Emphasis is heavily on mathematics and science. Ostensibly open now to the sons of all members of the Armed Forces, living or dead, in practice most of the places are reserved for sons of the regular officer corps or of those Communist Party functionaries with sufficient power or influence to arrange entrance. Boys are admitted to these schools at ten or eleven years of age, follow a six-year course and, provided they pass their examinations and display some officer-quality, they have the right to enter the Higher Military Institute of their choice without further examination.

Academic achievement is however only one of the hurdles in front of the would-be airman. He must also be recommended by his local government and Party officials as being politically reliable and properly motivated. He will obtain this recommendation only if his record in the Party youth programme has been spotless throughout all his years of childhood and adolescence. But mere conformity will not have been enough. The local selection board comprising educationalists, Party officials and retired military officers, will extort a blackmail price for their endorsement of political reliability and an applicant who has not devoted many voluntary hours to labour for the community is unlikely to be successful no matter what aptitude for flying he might have shown. Labour for the community includes all forms of civil project – harvesting, street cleaning, traffic control, painting and decorating, or even part-time work for the KGB. There is also the DOSAAF commitment. DOSAAF allows young people the pleasure of expensive sports such as flying, gliding, parachuting and off-shore sailing. It would be difficult for an applicant for air force service to convince a selection board of his suitability if he could not claim relevant DOSAAF experience. In developing the basic military codes and skills in both conscript and officer entrants to the Soviet Armed Forces, DOSAAF relieves pressure on the regular schools as well as ensuring that maximum benefit is gained from the conscription period. An entrant to a Higher Military-Aviation Institute will, for example, in all probability have completed 300 hours of basic flying training before ever he dons the uniform of a regular cadet.

Presuming that our airman has the prescribed educational qualifications, is medically fit and politically acceptable he enters upon his four-year course at the institute. The local Military Commissariat will have arranged a hero's send-off for him with his weeping relations, speeches from local dignitaries and a brass band. It is a fleeting moment of glory before he embarks on four arduous years during which his mind and body will be tested to their limits in a framework of a rigorous and often petty discipline. Four years may seem a long time by Western standards to reach the status of a qualified service pilot considering that our man has already flown 300 hours and is only required to fly another 240 hours, a mere 60 hours a year spread through the whole of this long course. The explanation no doubt lies in the heavy concentration on mathematics, science and engineering that the course entails as well as lengthy study of the Soviet-style 'humanities'. Students are required to research the history of military science, political economy, the science of Marxist–Leninism and the history of the Communist Party. In addition one foreign language (English or German) is an obligatory study. It thus becomes clear that four years is not an excessively long course if all these subjects are to be covered in sufficient depth to satisfy the examiners. Exactly what levels of attainment do satisfy the examiners are not easy to gauge. Those few Westerners who have seen inside one of these institutes have not been impressed by what they saw. They speak of a heavy emphasis on rote learning, having observed that cadets are heavily dependent on their brown rexine-covered notebooks filled with copious, closely written notes taken at all their lectures. Apparently the custom of issuing lecture precis notes is not followed in Soviet military institutes and, therefore, according to the students, success in examinations is related to the quality of the notes they take and their ability to recall these verbatim for the examiner. En route to the final examinations there is a progressive self-examining system based on multiple choice questions. As in children's games, a lamp is switched on when the student selects the correct combination of question and answer. This again indicates an emphasis on rote learning, a training system not vastly different from that used for much theoretical instruction in the British 'Empire Air Training Scheme' of World War II.

A somewhat different impression of academic prowess is created by Soviet technical periodicals. Drawing an inference solely from *Aviation and Cosmonautics*, the Soviet Air Forces' own journal, it would seem that the Soviet officer is capable of absorbing technical articles probably a little beyond the capacity of the average General Duties officer of the Royal Air Force, but again the danger of such inference is acknowledged. For all that we in the West know, the articles may be beyond the capacity of Soviet officers too. It is worth noting however that this sort of journal is a little closer to being a basic textbook than comparable Western aviation journals for the reason that detailed practical textbooks are scarce throughout the Soviet Armed Forces – presumably they would constitute an unacceptable security risk if distributed in large numbers. There is of course a prolific output of books on the purely academic aspects of aviation – the principles of aerodynamics, meteorology, cartography, engineering, etc. Only occasionally – and then very sketchily – are they illustrated with reference to current Soviet equipment. If concrete examples are necessary, they are mostly culled from Western publications. An aero-engine detail, for example, might be illustrated with a drawing of a Rolls-Royce engine; an armament question might be answered with a reference to *Sidewinder*, or a matter of performance related to F-111 or *Tornado*. Rarely do they illustrate with their own Soviet equipment and, when they do, they select only long-obsolete systems or systems already sold to foreign countries. There are signs that this approach to education has bred in many Soviet officers a level of respect for Western technology that in absolute terms is markedly higher than is perhaps warranted.

After the newly-fledged lieutenant graduates from the Institute, as might be expected, he commences his operational service, but his academic education is not necessarily finished. There are further opportunities for higher education through attendance at one of the 'Military Academies'. It would be wrong to equate these with Western staff colleges as one can the true service establishments such as the Frunze Military Academy or the Zhukovskiy and Gagarin Academies specifically associated with the training of Soviet Air Force officers for higher staff appointments. The true nature of the plain 'Military Academies' cannot be accurately construed from Soviet journals but they would seem principally to be academic establishments, connected with universities and concerned with the sinews of war only in an oblique way. There are no clues moreover to entrance requirements except that candidates must have completed more than two years' commissioned service. Nor is it easy to measure the scale of this training. Twenty-two academies are listed openly but they are located near large towns and each controls a number of 'filial' or provincial offshoots, e.g. the Moscow academy may have up to 30 filiali. It is known that the academies do produce real experts for appointments in research and development or weapons procurement staffs. The courses offered are usually long, e.g. five years for an engineering course, three years for jet propulsion, etc. Graduates receive fully recognised civilian degrees including doctorates. The military academy system probably explains why visitors to Soviet universities frequently find uniformed officers among the student body at lectures or seminars. It is impossible to estimate the number of officers who actually obtain diplomas or degrees in this way nor are there any firm indications of the standards of these qualifications. Courses can be arranged through garrison officers' clubs and tuition is free. Officers are allowed liberal time off for study – more than likely this is the main incentive.

The curriculum appears to be taught in mixed fashion, periods of full-time attendance interspersed through what is fundamentally a correspondence course. A few years ago, judging from the press, external study reached craze proportions but now, although many officers take advantage of the opportunity for further education, a gadarene rush to enrol is not these days so noticeable. The academy scheme is designed to elevate the general academic level of the officer corps with an eye to a resultant greater technical efficiency but the subjects studied are not exclusively technical and, considering the advanced age of some students, it looks very much as though their eyes may be focused more upon improving their prospects for a retirement job than upon extending their usefulness to the Armed Forces.

Do the foregoing paragraphs on general education tell us anything about the nature of the Soviet airman that we did not know before? Perhaps if nothing else it suggests that he may not be quite so unlike his Western counterparts as is often supposed. It may also have given some slight form to our usually amorphous perception of the human element of the Soviet air threat. At the heart of things can be discerned a young man with a burning ambition to fly, a goal held in common with many young men in the West. The distinction is that he is the product of a radically different education pattern which, although its structure is not unlike Western patterns in essence, succeeds by means of heavy political indoctrination in making him not so much a fanatical supporter of the communist regime as a believing, unquestioning one. Its great pressures towards conformity and its concern for the group rather than the individual tend to make him rather incurious and parrot-like in his approach to study. Not the best preparation for a career in aviation perhaps, but DOSAAF training and a protracted grounding in the aeronautical sciences at the Higher Military Aviation Institute will endow him with competence.

The newly qualified lieutenant will graduate from the Institute as a 'Pilot Engineer Third Class'. His training will have made him a safe pilot. Every flight he had made will have been prepared in advance to an extent that Western flight students would find surprising. For several days before an exercise the Soviet pupil is encouraged to study his task in great depth, filling his notebook with route details, engine settings, fuel loads, frequencies and call-signs, circuit patterns and other such details. As if this was not enough he also spends a lot of time with his instructor or fellow-pupils walking through the projected exercise with plastic models. The model has its uses in Western air forces of course, but not, it would seem nearly to the same degree.

If preparation is a lengthy process it is not nearly so protracted as the after-flight post mortem can be. This can last several days, mostly spent in the flight-recorder reading room examining the carbon traces. The pupil must establish just how accurately he executed his turns, loops or rolls, and how near the mark he was getting his undercarriage down in the right place and at the right speed. All his research must then be written up as a test-pilot might and the conclusions must, like a doctoral thesis, be defended to his instructor's satisfaction. Little wonder that they manage to fly such a comparatively small number of hours over the whole four year course. As a flying training system there is not enough evidence to assess its quality with full confidence but it seems to produce a theoretically well-qualified pilot and moreover a disciplined and safe pilot equal to the daunting USSR weather and its exacting demands. At the same time it probably makes for a procedure-dominated pilot with little of the imagination and flexibility required in a combat pilot. He will be slow to adapt to technological change but, as his compatriots in all walks of Soviet life continually demonstrate, he will get there in the end.

The final weeks at the Institute are occupied in flying somewhat more complex aircraft, e.g. the MiG-17, a preparation for flying the operational types found in the front-line regiments. Lieutenant Belyenko[10] tells of his days in such an advanced training regiment at Tikhoryetsk in the North Caucasus region. He describes a very rigorous routine commencing at 4.00 a.m. with a pre-flight breakfast. He then flew until it was time for a second breakfast about 9.30 a.m. Lunch was at noon and followed by a siesta, with ground school during the afternoon and early evening. Aviation subjects were interspersed with political studies – the science of communism, Marxist–Leninist philosophy, etc. The cadets, although not yet commissioned, now enjoyed greater privileges but even so their freedom was very restricted. Saturday evenings and Sundays were normally free unless, as Belyenko reports, 'they were called to clean factories or work in the fields . . . requests which occurred roughly every other week'. Such extra work is not rewarded with extra pay and is no more popular than it would be in Western air forces.

At the end of his course the graduate is not considered to be a combat pilot. He is usually posted direct to a squadron of an air regiment – loosely, a wing in Western air forces – and it is the responsibility of the regiment to turn the fledgling into a real combat pilot. He will remain with this squadron, or at least with this regiment for about eight years or longer perhaps, steadily working his way up through categorised stages to the grade of 'Pilot-Engineer – First Class' probably with the rating of 'excellent'. At that point in his career he might be selected for higher staff or technical training at the Air Forces' 'Zhukovskiy' or 'Gagarin' Academies. In the meantime he settles down to the task of making himself a highly specialised combat pilot and gaining experience in the manifold executive appointments within the air regiment. His progress is directed and monitored by the regiment's own organic instructional staff who will re-classify him by stages and when he merits it.

Motivation has been a problem in the Soviet Air Forces. Beyond a pure love of flying with its natural compulsion to improve, how can the young pilot be spurred to strive for that 'excellent' grading? Western air forces unashamedly develop aircrew skills and maintain morale within their squadrons by the encouragement of various forms of competition in weapon delivery, navigation, sport, etc. These are powerful aids to morale and greater effort. They are equally so in the Soviet book but for doctrinal reasons the approach is different. Individuals in a society where individualism is eschewed as a social vice cannot compete one against the other even in friendly or sporting fashion. In logical extension neither can groups of individuals compete, as sections, squadrons or regiments. It would be anti-social to do so and productive only of that supreme anathema – the personality cult. The individual, the primary group and sub-sector, all must remain undistinguished and subordinate to that glorious larger entity, Soviet society as a whole. Ever since the Revolution this awkward doctrinal nicety has had a stultifying influence in all walks of Soviet life but in recent years to some extent it has been by-passed. The stimulating effects of individual human rivalry are now enjoyed in the Air Forces no less than elsewhere. The solution lay in the discovery at the time of the Twenty-Third Party Congress of the phrase 'socialist competition', attributed of course to Lenin. Socialist competition is encouraged as the healthy spur to socialist progress and the only true measure of a citizen's contribution to the corporate society. Theoretically it is a matter of competing only with oneself. The airman is persuaded therefore on almost every page of *Aviation and Cosmonautics* to compete; with his own earlier achievements, with his seniors and instructors in striving to match their standards and by implication, with his contemporaries in order to guarantee the highest standards of mutual reliance in combat situations. In practice, competition is as unbridled as it is in free societies now that the ideology has been squared with this casuistry. Very conveniently, the Russian word for 'competition' also means 'emulation'. It need not therefore offend the communist ear. Moreover it is used to endorse the need for individual initiative in air operations to correct the faults of rigidity and lack of imagination which have been characteristic of the personnel of the Soviet Air Forces since their foundation. These shortcomings are always implied rather than admitted but from the sheer weight of words devoted to them in the military-aviation press it is beyond doubt that they exist and that they are a matter of serious concern for higher commanders.

Whether socialist competition can eliminate these faults and generate a greater flexibility of mind in Soviet pilots remains to be seen. A change is unlikely to occur overnight but change there will be nevertheless. With some of their former inhibitions removed, individuals, squadrons and regiments now compete madly for the coveted label of 'excellent'. Entitled squadrons have the word 'excellent' stencilled on their aircraft and most issues of *Aviation and Cosmonautics* and *Red Star* carry the names and photographs of the successful. There is evidence that this drive for initiative is having some positive effect and Western air forces would be ill-advised to count much longer on holding their current superiority in this direction.

TACTICAL FLYING EXERCISES

With this hurdle of doctrine cleared the way was open for the setting of realistic training standards and the establishment of authorities to maintain them. From references to 'Tactical Aviation Exercises' and descriptions of their form it is evident that the Soviet Air Forces have evolved monitoring systems not unlike NATO's tactical evaluation of operational units and the Royal Air Force's categorisation of aircrew. Both aspects appear to be controlled by 'inspector-pilots' or 'flight-inspectors'. As in NATO it seems that these gentlemen can descend unheralded upon the hapless regimental commander to examine everything from the competence of his pilots and instructors to the quality of his direction in operational exercises. No sector is left unprobed. Engineering staff, air-traffic control, security arrangements and NBC defences are tested equally as rigorously as are the pilots. At the same time the inspecting team categorises aircrew and regimental instructors. The departure of the inspectors and the end of the exercises is usually cause for rejoicing anyway, but especially is it so if a satisfying number of 'excellent' gradings have been conferred, individually and corporately.

An 'excellent' grading is far from automatic, as an article by Colonel Kovrizhkin, senior inspector-pilot group of Soviet Forces Germany proves. His opening sentence sets the scene:

> The group of missile-armed aircraft headed by first-class military pilot Lieutenant-Colonel Yuri Yurin was already on the approach to the target when 'enemy' fighters appeared in the air . . .[11]

According to custom in such articles many lines are devoted to a recital of Yurin's fine qualities of leadership in the air and to the high standard of combat efficiency achieved by the aviators under his command. The training mission is then briefly described, again emphasising the accuracy of the flying, the cohesion of the formation and the precision of the attack. The enemy's opposition was determined and skilful but in vain. The attack succeeded. But also according to custom the praise for Colonel Yurin is merely the prelude to serious criticism. To herald this there is always a paragraph in these articles beginning with 'unfortunately' or, 'however'.

In this case an 'unfortunately' clause tells us that in spite of the brilliantly conducted attack, Colonel Yurin had not made the optimum use of his resources and therefore the outstanding grade for overall performance was withheld. The problem was that a fighter screen had been allotted to the attacking group to ensure more effective penetration of 'enemy' air defences. Yurin himself had personally assigned these screening fighters and had rehearsed the plans for coordination with them in great detail. But that was on the ground. Once in the air Yurin concentrated exclusively on controlling his own wingmen. Having assured himself that the attached fighters were proceeding on the correct heading he forgot about them and became utterly absorbed in his more immediate concerns. When the 'enemy' fighters appeared, instead of involving the screen he committed his own group to engaging them. The opposition was successfully dealt with – Soviet journalists never lose battles – and the group flew on to attack their target as planned, but Yurin is roundly criticised by the author for his failure to make the best use of assets at his disposal. Above everything else he was guilty of neglecting to coordinate these assets.

Failure to do anything in the Soviet Air Forces is ascribed to a breakdown of personal discipline. Soviet discipline is considered to stem from the individual's oath of allegiance to the Soviet state and the Communist Party. Breaches, other than criminal breaches, are dealt with by massively increased doses of ideological indoctrination or by psychological examination. The word 'psychology' in Soviet aviation journals is used in its straight clinical sense referring to the coordination of physical faculties but also it is used in a far wider sense in connection with morale and spiritual factors. *Aviation and Cosmonautics* carries in every issue at least one article concerning the correct psychological preparation for flight – or for war – and all contain a practical example, relating perhaps to a young pilot with a serious problem and how he has been helped by an older and more experienced colleague who takes the trouble to diagnose his junior's difficulty. A typical scenario might involve a worried young pilot who cannot get his bombs down within the acceptable accuracy limits. His mentor, an instructor or flight commander, after much patient psychological study is able to define the young man's condition and correct it. This he does by taking him off flying and talking to him exhaustively – as only Russians can – and then demonstrating the cause of his errors using the flight simulator. After this the young man is again allowed to fly and – who would have guessed? – the bombs go straight into the centre of the target.

So far this is not very different from the training patterns followed in Western air forces, but then we learn that the hero of the story is not the younger man who has persevered to eliminate his faults of judgement, but the older, wiser teacher. And when the question is asked, 'where did the flight commander or instructor obtain his liberal understanding views and his shrewd psychological knowledge of people?' he answers laconically, 'I am a communist, I got it from the Party, the Communist Party without which no Soviet endeavour can succeed'. Again the circle is squared and the supreme value of Marxist–Leninism as a discipline is proved. These stories taken at face value suggest that a wide cultural gap exists between the Soviet airman and his Western counterpart but credible defector evidence claims that these stories and the prescribed doctrinal remedies are treated with the same amused contempt as they would be in the West. On the other hand this almost metaphysical relationship between practical skills and Marxist–Leninist doctrine so permeates Soviet society that it cannot be without its effects on the psyche of their airmen. In an article to commemorate the Anniversary of the October Revolution, Marshal of Aviation Yefimov, now Commander-in-Chief of the Soviet Air Forces, wrote:

> It is essential to approach the evaluation of the results of the military aviation effort in a more demanding and exacting manner and resolutely to eliminate all things which impede the development of combat efficiency of the winged defenders of the homeland, their training and indoctrination. At this moment, on the threshold of the new training year, each and every Air Forces' military collective, each and every aviator must focus on achieving new performance levels in combat and political training. They must be deeply conscious of their rôle and their personal responsibility for strengthening the defences of the homeland, for the future of genuine socialism and life on our planet.[12]

In this issue of the journal there is another article, typical of those which are free of ideological exhortation and aimed simply at eliminating combat deficiencies. Lieutenant Colonel Novikov writes that 'Lack of Imagination and Innovation are Incompatible'.[13] This title reflects the West's long-held suspicion about Soviet fighter-pilots; that they are well-practised in routine ground-controlled interceptions but lack experience in making tactical decisions when the controller on the ground can no longer provide guidance. The colonel tells us that one Captain Smirnov was scrambled during a tactical air exercise to intercept an 'aggressor'. He followed the controller's directions precisely and very soon he reported that his target, an 'enemy' bomber, was in sight. 'Permission to destroy the target', replied the controller. Smirnov moved in closer for his photographic victory.

But, suddenly, the bomber disappeared from his radar screen. All his efforts to regain contact failed and he was unable to make his attack. What had gone wrong? Interceptions had always worked out before. Why not this time? Smirnov's superiors discovered that all his squadron's practices had been conducted in exactly the same routine fashion. The target always flew on the same heading, took predictable evasion manoeuvres, first to the right and then to the left and the fighter-pilot merely had to follow the tactical control officer's commands for an assured camera-gun kill. 'Do these exercises represent what might happen in actual combat?' they asked. 'Of course not', they answered their own question, 'the enemy is not stupid. He also has been taught to fight and would try always to evade the fighter with unpredictable manoeuvres'.

The target bomber pilot from the neighbouring unit was commended for his simulation of the real thing and Smirnov and his comrades sat down with their squadron commander and the flight-inspector to learn the lesson and work out how they might deal with an enemy who is actually aggressive. They decided that the answer lay in initiative and imagination, that 'even with an excellent aircraft and formidable weapons, if a pilot does not have a mastery of the great diversity of technique and modes of air combat conduct, he will be unable to make use of the advantages of his aircraft to defeat the enemy'. The lesson is learned and in the next tactical flying practice the squadron is 100 per cent successful in spite of the brilliant tactics of the resourceful bomber 'enemy'. Lieutenant Colonel Novikov in drawing the moral of this story writes:

Of course it is no easy task to improve the tactical proficiency of pilots and to develop first-rate fighting qualities in them. It requires constant and full exertion of effort, close coordination and mutual understanding with tactical control officers. A pilot should put all his capabilities into play in flying a training mission in a combat simulator. Some however, in their desire to receive a high mark, seek to avoid unnecessary risk and in doing so, they adhere to the simplest operational manoeuvres. To do this for the sake of the camera-gun record losing sight of the fact that in actual combat they will be dealing with a crafty adversary who is well trained and equipped with the most advanced hardware, such oversimplification is intolerable.

The tale of Captain Smirnov is only one of many success stories offered to readers of *Aviation and Cosmonautics* every month throughout the year. They reveal the fundamental concern that the High Command of the Soviet Air Forces has about the defects plaguing their organisation; that their personnel lack initiative and, insofar as they consider the examination result is an end in itself rather than a reflection of the skills and standards necessary for the successful prosecution of war, they lack moral conscience. And this is especially worrying since it represents a contradiction in Marxist–Leninist terms.

The proposed remedy is exhortation to more cooperative self-improvement in operational skills and – the cry for the last 65 years – more intensified political education. In a society where the national education system itself is corrupt, where from the kindergarten onwards the drive is for marks of approval rather than for real knowledge, it is unlikely that the Soviet Air Forces will have any more notable success than do other sectors of Soviet society in the development of social conscience. The attitude of 'don't stick your neck out – do just enough to get by' is likely therefore to persist, although the increasingly complex aircraft and weapon systems that the air forces have been acquiring in recent years are making ever greater demands on their human sub-systems. These cannot be denied. They will be met in spite of outmoded social attitudes or ideology. The Soviet nation as a whole from long experience knows exactly when ideology has to defer to expediency, a point not always understood by Westerners.

What they have greater difficulty over is initiative. The general lack of it represents a Russian character weakness. The absence of real initiative is compensated to some degree by the defensive practice Soviet commanders follow of framing comprehensive operation orders covering every conceivable contingency. Nothing as far as is humanly possible is left to chance. Written orders are supplemented at every level by exhaustive oral briefings to reduce the possibility of the unforeseen to virtually zero.

This is still not enough for the peace of mind of the High Command who continue to clamour for more and more initiative and independence of action. An understandable requirement this to be sure, but it creates a dilemma of choice in a system where collective discussion and corporate decision-making are *de rigueur* and all individual initiative is strongly discouraged if not actually suppressed in the interests of political cohesion. We are unlikely ever to be fully informed of the decision-making sequence which decreed the shooting down of the Korean Air Liner 007 aircraft over Kamchatka in September 1983 but it is not difficult to imagine the progressive indecision at ascending levels of command, culminating at some lower altitude than the Politburo in a rash order to shoot it down.

In any interpretation this incident suggests a sclerosis in the Soviet Air Forces' command and control structure. For routine exercises or in actual operations where all develops according to plan it might not be a serious disease. On the other hand, in war, it could perhaps give rise to a structural failure of the whole plan, a coming apart at the seams leading to failure and defeat. Soviet commanders fear this 'coming apart of the seams' – they call it *ractyerranost* – hence their insistent demands for a higher quality of initiative generally in their subordinates. From the tenor of writings in the aviation press it is more than clear that an intensive drive is in train to inculcate this quality of initiative, if necessary to the detriment of discipline in its traditionally rigid form. The political price of this will have to be paid if the Soviet Air Forces are to become truly efficient in this technologically demanding age. The more centralised command and control organisation adopted in recent years and a significantly enhanced communication system are probably considered a sufficient bridle to prevent any development of individual initiative straying beyond the desired operational boundaries.

Not all the personnel of the Soviet Air Forces are aircrew. Of almost equal importance are the engineers and groundstaff, the airmen – or more accurately – the soldiers. These can be dismissed briefly since the process of their recruitment, background and subsequent conditions of service are almost identical to those of their fellows conscripted into the Army and Navy. They are two-year conscripts and therefore not of great value in the advanced technical trades although indispensable for the ancillary tasks such as driving, cooking, hangar-sweeping, snow-shovelling and perhaps, storekeeping. The general unpopularity of military service, in spite of the glorious tone of official propaganda, means that comparatively few stay on beyond their term to become long-service NCOs. Those who do stay tend to be the mediocrities and bad-hats who would not get far in respectable civilian careers. As a rule they do not progress to become advanced tradesmen but are content to carry on driving or cooking, enhancing their life-style only by persecuting and blackmailing successive generations of new conscripts, extorting from them the little they receive by way of pay.

The Air Forces do however need men of some intelligence who are able to assist in complex, technical spheres such as aircraft maintenance, air traffic control, communications, and the operation and servicing of electronic and computer systems. Personnel destined for these functions are recruited from among the more intelligent of the annual cohort, the Soviet Air Forces having priority of selection second only to the Strategic Rocket Forces. Men already trained as radio operators or mechanics, or with DOSAAF experience before call-up in aviation-related subjects are obvious choices as are the many who have studied at institutes of higher technical education, failed to graduate and thereby lost their conscription exemption.

It is not so much therefore that the Air Forces find it difficult to select recruits of acceptable IQ as the straitjacket of the short conscription period which restricts the utility of the available manpower. Before trainees reach a stage of efficient development it is time to release them. The Soviet Air Forces are not alone here. Other air forces based on conscription face the same problem. The whole task of getting the aeroplane into the air and keeping them usefully flying rests heavily on the commissioned engineer officers.

As for aircrew, engineer officers having satisfied similar entry standards are trained in Institutes but on five-year rather than four-year courses. The syllabus at the Higher Military-Aviation Engineering Institutes is again a mix of technical and political instruction. The large numbers trained each year – there are no less than seven of these engineer officer–factories – are necessary to counterbalance the inadequacies of the conscript intake. The officer–man ratio is very close with lieutenants and captains carrying out the less complex duties that Western air forces would confidently entrust to lower enlisted ranks. The products of these Institutes, engineers highly trained both in theory and practice, are awarded degrees on graduation but nevertheless they must expect to spend a goodly number of years on the flight-line of an air regiment with their jackets off and spanners in their hands. Whereas in the West aircraft crew-chiefs are senior NCOs, nothing less than captains would be encountered in the Soviet Air Forces but the customary rank for a crew-chief is major.

In addition to the seven Higher Military-Aviation Engineering Institutes there are also four Aviation Technical Schools training aviation-technical officers. Courses here run for three years only and obviously the product is of a lower standard than that of the Institutes, successful students gaining diplomas rather than degrees, but information is too scant to allow a comparison of their performance and promotion prospects. It can be assumed only that they are likely to hold the spanner-wielding jobs on the flight-lines for longer than their Institute-trained colleagues.

Like the Army and Navy, the Soviet Air Forces some twelve years ago adopted the 'ensign' (*praporshchik*) rank in an attempt to bridge the gap between soldiers and officers and thereby improve the quality of a NCO corps that had long been notoriously lacking. The experiment at best has been only partially successful. Ensigns certainly have come to be regarded as right-hand men by the junior officers they assist but they do not appear to have erected a structurally reliable bridge either to the conscripts or to the NCOs of doubtful quality. The problem would seem to be one of association. As officers are commissioned so are ensigns granted their senior rank at an early age immediately following training in their own academy. They dress in officers' uniform with rank insignia only subtly different from that of a lieutenant and they enjoy most of the privileges of junior officers. Officers' clubs are open to them and they receive time promotion to lieutenant, so to all intents and purposes they are officers. The scheme has therefore been self-defeating and the problem remains.

Engineers are no less vulnerable to criticism than pilots and their errors or shortcomings are given wide publicity in the military press. The pattern of exposure is the same. The writer opens his critical article with unbounded praise for a particular unit, citing its second to none record in war and peace. Then, with a sentence beginning, 'Unfortunately . . .', it focuses on the offending individual or individuals, pillorying him or them for inefficiency or indiscipline.

Not long ago *Red Star* carried an article describing the severe problems that the slush of the Spring thaw can pose for aircraft operating at temperatures around zero. The article is sober and useful, giving good advice to help ensure that such conditions do not affect aircraft sortie rate, in training or in war. Suddenly however the spotlight is directed on to Major Silvanovich, a crew-chief who had allowed his pilot to take-off with ice in the undercarriage preventing its retraction. This, on the front page of a national daily is unlikely to have enhanced Silvanovich's career prospects.

If Silvanovich's sin was a lapse of personal discipline, Major Sakhautvinov's crime was failing to supervise a subordinate. According to *Red Star* one of Sakhautvinov's aircraft technicians, one Senior-Lieutenant Dubinin, taking advantage of his superior's lax supervision, took short-cuts and violated all the rules for replenishing aircraft for a battle sortie to the extent that he even omitted to refuel a missile-armed aircraft. For this he was publicly reproached, the name of Dubinin being brought not only to the attention of all ranks in the five branches of the Armed Forces but also to that of every citizen in all the fifteen Republics of the USSR. But the editor of *Red Star* makes it clear that he exposes offenders in this way not in a punitive spirit but simply in the good cause of eliminating 'technical errors' and thus enhancing 'war-preparedness', the great national aim. The practice, insofar as it succeeds in breeding a fear of this kind of publicity, is probably more effective than the officially-recommended remedy for flight-line indiscipline. Once again this is the usual reflex demand for more indoctrination:

> Commanders, political organs of the Party and the KOMSOMOL must pay unremitting attention to the training of the highly-qualified aviation engineers, technicians and junior specialists who love their profession. They must employ all methods of Party-political indoctrination to instil in them a sense of responsibility for the performance of their assigned task to maintain the aircraft and equipment in their charge in a state of constant combat readiness.[14]

Soviet security ensures that it is even more difficult to assess the quality of their Air Forces' ground personnel than to judge their pilots. Glimpses of their aircraft are vouchsafed to foreigners but the activities of engineers inside their airfield perimeter fences are totally hidden. But if Soviet journals in the main paint a picture of unrelieved perfection, of Air Forces finely tuned for war at any moment, it is perhaps reassuring to note just how many Silvanoviches, Sakhautvinovs and Dubinins there are to mar the canvas with their testimony of human fallibility. On the other hand it has to be conceded, in spite of all the warts, the suffocating political indoctrination and the rigid training system producing pilots without initiative and engineers who fail to service their aircraft, that the corporate whole, Soviet air power, is with little doubt greater than the sum of the parts. From actual evidence and from inference it does seem that both engineers, pilots and officers of other branches carry out their respective tasks with a good degree of confidence. Some of the operational practices might give Western professionals cause to wince but against their extreme climate and the built-in head winds of their political system they do keep the aircraft flying, the turbines turning and the guns firing. In recent years the Soviet Air Forces have developed to a size and quality posing a threat that the West might underrate only at its peril. They have already acquired capabilities approaching those of Western air forces and are continuing to develop at a disquieting rate.

Finally, it should be noticed that it is the Air Forces that are driving the Soviet nation into space. Their professional journal is not concerned simply with aviation but also devotes many of its pages to the cosmic tracts beyond the stratosphere. For many years it has been styled *Aviation and Cosmonautics.* Young Soviet men dream of becoming cosmonauts as once their forefathers dreamt of flying aeroplanes. The crowds seen on Sundays in the Moscow space museum testify that the whole nation supports their ambition. Since their dramatic first, *Sputnik 1* in 1957, space achievements have been a matter of enormous pride for Soviet people, a patent validation of their claim to Superpower status. The exploration of the cosmos they regard in the same symbolic relation to perfected communism as hitherto they have related aviation to The Revolution and Socialism – i.e. as the key to the future. It remains for that future to prove whether the pseudo-scientific Marxist–Leninist teachings stood up to the journey.

6 The Soviet Sailor

J. E. MOORE

While all military service in the Soviet Union is described as an honourable duty and a privilege for those doing it, naval service has always held a special place in the esteem of the general public. This is not entirely due to the continuous and fulsome praise heaped upon the navy by the political leaders and the press. A lot of credit and respect is based on the part the navy played in the Revolution and the subsequent setting up of the Party, and the 1921 Kronshtadt rebellion does not appear to have affected that, but the prime factor seems to be that the navy travels to foreign countries – a tantalising thought for the great majority of Soviet citizens to whom any foreign travel remains a dream.

Roughly 20 per cent of the navy consists of officers, with a further ten per cent made up of warrant officers and volunteer extended servicemen. The remaining 70 per cent is entirely conscript, serving for two years ashore or three years afloat. Women may volunteer for shore service as clerks, communicators, caterers or medical staff and the recent spate of press coverage probably indicates their growing importance in keeping the Navy running.

Currently the navy has approximately half a million men in uniform. Of these almost 200 000 are at sea, 60 000 are in naval aviation, 16 000 are naval infantry with 8000 in coastal defence and a further 4000 manning coastal observation posts. Some 58 000 are engaged in training and about 125 000 provide shore support. Large numbers of civilians also furnish support and man many of the auxiliary ships, although a naval presence is always included. A separate Border Guard navy under the control of the KGB carries out the functions of the British coastguards Customs and Immigration Services as well as preventing illegal emigration.

PRE-SERVICE TRAINING

The indoctrination of the Soviet child has already been discussed but it is worth noting once more that, from pre-school days, these children are exposed to a steady flow of nationalistic propaganda. The elevation of certain courageous military characters to the status of heroes and the dissemination of tales of their valorous deeds is a major part of this early training which soon has more practical additions. These include mock battles and military manoeuvres supervised by professional officers, occupations designed to instil in the young the patriotism, discipline, obedience and sense of duty which is necessary for future members of the armed forces if the latter are to remain cohesive organisations within the numbing constraints of the Soviet system.

In 1967 the amended Universal Military Service Law lowered the age of conscription to eighteen and also reduced the terms of service by one year to two years for all the armed forces but three years for those serving afloat. To make up for the lost year a system of compulsory pre-military training was introduced. This comes under the direct control of the local military commissions who are also responsible for conscript registration and call-up as well as for maintaining lists of reservists and running the mobilisation programme. For those undergoing a ten-year high school course or attending a technical school, military training is carried out in school during the final two years. For those leaving school in their eighth year the training is carried out at their place of work. This consists of 140 hours of instruction over two years and includes basic military skills, weapon training and military indoctrination.

In 1977 a change in the law increased the time to be served by those who had been deferred for educational reasons to one year (18 months afloat) after they had completed their course of study. Recent indications are that only Medical and Agricultural students are getting deferments and that all other students have to complete their conscripted service before embarking upon a course of further education.

In addition to this compulsory training and the activities of the Communist Youth League KOMSOMOL, paramilitary specialist courses are run at clubs organised by the All Union Voluntary Society for Assistance to the Army, Air Force and Navy

(DOSAAF). The clubs and courses are normally aimed at a particular service and will be supported by it. They carry on the basic training of the individual but also provide specialist training in various fields on behalf of their sponsor service. Training in radio operating, diving, driving, parachuting and flying have been noted and it has been claimed that some conscripts are sufficiently well trained on induction to be able to proceed direct to their ships, but the main reason for the popularity of the clubs is that they provide facilities which are not available anywhere else in the Soviet Union. However, the whole system regularly comes in for strong criticism in the press for producing an unsatisfactory balance of skills, so all is not perfect. Nevertheless any training in advance of conscription must assist the services in their tasks as do the activities of various sporting clubs involved in swimming, parachuting, musketry and other military activities.

On completion of conscription naval ratings have to register again with their local military commission as reservists. They remain eligible until the age of 50. With some 130 000 entering the reserves every year there is a vast pool of training manpower available but, with only sporadic reserve training, those more than three or four years out of date would not be suitable for sea service. Nevertheless the figures, particularly when compared with numbers available in Western countries, are impressive. Approximately 6.5 million naval reservists remain on the books – of these half a million would be suitable for call-up to their original service. Most of this huge number, in fact, are earmarked for the army, whatever their previous service, but even here the authorities must be somewhat selective if mobilisation is not to bring the country to a complete stop.

RATINGS

The Soviet naval rating is a conscript with very limited training and with little desire to do more than complete his service with the minimum of fuss. The navy is fortunate in being able to select the better type of conscript (together with the Strategic Rocket Forces) so is less burdened than the army with men speaking Russian as a second language or not at all. However some 65 000 are inducted every six months, a change of 18 per cent twice a year, a mammoth task of assimilation and training necessitating a constant return to the most basic stages of ship operation.

The conscript undergoes a nine-week basic training programme where he is either selected for further specialist training or goes directly to a ship. Some three-quarters of all conscripts receive extra specialist training before joining the fleet. Those who are considered incapable of benefiting from this training are placed in such tasks as construction worker or security guard.

Specialist training takes from four to six months depending on the complexity of the subject. It is based on learning by rote and produces men who have a basic understanding of the theory of their equipment but no practical experience. They are not cross-trained in other roles and usually only study the equipment to be found in the ship they are destined to man. On-the-job training begins only on joining the ship. Here the conscript understudies his predecessor whose discharge will, if necessary, be delayed until the relief rating has reached a satisfactory standard. Once this stage has been reached the Officers and Warrant Officers of his department will give him further practical training to enable him to qualify as a third-class specialist. If he is suitable and is prepared to study by himself the conscript can, without any further training ashore, proceed to qualify on board as a second- and then a first-class specialist. It is claimed that it is possible to pass from third- to first-class in one year, so a conscript could be rated first-class after only 18 months service – a fair indication of the lower standards required *vis-à-vis* Western navies. The differentiation between substantive (e.g. AB) rates and non-substantive (e.g. Layer first-class) is much the same as existed in earlier years in Western fleets. Thus an able seaman could be captain of a gun. A senior substantive rating is, therefore, not necessarily more qualified technically although this may be the case on a number of occasions.

In parallel with specialist or combat training goes the political training required by the Party. Each ship has a fully trained political officer as the Deputy CO for Political Matters as well as carrying a KGB officer and each department in the ship has an officer appointed as the deputy department head for political affairs. In addition there is a Party Bureau and a Young Communist League (KOMSOMOL) organisation. All these attempt to get the conscript into the Party. As a side product they run the various forms of socialist competition without which nothing seems to happen. Satisfactory Party activity and a third-class rating will enable the Captain to award the 'outstanding' badge. The number of specialists and 'outstanding' ratings in a ship are taken into account in judging its performance against other ships of similar class in the annual search to find the best ship in the navy for each type of activity.

This system of standardised competitions, working against set goals, has led to many abuses. These range from setting low targets of achievement to outright cheating. One watch of a ship's crew will tend to have all the best ratings posted to it so that, whenever there is a competitive drill, this team can perform and gain high marks. This overlooks the fact that the other watches are not getting the training or practice to enable them to work well and raises doubts as to the ability of the ship to operate in war for very long at peak activity. The authorities are aware of this but do not yet seem to have found a way out of the dilemma.

Pay for the conscript is very low. Basic pay is 7 roubles (about £7) per month with an additional rouble when serving in an operational ship. There is no extra pay for higher ratings up to Petty Officer first-class but extra allowances of 2½ and 5 roubles are paid for second- and first-class specialist rates. Extra money is awarded for positions of responsibility such as team leader on a gun or sonar set, but the maximum amount will not exceed some 40 roubles a month. Alcohol is forbidden for the sailor in a ship and leave is very much a privilege – none in the first year of service, a maximum of 10 days plus travelling time in the second and third years. Many conscripts complete their service without ever having had home leave. It appears that no conscript may serve within 620 miles of his home, so short leave is insufficient to enable them to get home, unless travelling time is extended. On long deployments ships often spend lengthy periods at anchor and only rarely is shore leave granted to small supervised parties. However, there is some alleviation of the lot of the sailors' families – exemption from marriage tax, housing assistance as well as ensured employment for wives and discharged conscripts.

Living conditions on board are poor by Western standards but the more modern ships provide standards which are higher than many conscripts will have enjoyed ashore. Nevertheless the filthy conditions of the heads, the inadequate toilet facilities and frequent 'hot-bunking' (the use of the bunk recently vacated by the man relieving the watch) must have some effect on the more enlightened members of the crew. When compared with the comparatively sumptuous accommodation provided for the officers, the gulf between standards is strangely reminiscent of the situation in the Tsarist navies. Food is dull and monotonous but that applies all over the Soviet Union. Its stowage and replenishment clearly present fewer problems than those facing NATO navies.

But from early childhood these sailors have been brought up on stories of the sacrifices of the Revolutionaries and the fighters of the Great Patriotic War and these tales, coupled with centuries of hardship and natural Russian fatalism, seems to make them reasonably happy with their lot.

WARRANT OFFICERS

Prior to 1971 ratings could volunteer to extend their service in the rate they held and could rise to the rank of Chief Petty Officer. Given sufficient time they might even attain Master Specialist rating. On the whole the wrong type remained and set a bad example to the young conscripts. To overcome the problem the Warrant Officer (Michman) rate was reintroduced, giving better uniform as well as pay and conditions similar to those of the junior officers. At the same time all other extended service rates were abolished so that many of the old element became Warrant Officers overnight. New ones were required to engage for a period of five years and could continue to extend by increments of five years. They received better training and were written up as the indispensable assistants of the officers. At sea they undertook some of the more routine maintenance of equipment and even filled some of the billets previously occupied by junior officers. It is an interesting comment on the approach of the new Soviet navy that, ten years after the humiliations off Cuba, the management was only just appreciating the fact, so well known for generations in Western fleets, that the backbone of a ship lies in the Chief Petty Officers' mess.

In spite of this not enough suitable candidates came forward and it was necessary very soon to reintroduce the old extended service rating structure again, extensions being for two, four or six years. Even this was not enough and, in 1980, the new rate of senior Warrant Officer was introduced for those who were filling officer type posts. It is too early yet to tell if this has been effective. Under the previous rules many of the better warrant officers had already progressed to officer status. Press articles suggest that many officers are still not employing the warrant officers correctly and that they are not always allowed to use their initiative or to take charge in a satisfactory way. That is probably a fault of the system rather than of individual officers.

The total pay of a warrant officer starts at the national average wage of about 170 roubles (about £135) per month and can go up to about 250. Leave, to a maximum of 45 days a year, depends on the area of service and the length of service, but starts at 30 days a year in the same way as for junior officers.

OFFICERS

The position of the Soviet naval officer has changed little since the days of the Tsar. He is still a valued and respected member of society, well paid and looked after; a member of an élite. His attitudes towards his ratings are often not much different from those of his forebears and his treatment of them bears this out. In a so-called egalitarian society his pay, position and conditions of service are so far in excess of anything his subordinates can expect that they call everything about the Soviet system into question.

The average naval officer, a volunteer career man, is likely to be the relative of another naval officer or of a Party official. He will have been carefully selected and well trained in his specialisation. He will almost certainly be a Great Russian or Ukrainian. Most start their careers with a five year training course at one of the eleven Higher Naval Schools, although a few will have made their way up from the ranks or will be reserve officers who have completed a naval course during their main course of instruction at college.

The favoured method of entry, used by a large proportion of the present senior officers, is through the Nakhimov Naval School, where they undergo a special three-year course aimed specifically at entry into a Higher Naval School. This school is the only one left of three originally opened during World War II for the sons of those killed in action. This requirement was later dropped and by

1955 the schools at Riga and Tbilisi had closed, leaving only that at Leningrad to carry on the name.

Candidates for the Higher Naval Schools have to pass a rigorous written examination and then satisfy a selection board that they possess the necessary attributes for a naval career. Competition is fierce and most places are oversubscribed, especially at the more popular schools. In fact recent articles by senior officers have suggested that the standard of candidate being attracted is not high enough and advise the schools to embark upon a much more aggressive policy of selling themselves to the youth of the country by means of open days, sponsorship of clubs and provision of sea trips. They are also using selection tests to a much greater extent in order to cut down an unknown but obviously significant failure rate.

Selected candidates for officer school enter as cadets and serve for five years. At the end of this period the best will receive an Engineering Diploma and a commission as Lieutenant. They will already have been selected for their future speciality and those passing out at the top of their year are allowed to express a preference for their area of duty. The rest go where they are sent but it seems that only the better qualified cadets can hope to get to sea. After graduation officers join a ship and, in a destroyer or below, remain onboard while they work up through their department to becoming Head of it as a senior lieutenant or captain lieutenant after five to six years. In this time they will take various examinations to enable them to stand watch, to obtain a higher rating in their speciality and be certified as a supervisor. Not only do they act as managers of their departments but also undertake the role of technical specialist. A satisfactory officer is involved in the supervision of his sailors' duties, their political well-being and all but the most elementary maintenance tasks. With such a heavy work load it is somewhat surprising that so many junior officers still manage to find the time and effort to study for promotion as well.

COMMAND

In the Soviet navy the Commanding Officer frequently selects his own successor. This will normally be one of his departmental heads and favours those who specialise in navigation or gunnery and missiles. Having been chosen, an officer is appointed as executive officer and begins a programme of study to broaden his experience and to fit him for command. When ready he will take a test for command and ultimately will become CO of the ship or of one of a similar class. He will remain in command for some three to five years during which he, too, will train his successor. Even in command there are several levels to pass through before being allowed to take a ship to sea independently, and yet more tests and examinations before being qualified to lead a group of ships at sea. All this certification takes time and can lead to various forms of nepotism as senior officers advance their favourites.

Those officers not selected for command usually return to their specialisation schools for advanced training in their subject before going on to become staff officers or instructors. In an attempt to improve standards of expertise and to cope with certification of officers many ships carry staff officers with them at sea advising, instructing and checking. In fact it is possible to arrive at a situation in a ship where every officer from the CO downwards is duplicated by a staff officer. This could result in a fair measure of overcrowding in a ship such as a *Kashin* class where the normal wardroom is 20–65 officers out of a complement of 280–300. In a ballistic missile submarine, with many more officers, the conditions would be unbearable.

SENIOR OFFICERS

Throughout his career the naval officer is encouraged to undertake postgraduate study. This may be done by correspondence course or, for the favoured few, at special schools. An advanced degree is almost mandatory for the more senior command posts. Thus, usually after their first command, officers attend the Marshal Grechko Naval Academy in Leningrad for a two year course designed to fit them for higher responsibility. Following staff and further command experience those selected for advancement to flag rank will normally attend the Academy of the General Staff, a joint service organisation in Moscow. From this it can be seen that the Soviet navy recognises that its system has deficiencies. From the beginning the officer is trained as a narrow specialist and all this special effort to broaden the experience of the chosen few getting to the top emphasises that narrowness. By Western standards the average Soviet officer is not a very balanced product.

PAY

The Soviet naval officer is very well paid and is on average better paid than his colleagues in the other armed forces. Rank pay is added to position pay to form base pay. This can be doubled or even trebled depending on the area and conditions of his service and also attracts climatic pay, length of service pay and, in some cases, extra specialist pay. The outcome is that most officers receive far more pay than their peers in civilian life and probably explains the desire of the young to join. Service also qualifies the officer for a state pension and again certain types of service can count as double or treble time for pension purpose although the time actually served remains a minimum of twenty-five years including cadet training.

The following is a rough example of the complexity of this system:

		roubles
1.	Rank pay	100
2.	Position pay (3× rank pay	300
3.	Base pay (1 + 2)	400
4.	Increments (+5 per cent after 2 years, 10 per cent after 5 years, 15 per cent after 10 years and so on at 1 per cent per year)	440 (after 5 years)
5.	Specialist pay for submariners and others such as *Spetsnaz*. (Add one-half to base pay)	640 (submariners)
6.	Add also sea pay on a daily rate and, sometimes, climatic pay.	

The trebling of base pay is technically reserved for war service; doubling is used for service under what the Western sailor would consider 'unsocial' conditions.

HIGHER NAVAL SCHOOLS

Location	School	Speciality
Leningrad	Frunze Higher Naval School	Executive Seaman Branch
Vladivostock	Makarov Pacific Ocean Higher Naval School	Executive Seaman Branch
Baku	Kirov Red Banner Caspian Sea Higher Naval School	Executive Seaman Branch
Sevastopol	Nakhimov Black Sea Higher Naval School	Executive Seaman Branch
Kaliningrad	Kaliningrad Higher Naval School	Executive Seaman Branch
Leningrad	Leninskiy Komsomol Higher Naval School of Submarine Navigation	Submarine Officers
Leningrad	Dzerzhinskiy Order of Lenin Higher Naval Engineering School	Ship Engineers
Sevastopol	Sevastopol Higher Naval Engineering School	Ship Engineers
Leningrad (Petrodvorets)	Popov Higher Naval Radio Electronics School	Radio Electronics
Leningrad (Pushkin)	Lenin Higher Naval Engineering School	Shore Engineers
Kiev	Kiev Higher Naval Political School	Political Officers

All except the political school carry out a five-year training programme. The Kiev HNS gives only a four-year course.

Postgraduate courses are held at the following:

Leningrad	Order of Lenin and Ushakov Naval Academy named after Marshal of the Soviet Union A. A. Grechko	Advanced Technical & Staff Training
Moscow	Higher Military Academy of the General Staff	All Services General Staff Training
Kronshtadt	Naval Officers Technical School	Officer Technical Training
Leningrad	School for Higher Naval Courses	Officer Technical Training

All flying training is carried out by the Soviet Air Forces and it is not at all clear whether the naval aviator starts in the navy or is merely selected for the service at the end of his flying training. It is not until the level of operational flying training is reached that we see a separate naval training section.

In medicine, transport and supply the navy again relies upon all service schools and academies for training but it is believed that some of the officers are selected for this training by the navy beforehand. Medicine is the most likely area for recruitment of women.

The naval infantry officers undergo their training for infantry, tank or artillery units with the army schools and academies. It is not known at what stage they are selected for this arm of the service. However, there is some evidence that the conscript volunteers for the naval infantry are often influenced by the fact that they have to serve for a period of only two years, even though the training and service are so much more arduous.

LEADERSHIP

The highest position in the Soviet Navy is that of Commander-in-Chief, which also embraces the political post of a Deputy Minister of Defence, in line with the Heads of the other four services. Thus the current incumbent, Admiral of the Fleet of the Soviet Union V. N. Chernavin, is both Chief of the Naval Staff and Minister for the Navy. Under him are two First Deputy Commanders-in-Chief responsible for the operation and administration of the navy. Below them are some eight Deputy Commanders-in-Chief responsible for the various training, technical, logistic and administrative functions. In addition the heads of the various directorates form a naval staff to assist with policy and planning.

Each of the four Fleets is headed by a Fleet Commander who had beneath him a very similar but smaller staff structure than that of the C.-in-C.

Soviet Admirals tend to remain in post for a very long time. Gorshkov until his retirement in 1985 had been C.-in-C. for over 29 years and terms of ten or more years are common even with Fleet Commanders. Over the years a pattern has emerged where the Commanders of the Northern and Pacific Fleets provide the top members of the central staff while the Baltic and Black Sea Fleets provide Commandants of schools and academics and fill the administrative posts for training and the like. This reflects the relative strengths and roles of the fleets. A perfect illustration is

Admiral Chernavin. Before his promotion to C.-in-C. he had served as First Deputy C.-in-C. and Chief of the Main Naval Staff, who is responsible for naval operations. After a career in Northern Fleet SSBNs he was then Chief of Staff and later Commander of the Northern Fleet.

POLITICAL AFFAIRS

Like everything in the Soviet Union the navy is subject to political indoctrination and monitoring of their activities by the Communist Party. Compared with other sectors of the community a very high proportion of officers belong to the Party but, since membership is a requirement for promotion beyond Commander, this could reflect the facts of life as much as any deep commitment to the faith. The Party in turn is determined to ensure that its main support remains subordinate and unable to obtain power on its own.

Throughout the navy the command structure is paralleled by a political structure and the Political Directorates of the various branches of the Armed Forces are all subordinate to a central Armed Forces Main Political Administration (MPA). At the lower levels a lot of the effort of the junior political officers is devoted to the ubiquitous socialist competition without which the navy seems unable to operate. In this way the interests of the CO and the Political Officer become the same and so many of the grounds for difference which previously existed between them have been removed.

COMPARABILITY

Any comparison of ranks between the Soviet and Western navies is difficult. The former has made a point of giving basically equivalent ranks one badge of rank higher than the latter so that a Captain wears a Commodore's thick stripe. Additional levels of rank have also been introduced. The following list is a rough approximation of the various equivalents:

SOVIET RANKS	BRITISH RANKS
Admiral of the Fleet of the Soviet Union	Admiral of the Fleet
Admiral of the Fleet	
	Admiral
Admiral	
	Vice Admiral
Vice-Admiral	
	Rear Admiral
Rear Admiral	
	Commodore
Captain 1st Rank	Captain
Captain 2nd Rank	Commander
Captain 3rd Rank	Lieutenant Commander
Captain Lieutenant	Lieutenant over 6 years
Senior Lieutenant	Lieutenant under 6 years
Lieutenant	Sub-Lieutenant
Junior Lieutenant (only reserve officers and retired Michmans on reserve)	
Senior Warrant Officer	
Warrant Officer	Fleet Chief Petty Officer
Ship's Chief Petty Officer	
	Chief Petty Officer
Chief Petty Officer	
Petty Officer 1st Class	Petty Officer
Petty Officer 2nd Class	Leading Seaman
Senior Seaman	Able Seaman
Seaman	Ordinary Seaman

No attempt has been made to differentiate between the various badges of rank and the branch distinguishing colours. This is a complex subject more suited to a separate study, but it must be emphasised that, though there is a superficial comparability in the lower grades, the Western equivalent is of a vastly higher professional standard.

CONCLUSION

There can be no direct comparison between those who man the Soviet Navy and those in the navies of the rest of the world. This stems from the fundamental differences between the Soviet system and the administration of any other fleet and is typified by the fact that the head of the navy in the USSR holds both a political and a professional position.

In a different way this duality permeates the whole Soviet Navy. Political indoctrination is continuous and combines in an extraordinary way with the conduct of a ship's business. Ordinary naval officers are responsible for the political guidance of those in their department while the ship's Political Officer is in overall charge of this aspect of affairs, as well as its coordination with operational matters and is a very basic welfare officer.

The fact that 70 per cent of the navy's personnel serves for only three years and one-sixth of this huge number changes every six months requires a gigantic training effort, causes considerable manpower turbulence on board and throws a considerable burden of maintenance on the officers and warrant officers.

Of these none has ever been engaged in active hostilities except for a small number of the more senior admirals. This may be one of several reasons which lie behind the close central control, a grip which has recently undergone certain minor relaxations.

The Soviet sailor lives under conditions unseen in Western fleets for fifty years, is miserably paid, harshly disciplined and subjected to a constant stream of party indoctrination. The variations in population throughout the USSR are tilting the balance away from homogeneous ships' companies and this change is accelerating.

It is impossible to predict how the men would react under battle conditions. Their officers are probably too highly specialised, the warrant officers generally with inadequate experience. We must hope that the truth will never emerge from the fact of conflict but were it to do so a personal opinion is that the high command would function with speed and efficiency, squadron and ship commands would still seek guidance from above and those in the ships would fight with courage and tenacity. How all this would stand up to the terror of action, casualties and ship damage is an open question.

7 Some Current Considerations

The continuing Soviet campaign in Afghanistan is the obvious 'behavioural laboratory' for the testing of theories concerning the morale and motivation of their Armed Forces or the efficiency of their political indoctrination system.

Soviet troops invaded Afghanistan in force as long ago as December 1979. Unfortunately, intelligence on the conduct of their campaign has proved relatively difficult to obtain but a body of evidence of morale and troop behaviour has been gathered from various sources sufficient to indicate that conditions there have not successfully united soldiers in a selfless common effort against socialism's enemies. The chronic cycle of depression and crime appears to operate in this active theatre much as it does inside the USSR peacetime bases but the backcloth of war adds greater drama both to cause and effect. Criminal violence appears to have become prevalent.

The greater bulk of the available evidence has been gained from Soviet soldiers who have defected either directly to the Mujahedin forces or who have done so after capture. They have testified to their captors and, later, to journalists or representatives of *émigré* and other organisations. Reports of this testimony by NTS[1] and some other *émigré* groups show an understandable bias towards the Russian *émigré* cause but the general tenor of the defectors' stories is consistent and largely credible. At the time of writing the number of witnesses is small. A *Daily Mail* story of two defectors who have managed to reach the West claimed that they are the 'first of hundreds'. The claim has not so far (May 1986) been borne out.[2]

The number of witnesses is comparatively small but a composite picture emerges of steadily decreasing morale among the troops. The familiar problems of boredom, bad discipline, primitive hygiene and poor living conditions generally are present

176

in Afghanistan. Unusually, drunkeness does not seem to be quite the problem it is in the USSR, as a result it would seem of a dearth of liquor, but its place has been taken by hashish or, according to some journalists' reports, harder drugs.

Typical of deserters' stories is that told by Private Zakharov in a convincing interview conducted in late 1982. Zakharov, a nineteen-year old farm-worker from Mordovia claimed that disaffection is now so rife that officers and NCOs have been shot by their own men:

They did it to make us submit to everything. The sergeants, told us "We were beaten, so now we beat you". Sometimes it got so bad that soldiers would try to defend themselves with their guns. Such shootings are happening more and more often all over Afghanistan. The usual punishment is a minimum of fifteen years in a military prison. There is not only lack of enthusiasm for service in Afghanistan but also a total absence of loyalty to those in command and to the government itself.

Zakharov and others complained similarly about living conditions. Accommodation is in tents – 30 men crowded in each tent. Poor and inadequate food is the soldier's lot. Some units it seems do have special shops selling foodstuffs, but only for officers. Conscript soldiers have no such facility. The cramped conditions, low standard of hygiene and poor food result in serious epidemics of hepatitis, cholera, typhoid and a high suicide rate.

In such conditions it is scarcely surprising that troops seek solace from vodka – except that there is no vodka. A drink could be made from hydraulic fluid and water, but a bottle of real vodka bought on the black market would have absorbed six months' pay. Hashish is a readily available substitute and other drugs are obtainable. Zakharov says that drug use is widespread, in many cases to the point of addiction, some soldiers becoming so desperate that they would barter arms with the local population for drugs. He mentioned a case of three soldiers who were given sentences ranging from six to ten years for 'selling bullets' to civilians.

These conscript tales cannot be relied upon implicitly but much of what they say is credible. It seems that the Soviet military authorities cannot trust the ideological training programme to offset the deleterious effect on morale of these conditions however much they sharpen up the image of the external enemy. Sergeant Povarnitsyn, another Soviet soldier captured by the Mujahedin intimated that he had been told that Soviet troops had been invited into Afghanistan by the lawful government of that country to repel counter-revolutionary bandits from China and the United States. In a broadcast to his erstwhile colleagues over Radio Free Kabul he dismissed the claims as rubbish. 'It becomes obvious to every Soviet soldier', he said, 'that the Mujahedin enjoy widespread national support and Soviet troops are only there to do Babrak Karmal's dirty work.'[3]

Povarnitsyn conceivably was under pressure from his Mujahedin 'hosts' to declare himself in such terms but he is by no means a lone voice. Privates Ryzhkov and Voronin, interviewed in a less, apprehensive environment, in Brussels,[4] tell of a briefing they received before they were sent to Afghanistan, 'It was very inspiring, they told us we were going to Afghanistan to defend our homeland. The two great enemies of our country, America and China, were working together, building aggressive bases in Afghanistan in preparation for the invasion of the Soviet Union. The Soviet Army could not stand idly by while these imperialist plans were so blatantly carried out. The Defence of the homeland must take place in Afghanistan itself. We were to be among the troops honoured to carry out that sacred mission.'

Ryzhkov and Voronin like many others were soon disillusioned. Not only were they demoralised by the wretched conditions already described by Zakharov, they began to realise that their briefing had been a little wide of the mark. As reported by Bethell they soon came to the conclusion that:

> We were ordinary soldiers with no great education but we knew we were not fighting Americans or Chinese. What they had told us was not true. We knew we were fighting the Afghan people but, even more important we knew they were not going to invade the Soviet Union. They were only defending their country the way we in Russia did in 1941.[5]

Coming on top of the bad living conditions, the sickness, the lack of discipline and the corruption, this crumbling of the ideological defences completed the demoralisation of these young men. The *Zampolit* had failed. It is impossible at present to assess the extent of this collapse of morale among Soviet troops in

Afghanistan but there are indications that, while serious, it is far from total. The campaign there and the behaviour of the Soviet soldier – and airman – need close attention when forming any judgement of the likely performance of the Soviet Armed Forces in other settings.

It is becoming fashionable in some quarters to compare Afghanistan with Vietnam and conclude that the troop behaviour of the respective invaders has been similar. Certainly there are common factors; drug abuse, the 'fragging' of officers or NCOs, a high crime-rate and, above all, an unclear mission. However, low morale is both cause and consequence when these conditions operate and much of the comparison is valid. The longer-term effects of Afghanistan are not easy to predict. The Soviet Union will not be able to purge itself in the way that the open society of the United States was able to do, however painfully. It will on the other hand be able to rewrite history and expunge the uncomfortable facts of Afghanistan from the Soviet folk-memory. Military morale will be another problem. Until they re-shape their disciplinary system to a pattern of mutual respect between all ranks and strong primary group loyalties, the Soviet Forces will, as they did after Hungary in 1956 and Czechoslovakia in 1968, have to rely on a massively increased dosage of 'political enlightenment' to repair the damage. The method has not been without its successes.

MORALE AND MOTIVATION – A GENERAL SUMMARY

From the foregoing paragraphs it is clear that the gauging of morale in the Soviet Armed Forces is no simple task. The imponderables are many. Dissidents, defectors and *émigrés* say it is low and their claim is supported by a considerable weight of collateral evidence. On the other hand the structure of the various arms is holding up, albeit with difficulty even in Afghanistan, almost certainly on account of the continued, conforming co-operation of the silent majority of Soviet-educated officers and conscripted men who, as Kravchenko said, have that yearning desire to believe the Marxist–Leninist philosophy and will go to any length to explain and justify its excesses.[6] The Marxist–Leninist faith, or at least a faith proclaimed in the knowledge that there can be no prospect of a tolerable life in the Soviet Union without expressing it, coupled with a determination to defend Mother Russia – and, arguably, Mother Uzbekistan – against barbaric external enemies, motivates the bulk of Soviet officers and soldiers to serve loyally in peacetime. This apparently holds true in Afghanistan despite the proven desertions.

How long this majority will conform and remain docile depends on the development of internal politics within the whole Soviet nation. That is a question beyond the scope of this book but there are definite signs of disquiet among the leadership over current social trends. As the October Revolution recedes into history a younger generation, bored and disenchanted with many aspects of the official Party message is beginning to question the paramount importance of ideology. Impatient at the non-arrival of the golden era of communism and fascinated by the artefacts of Western culture, the clothes, music, books and ideas, many young people are becoming less ready to conform and their growing antagonism to the outmoded slogans of earlier days is expressing itself not only by criticism of the sacred Marxist–Leninist tenets but also slackness at work, vandalism, drunkenness and a lack of interest in military affairs. The current generation of *Zampoliti* have not escaped contamination. Andropov, Chernenko and now Gorbachev have brought these trends forcefully to general notice while very senior Soviet officers continually address the military on the problem. They have called for better educational, technical and ideological preparation for call-up. They describe as naive the inclination of young people to believe what they hear from foreign broadcasting and, as a consequence, to underestimate the threat of war. Yepishev expressed concern that new recruits to the Army were showing symptoms of 'passivity and an indifferent attitude to the threat posed by our class enemies'.[7]

The suggested remedy for these regressive tendencies is more and yet more ideological training, the Soviet cure-all for every ill. If the self-discipline system is failing in any respect it can only be attributed to the slipping of 'ideological steeling'.[8] The Party and its organs could never admit that it might be the ideology itself that cannot any longer satisfy the intellectual demands of youth. The more percipient great-grandchildren of the Revolution are just beginning to question the fundamental articles of the Leninist religion and are finding it wanting. Their dissatisfaction is manifesting itself in various forms ranging from Samizdat articles on anarchy to a return to the old Orthodox religion. But even if it continues, the movement will be slow and it is no immediate threat to the present state of morale and discipline within the Armed Forces. The external ogre is still painted in sufficiently strong colours to ensure that there will be no rapid erosion of the morale base in the shorter-term future.

The important question however is – do morale and motivation crucially matter? Obviously they must do to a significant degree. Forces reduced to unruly mob status present a much reduced threat to the potential enemy. Soviet forces are far from that state. They might find themselves beset by man-management problems exemplified by divisive ethnic divisions, drunkenness and other serious expressions of ill-discipline but they are doubtless confident that the coercive system of the KGB and the penal battalions will contain dissaffection when troop welfare and leadership fall down. Suvorov's description of the completely moronic conformity of the recalcitrant soldier returned from the penal battalion is chilling in its implication.[9] As for KGB methods of persuasion there is no shortage of examples of their ruthless nature. Gilmore witnessed the clearance of German butterfly anti-personnel mines from the United States Army Air Corps base at Poltava during World War II. Under compulsion from KGB machine-guns, parties of groundstaff, female as well as male, were forced to walk over the airfield, either collecting or exploding these nuisance weapons. The wailing cries of protest went unheeded.[10]

Such tales of inhumanity abound, all serving to emphasise that when it comes to military necessity the KGB will play for keeps. In World War II the Soviet Union soon realised that it was playing for keeps. Much has been made of the massive desertions of Soviet troops to the German enemy in the early days of their 1941 invasion. The unspoken Western hope that the Soviet High Command might be deterred from major military ventures by the fear of history repeating itself in this regard has been encouraged by Suvorov and other defectors, but the facts of World War II must be recalled.

There is no doubt that the Soviet Army deserted to the enemy in large numbers in the early days of the invasion. Dallin suggests two main reasons. The surprise shock of the attack which engulfed whole formations giving them no option but to make the best deal they could with the Germans and, since most of the defectors were Ukrainian or Balts, they seized what they saw to be a heaven-sent opportunity to secede from the Soviet Union, collectively or personally.[11] In spite of this blow to the heart, the true Russians did not desert and the Soviet Army was able to recover the position and in less than three months successfully held the Germans in front of Moscow and Leningrad before the onset of winter gave them a respite. In the face of all the adverse factors, the 1936–38 purge of the officer corps, the Finnish disaster of 1939 and the demoralising legacy of Stalin's collectivisation of agriculture programme on a mainly peasant army, an appeal to patriotism was answered. The nation and the system were saved.

The Germans' experience of their Soviet enemy in World War II was obviously wide and deep but, curiously, their impressions have not been studied as closely in the English-speaking West as perhaps they should be. A backward glance to that period is very relevant to today's study. Graham Vernon in recent research has discovered in what he calls 'the dusty stacks of the National Archives' the debriefing reports of a group of ex-Wehrmacht officers who served on the Eastern Front.[12] They contain a wealth of first-hand experience which, although over forty years old, cannot be ignored as an indicator of how the Soviet soldier of today might behave in battle. Vernon's study is very revealing of Soviet national characteristics and there is no reason to believe that they have altered much since 1945. He has exposed the tip of an iceberg and hopes that further research effort will lead to the full exploitation of this valuable source material.

Contemporary studies suggest three tiers of leadership quality exist in all works of Soviet life; a zealous, inspired higher direction with clear aims either uncoordinated and uncontrollable enthusiasm or total apathy at the bottom, with a conscientious but inflexible middle management recognising the difficulties and trying to reconcile the two ends of the scale. The German appraisals make interesting comparisons. Vernon notes that they found a qualitative difference in the several echelons of Soviet command:

> In Soviet Russia the top level leadership was purposeful and capable while the intermediate and lower echelons were, at least in the beginning, slow to take the initiative and unwilling to deviate from a set pattern of battle.[13]

The lower rank levels were judged in another manuscript to be 'inflexible and indecisive, avoiding all personal responsibility'. In their view the explanation was:

> . . . the rigid pattern of training and an over-strict discipline so narrowly confined the lower command within the framework of existing regulations that the result was lethargy. Spirited application to a task, born of the decision of an individual was a rarity . . . the Russian small unit commander's fear of doing something wrong and being called to account for it was greater than the urge to take advantage of a situation.[14]

A 'fear of doing something wrong' is probably as strong in the Soviet officer's breast today as it was in the 1940s. It is engendered primarily by the national understanding – or misunderstanding – of the word 'initiative', paralysing in its effects throughout all walks of Soviet life, not least among the military. The Russian word *initsiyativa* does not translate simply. To Western minds 'initiative' suggests the willingness of an individual to react in accordance with the apparent logic of the moment in circumstances beyond the vision or control of his superior authority. The Soviet interpretation is not quite the same. 'Initiative' to them means the ability to divine from Marxist–Leninist principles precisely what a superior's plan for the present contingency would have been. Such a plan must have existed since Soviet training admits no possibility of the unforeseen event. A dread that he might read his commander's mind incorrectly results very often in the Soviet officer taking no action at all, the consequent breakdown of control leading to failure of the mission with heavy collateral damage to unit morale.[15] This difference in definition is slight, a subtlety of nuance rather than substance, but it has deep implications. It represents a deficiency that senior Soviet military authorities have been aware of for many years but seem unable to remedy. Again their great fear is of *rastyeranost*, a corporate loss of will, paralysis and disintegration. To prevent this collapse of discipline they wisely teach that operation orders should be as all-embracing as possible, covering the remotest contingency, but for the encouragement of true initiative their only prescription thus far has been – again, exactly as for all other deficiencies – periodically to call for yet more intensive ideological training.

If the fear of taking the initiative is potentially demoralising, the fear of death or injury is probably less of a threat to morale that it would be to Western armed forces, especially with regard to ground troops. As mentioned earlier, *dulce et decorum est pro patria mori* is a prominent theme in the ideological instruction of Soviet youth from the earliest days of schooling and throughout military service. Once a young man is conscripted, the 'steeling of the will' process involves the steeling of the young man's body as well as his mind. He is exercised incessantly and realistically, the sound and fury of the simulated battlefield being hardly less testing to nerve and sinew than the real thing. Realism is not difficult to inject into exercises when training casualties are not of great concern. Though lack of initiative on the part of officers, especially junior officers, might make for some inertia in the command and control system and a consequent loss of cohesion among units or even formations, it would be unwise to expect that the soldiers' wooden discipline would collapse merely from the strain of battle although as German evidence suggests, herd instinct panic might well affect the units bereft of leadership or direction.[16]

Of itself, a reverse would be unlikely to develop into a rout. The Germans, their quick 1941 victories notwithstanding, appear unanimous in assessing the Soviet soldier as a tough enemy, courageous and enduring beyond the normal human measure:

The stoicism of the majority of Russian soldiers and their mental sluggishness make them insensible to losses. The Russian values his own life no more than those of his comrades. To step on walls of dead, composed of the bodies of his former friends and companions makes not the slightest impression on him and does not upset his equanimity at all; without so much as twinkling an eye-lid he stolidly continues to attack or stays in the position he has been told to defend. He is immune to the most incredible hardships and does not even appear to notice them; he seems equally indifferent to bombs and shells.[17]

The Germans were not bemused by a 'ten-foot' image of their enemy. They were equally aware of his warts and judged him objectively. Von Mellenthin continues:

It must be pointed out however that there were cases when battle-hardened Russian formations panicked or showed nervousness under light shelling. But such cases were few and far between. It will be much better to overestimate Russian toughness; softness is the exception and nobody can ever depend on the lucky case when the Russian will prove soft.

Alan Clark in his excellent study of the Soviet–German conflict describes how the quality of the Soviet soldier gave rise to an uneasy feeling among German troops that they were fighting something of almost supernatural strength and resilience. Myths grew among them that a Russian always has to be killed twice over; that the Russians could never be beaten and that no man who drew blood there ever left Russia alive. They were above all impressed by the conduct of the wounded:

They do not cry out, they do not groan, they do not curse. Undoubtedly there is something mysterious, something inscrutable about their stern stubborn silence.[18]

Without much doubt the legend of the 'ten-feet tall' Soviet soldier came originally from the Germans, a compound probably of their genuine astonishment at his performance and a reflexive need to cite the superhuman nature of the enemy as an excuse for their defeat. Today it is important only to consider the extent to which the heroic characteristics of his grandfather – 'the liberator of Europe' – are present in the genes of the grandson, the officer or conscript soldier serving at the present time. Some argue that the situation is vastly changed from the days of World War II, that today's generation of conscripts, 60 per cent of which now comes from an urban rather than a peasant background is softer than its predecessor and it could not be expected in war to display the same degree of stoic endurance or indifference to pain and death. Moreover, growing disillusion with the Marxist–Leninist ideology would make young men less willing to leap to the defence of their homeland than were the earlier generations. Neither claim can be entirely discounted. They have to be considered in weighing the balance.

It is abundantly clear that many factors are likely to have a bearing on morale in the Soviet Armed Forces, most of them common to the Armed Forces of any nation. An attempt has been made here to examine the principal factors, recognising that there are subsidiary influences likely to have appreciable negative or positive effect on morale, i.e. it is not a constant which can be credited or debited to a military balance in the same way as ships, tanks or aircraft. In peacetime it is acutely sensitive to living conditions and certain aspects of discipline such as have been illustrated in the Soviet context where they are generally depressive. The quality of food, the personality of the sergeant-major, the thraldom of the repetitive training programme, the ethnic origins of one's comrades or the proximity of fleshpot diversions are among the issues which loom large. They may not be important at all in war.

All these factors appear to have had an adverse effect on the morale of Soviet forces in Afghanistan, some exacerbated by specific features of the campaign, none as far as can be judged ameliorated by the experience of active service. Inter-racial quarrels have continued to flare, drug abuse has become serious and slack discipline has called forth severe punitive remedies, all this resulting in operational inefficiency. Notwithstanding some signs of a hitherto unsuspected capacity for technical innovation, command and control continues inflexible and slow in response to the demands of rapidly changing situations. Does this evidence suggest that an outbreak of war on a grand scale against NATO in Europe would see the early collapse of Soviet military morale?

It would be unwise of the NATO powers to bank on it, and estimates of morale made from extrapolations of the peacetime state could be dangerously unsound. Much would depend obviously on the fortunes of the war. The political and military indoctrination of Soviet youth, not only as it is refined by the *Zampolit* during their period of service but also as it is cultivated throughout the whole of their education, has been described above in some detail because it seems to be the keystone of morale. It is obvious from the sheer weight of resources devoted to it that the Soviet authorities themselves regard it so. There is little doubt that 'the ideological steeling of the will', the inculcation of a love for the communist homeland, with the counterpoint notion of hate for the capitalist–imperialist enemies who encircle and threaten that homeland, is calculated to transcend all the irritants of peacetime military service and create a morale, durable enough to outlast that of the opposition. Crowded rooms, spartan rations and the injustice of NCOs will be forgotten when the enemy is engaged in the field and all will rush forward in noble self-sacrifice to rid the world of evil at last and forever. Authority will take prudent precautions to ensure that it will happen this way. Ethnically sensitive elements will not be committed early to the battle, the *Zampolit* will prove the righteous nature of the Soviet cause using all available evidence, true or false, and KGB troops will be positioned to preclude the possibility of wavering or disorderly retreat. There is no reason to believe that such measures would not be effective or that morale would prove brittle in the crucial opening state of hostilities. Soviet troops are expensively acclimatised to the noise of battle, much more so than NATO troops, and as fully instructed as possible concerning the probable features of a nuclear battlefield. They are unlikely to be unnerved by fright on this account as long as their advance continues and enemy opposition to it is overcome in accordance with the plan. Should things on the other hand go wrong they would not find it easy to improvise and could possibly flounder in confusion and indecision. NATO should not only be conscious of this possibility but ready to exploit it should it occur. It is not however to be expected that they would flee the field or surrender *en masse*. The same brand of courage displayed by all ranks, soldiers and airmen, in the retreat of 1941 and the stand before Moscow would be demonstrated to NATO. That earlier determination to defend the homeland had not been extinguished by famine, collectivisation, the Great Purge or the Gulag. It is almost certainly still on call today. Owing more to a love for 'Mother Russia' than to the ideology of the *Zampolit* it must be expected that it would come to the surface naturally now as then – at least to Slavs – in spite of any fashionable cynicism towards the communist ideal.

The non-Slav elements of the Soviet forces are an enigma. The simple conclusion that a Soviet Russian success, though it might not be applauded by all the other Soviet constituent nationalities but for every reason of self-interest would be supported, would probably be borne out in the event. A Soviet Russian reverse would not necessarily have the opposite effect. It would depend on geography and its magnitude. If serious enough it could well rekindle dormant nationalist urges for independence and ultimately rend the fabric of the Union. There is sufficient indication that the Soviet General Staff is conscious of this possibility and that however remote they consider it to be it has for a long time now contributed to their extreme caution in the exercise of military power.

An attempt has been made here to show that no simple

stereotype of the Soviet Serviceman can be drawn. His morale can be expected to vary in accordance with variations of its many motivating influences. No assessment of the factors affecting the morale of non-Soviet Warsaw Pact Forces has been made here. It is considered however that their cohesion in war would depend on events in broadly similar fashion to their effect on the non-Slav Soviet Forces, i.e., they would support success but, if the circumstances of a Soviet reverse were favourable they would be likely to desert. Again, self-interest would be the motive but in either case the likely repercussions on Soviet morale are not difficult to imagine. In conclusion it is possible to endorse the conventional view that Soviet soldiers are never likely to be as strong as is often supposed – nor as weak!

Notes

CHAPTER 1   POLITICAL EDUCATION AND TRAINING

1. Marshal of the Soviet Union A. A. Grechko, *The Armed Forces of the Soviet State*, (Moscow: Military Publishing House, 1975).
2. General Svechin, *Military Strategy* (Moscow, 1926).
3. A. Inkeles, *Public Opinion in Soviet Russia* (Harvard University Press, 1950); Margaret Meade, *Soviet Attitude Towards Authority* (London: Tavistock Publications, 1950).
4. E.g. Suvorov, *The Liberators* (London: Hamish Hamilton, 1981); Belyenko, *MiG Pilot* (John Barron) (London: Readers' Digest Press, 1979).
5. Hedrik Smith, *The Russians* (London: Sphere, 1976).
6. Vladimirov, *The Russians* . . . (Pall Mall, London, 1968).
7. E.g. 'The object of education in a socialist society is the formation of a convinced collectivist, a person who does not think of himself outside society' (from V. M. Korotov . . . *Development of the Educational Function of the Collective*).
8. *Father's Old Army Tunic* (Moscow: Children's Publishing House, 1973).
9. *A Border Guard and his Dog* (Moscow: Children's Publishing House, 1973).
10. A. Gaidar, *Malchish Kibalchish and the Tale of the Military Secret* (Moscow: Novosti Publishers, 1978).
11. Allan Kassoff, *The Soviet Youth Programme* (Harvard University Press, 1965).
12. E. I. Monoszona, *The Formation of the Communist World Outlook in Schoolchildren* (Moscow: Pedagogic Press, 1978).
13. The word inculcate has been chosen carefully. The Russian *vospitaniye* beloved of Soviet pedagogues may be translated as 'bringing up' (of children), indoctrination or the inculcation of a doctrine. Only loosely does it mean 'education'. Monoszona writes almost exclusively of *vospitaniye*. The word for 'education' in the true sense is *obrazovaniye*.
14. A full description of the Soviet school system can be found in Nigel Grant's *Soviet Education* (Harmondsworth, Middx: Penguin, 1967).
15. L. A. Voskresenskaya *A Word about a Great Matter* (Moscow: Children's Press, 1981).
16. Mikhail Yefimov, *The USSR Constitution* (Moscow: Novosti Publishers, 1979).
17. S. Baruzgin, *A Soldier Walked Down the Street* (Moscow: Children's Literature Press, 1978).
18. World War I is also inconvenient for Soviet historians since, like the Crimean and Russo–Japanese Wars, the Russians did not win.

189

19. The myth of the Winter Palace battle, in reality a minor skirmish, has long been established as truth. Total casualties on both sides in the 'battle' were seven killed. See John Reed *Ten Days that Shook the World* (Harmondsworth, Middx: Penguin, 1981).

20. The author met many from various age groups who were not sure whether Britain was involved in World War II and some who were under the impression that she had fought on the German side. None of them had heard of the 'Battle of Britain'.

21. *The Soviet Constitution* (1977).

22. The wreckage of the American U-2 reconnaissance aircraft shot down over Sverdlovsk in 1961 is one of the most popular exhibits in the Armed Forces Museum in Moscow.

23. L. I. Brezhnev, *On the Communist Up-bringing of the Workers* (Moscow: 'Enlightenment' Publishing House, 1974) pp. 527–8.

24. Allen Kassoff, *The Soviet Youth Programme* (Harvard University Press, 1965).

25. The Voluntary Organisation for supporting the Soviet Armed Forces.

26. Kassoff, op. cit., p. 79.

27. Ibid., p. 79.

28. O. Volodin, 'Bringing up the Defenders of the Homeland' (*'Narodnoye Obrasovaniye'*), (Moscow: National Education, 1972).

29. Extract from poem by B. Dubrovin from 'February' in *The Scholar's Calender* (Moscow: Political House, 1981).

30. 'Zarnitsa, School of Courage', *Military Knowledge* (*Voyennoye Znaniye*), May 1974.

31. 'Ready for Labour and Defence', *Red Star*, 26 April 1972.

32. I. Ilinskiy, *What is the KOMSOMOL?* (Moscow: Novosti Publishing, 1978).

33. L. Pesterev, 'The Combat Examination', *Military Knowledge*, June 1974.

34. L. Pesterev 'Orlyonok is no Picnic', *Military Knowledge*, April 1975.

35. Kassoff, *The Soviet Youth Programme*.

36. Ilinskiy, *What is the KOMSOMOL?*

37. Ibid.

38. Y. Bogat, *Dumayushcheye Litso* (*The Thoughtful Reader*) (Moscow: Novosti Publishing House, 1978).

39. Ibid.

40. Ibid.

41. Ibid.

42. Ibid.

43. DOSAAF (*Dobrovolnoye Obshchestvo Sodyeistviya Armii, Aviatiya i Flota*).

44. *The Great Soviet Encyclopaedia*, Vol. 8 (Moscow: 1970–79).

45. Scott and Scott, *The Armed Forces of the USSR* (New York: Westview, 1979).

46. Ibid.

47. The main publication is a monthly illustrated journal *Voyennoye Znaniye* (*Military Knowledge*).

48. V. V. Mosyaikin, *The DOSAAF Organisation – Programme of Action* (Moscow: DOSAAF Press, 1978).

49. All published by the 'Badge of Honour' (Moscow: DOSAAF Press, 1977–80).

50. N. A. Kostikov (ed.), *The Complete Approach to the Training of the Pre-Call up Youth* (Moscow: DOSAAF Publishing House, 1980).

51. Mosyaikin, *The DOSAAF Organisation – Programme of Action*.
52. 'Internal regulations for the Armed Forces of the USSR-1977' as quoted in vol. 6 of *The Military Encyclopaedia*, Moscow, 1977.
53. R. Gabriel, *The New Red Legions* (New York: Greenwood, 1981).
54. 'Who Would Like to Become an Officer?', *Red Star*, 19 January 1982.
55. *Politicheskiy Rukovoditel* (Political leader).
56. L. Nemzer *Basic Patterns of Political and Propaganda Operations in the Soviet Armed Forces* (New York: John Hopkins University Press, 1953).
57. R. Kolkowicz, *The Soviet Military and the Communist Party*. (Princeton University Press, 1967).
58. V. Suvorov, *The Liberators* (London: Hamish Hamilton, 1981), as one example.
59. Observed on wall posters at Soviet military training establishment (1981).
60. *General Regulations for the Armed Forces of the USSR*, Articles 107 and 119 (Moscow: Military Publishing House, 1984).
61. The official journal of the Main Political Administration, published monthly.
62. A. Zaitsev, 'Communist of the Armed Forces', December Communist of the Armed Forces, 1976.
63. Colonel A. Migolatyev, 'The Stark Reality of Our Times', *Red Star*, 8 January 1982.
64. D. A. Volkogonov, *Handbook for Propagandists and Agitators in the Army and the Fleet*, (Moscow: Military Publishing House, 1978).
65. An interesting mirror-image of the widely-held Western view of the Soviet economy.
66. Zhilin and Bryul, *The Military Bloc Alliance Policies of Imperialism*' (Moscow: Military Publishing House, 1980). An exhaustive study of anti-communist military alliances traced from the Intervention of 1918 to the present day.
67. Marshal A. A. Grechko, *The Armed Forces of the Soviet State*, 2nd edn, (Moscow: Military Press at the USSR Ministry of Defence, 1975).
68. *Ideologicheskaya obrabotka.*
69. Major General V. Bruz 'The Brainwashing of USAF Crews', *Air Defence Herald*, July 1981.
70. It is presumed that Bruz is referring to the USAF 'Soviet Awareness' programme.
71. It is worth noting that this 1981 article appeared a considerable time after the proven use of anti-personnel, booby trap weapons in Afghanistan by Soviet forces – not before.
72. Colonel A. Ivanov, 'The Spiritual "Ration" of the Bundeswehr', *Red Star*, 20 May 1982.
73. That is, as conducted by the USSR.
74. Y. Polyakov, *A History of Soviet Society* (Moscow: Novosti Publishers, 1977).
75. 'USA–Latin America', *Izvestia*, 16 May 1982.
76. 'What They Teach Tommy' *Red Star*, 24 January 1977.
77. M. I. Kalinin as quoted in L. Nemzer, 'Basic Patterns of Political and Propaganda Operations in the Soviet Armed Forces' (New York: John Hopkins University Press, 1953).
78. Lieutenant General V. P. Novikov, *The Inculcation of Traditions* (Moscow: Military Publishing House, 1979).

79. Major General N. I. Smorigo, *Towards More Effective Propaganda and Agitation* (Moscow: Military Publishing House, 1979).
80. Address by General of the Army A. A. Epishev, then head of MPA, at the 19th All-Union KOMSOMOL Congress, reported in *Red Star*, 20 May 1982.
81. Major General S. N. Kozlov, *The Officer's Handbook*, ch. 3, (Moscow: Military Publishing House, 1971).
82. Colonel M. P. Skirdo, *The People, the Army, the Commander* (Moscow: Military Publishing House, 1970).
83. Y. Volkov, *The Truth about Afghanistan* (Moscow: Novosti Publishing House, 1980).
84. Major General S. N. Kozlov, The Officers' Handbook, ch. 3 (Moscow: Military Publishing House, 1976).
85. Marshal A. A. Grechko, *The Armed Forces of the Sovirt State* (Moscow: Military Publishing House, 1975).
86. A. M. Rumyantsev, *Dictionary of Scientific Communism* (Moscow: Political Publishing House, 1980).
87. V. I. Anikovich *The Army – a School of Culture* (Moscow: DOSAAF Publishers, 1980).
88. Anon., *The Soviet Army – a School of Internationalism and Friendship of the Peoples and a School of Courage and Discipline*' (Soviet Army Publications no. 1/70121-T6, 1981).
89. Y. I. Anikovich, *The Army – a School of Culture*.
90. Levin and Kamsyuk, *Bourgeois Culture in the Service of Reaction* (Moscow: Central Club of Soviet Army, 1975).
91. Lenin, *Collected Works*, vol. 6, p. 259.
92. Lenin, *Collected Works*, vol. 17, p. 418.
93. Dolgikh and Kurantov, *Communist Ideals and the Atheistic Indoctrination of Troops* (Moscow: Military Publishing House, 1976).
94. A. V. Kalachnikov, *The Inculcation of Vigilance in Soviet Troops*.
95. L. Nemzer, *Basic Patterns of Political and Propaganda Operations in the Soviet Armed Forces*' (New York: John Hopkins University Press, 1953).

CHAPTER 2   IS THE *ZAMPOLIT* EFFECTIVE?

1. J. H. Schnitzler, *Secret History of the Court and Government of Russia* (London: Richard Bentley, 1849).
2. A. Inkeles, *Public Opinion in Soviet Russia* (Harvard University Press, 1950).
3. General of the Army A. A. Yepishev, Address to 19th KOMSOMOL Congress as reported in *Red Star*, 20 May 1982.
4. 'I serve the Soviet Union' has already run on the Soviet TV network for longer than 'Coronation Street' in Britain.
5. V. Suvorov, *The Liberators* (London: Hamish Hamilton, 1981).
6. A. Myagkov, *Inside the KGB* (New York: Ballantine Books, 1981).
7. John Barron, *MiG Pilot* (New York: Readers' Digest Press, 1980).
8. Richard Gabriel, *The New Red Legions* (New York: Greenwood, 1981).
9. Gabriel's figures have been compounded here to give averages across the sub-divisions of his sample range.

10. Goldhamer, *The Soviet Soldier*, for instance.
11. Brezhnev and company taking the salute on Lenin's Mausoleum in Red Square.

CHAPTER 3   MORALE AND OTHER FACTORS

1. R. A. Gabriel, *The New Red Legions* (New York: Greenwood, 1981).
2. E.g. H. Goldhamer, *The Soviet Soldier* (New York: Crane, Russak, 1975).
3. See A. A. Yepishev, *True to the Ideals of the Party* (Moscow: Military Publishing House, 1981). A frank listing of moral shortcomings.
4. Except those who volunteer for officer service, whose higher education and Russian language competence reduces integration difficulties to almost negligible proportions.
5. Wimbush and Alexiev, *The Ethnic Factor in the Soviet Armed Forces* (Rand Corporation, March 1982).
6. Not only *DOSAAF* training is so limited; education generally is of a lower standard in non-Slav areas.
7. A. Sheehy, 'Language Problems in the Soviet Armed Forces', Radio Liberty research paper RL 196/78.
8. Included nearly all the officers and sergeants.
9. Rand R-2887/1, March 1981, p. 34.
10. Ethnic imbalance in units has itself often been the cause of trouble. Conscript selection is now more carefully regulated in an attempt to minimise the problem.
11. This irritates the Slav conscripts because construction troops receive more pay and have greater access to alcohol supplies. In many cases they become highly-skilled tradesmen, a marketable asset when they return to civil life, denying the cherished Slav belief that they are 'blacks' or 'monkeys'.
12. *The Ethnic Factor in the Soviet Armed Forces*, Rand Report R-2787/1, 1982, extracts from ch. 7. (Wimbush and Alexiev).
13. One witness stated:
    'After the first term [year] of service, the relationship among nationalities becomes more equal; all become more like brothers. During the first term of service, Uzbeks make friends only with Uzbeks, Russians with Russians, Jews with Jews and so forth. But in subsequent service this is levelled out.'
    Rand, R-2787/1, p. 39
14. Extracts from Rand R-2787/1, p. 40.
15. Rand R-2787/1, p. 45.
16. Rand R-2787/1, p. 13.
17. Rand R-2787/1, p. 46.
18. Rand R-2787/1, p. 13.
19. Admiral A. I. Sorokin, in *Voprosy Filosofi* (Issue 2, 1983). Not only Sorokin but Yepishev himself also raises this issue in his 'True to the Ideals of the Party' (1981).
20. R. A. Gabriel, *The New Red Legions* (New York: Greenwood, 1981) p. 43.
21. Ibid., p. 43.

22. The ambiguous framing of the question points to the somewhat dubious nature of parts of the study.
23. V. Suvorov, *The Liberators* (London: Hamish Hamilton, 1981).
24. P. Aleksandr, 'The Story of a Sailor', *Posyev*, no. 6, Munich, 1983.
25. B. B. Krabtsov, 'The Law against Drunkenness', USSR Minister of Justice, reported in *Tass*, 1 June 1985.
26. M. Tsypkin, 'The Conscripts', *The Bulletin of Atomic Scientists*, May 1983.
27. Myakgov, *Inside the KGB* (New York: Ballantine, 1981).
28. Belyenko (John Barron), *MiG Pilot* (London: Readers' Digest Association, 1979).
29. Suvorov, *The Liberators*.
30. V. Snezhko, 'The Code of Military Law', *Agitator of the Army and the Fleet*, Issue 18, September 1982.
31. H. Goldhamer, *The Soviet Soldier* (1976).
32. A. Zyryanov, 'Let's Discuss the New Military Regulations', *Military Knowledge*, no. 11 (Moscow: Military Publishing House, October 1975).
33. Belyenko, *MiG Pilot* (London: Readers' Digest Press, 1980).

CHAPTER 5   THE SOVIET AIRMAN

1. Inoshevsky, *Red Pilot* (1937).
2. V. Pinchyuk, 'The Business of All the People', *Aviation and Cosmonautics*, August 1983.
3. Ibid.
4. For a Soviet account of their involvement in Spain see A. Yakovlev's *The Aim of a Lifetime* (Moscow: Progress Publishers, 1972).
5. R. A. Kilmarx, *A History of Soviet Air Power* (London: Faber & Faber, 1962).
6. Ibid., pp. 151–3.
7. Ibid., p. 153.
8. Ibid., p. 177.
9. *Red Star* 28 February 1983.
10. V. Belyenko (John Barron), *MiG Pilot*, (London: Readers' Digest Association, 1980).
11. L. Khovrizhkin, 'Combat Demands Co-ordination', *Red Star*, 10 November 1983.
12. Marshal of Aviation A. Yefimov, *Aviation and Cosmonautics* Moscow, November 1983.
13. Lt. Col. Novikov 'Lack of Imagination and Innovation are Incompatible', Moscow, November 1983.
14. 'Pre-flight Checks must be Thorough', *Red Star*, 4 August 1984.

CHAPTER 7   SOME CURRENT CONSIDERATIONS

1. *Natsionalniy Trudovoi Soyuz* (National Labour Union) – the largest of the Russian *émigré* organisations.
2. *Daily Mail*, 25 November 1983.
3. 'Soviet Deserters Speak', *Soviet Analyst*, 26 January 1983.

4. Nicholas Bethell 'This Wasn't Our War – the Commissars Had Lied', *Daily Mail*, 25 November 1983.

5. Some of these men have since been repatriated and Soviet media have attempted to repudiate their testimony. See for example Tass, 1 February 1985, 'Die Welt's Dirty Inventions'. In spite of this the original evidence retain incredibility.

6. See p. 32.

7. Speech by General A. A. Yepishev at the KOMSOMOL Congress, Moscow, May 1982.

8. See 'The Business of the Whole Nation', by Admiral of the Fleet G. M. Yegorov, President of the DOSAAF organisation, DOSAAF Press, 1984. The book is a strong plea for the revitalisation and reform of DOSAAF ideological training. It implies that it has seriously deteriorated in recent years over the whole USSR.

9. V. Suvorov, *Inside the Soviet Army* (London: Hamish Hamilton, 1982).

10. E. Gilmore, *Me and My Russian Wife* (Slough: Foulsham, 1950).

11. A. Dallin, *The Germans in Occupied USSR 1941–45* (London: Macmillan, 1957).

12. Colonel G. D. Vernon US Army (retired), 'Soviet Combat Operations, in World War Two – Lessons for Today', *Military Review* March 1980 and April 1980.

13. Vernon, US National Archives, Manuscript P-145, p. 253.

14. Ibid., March 1980.

15. Illustrated best perhaps in the frequently-used phrase, *initsiyativa nakazuyema* (literally, 'initiative', is punishable) i.e. 'nothing ventured, nothing lost'.

16. See Vernon, *Military Review*, March 1980, p. 39.

17. Major General Von Mellenthin, *Panzer Battles* (University of Oklahoma Press, 1956).

18. Alan Clark, *Barbarossa* (London: Hutchinson, 1965).

Bibliography

Alexander, P., The Story of a Sailor, *Posyev*, no. 6 (Munich, 1983).
Anikovich, V. I., *The Army – School of Culture* (Moscow: *DOSAAF* Press, 1977).
——, *Badge of Honour* (Moscow: *DOSAAF* Press, 1977).
Barron, J., *MiG Pilot* (New York: Readers' Digest Press, 1980).
Baruzgin, S., *A Soldier Walks Down the Street* (Moscow: Children's Publishers, 1978).
——, *A Border Guard and His Dog* (Moscow: Children's Publishers, 1973).
Bethell, N., 'This Wasn't Our War', *Daily Mail*, London, 25 November 1983.
Bocas, Y., *The Thoughtful Reader* (Moscow: Novosti Publishers, 1978).
Brezhnev, L. I., *On the Communist Upbringing of the Workers* (Moscow: Enlightenment Publishing House, 1974).
Bruz, V., 'The Brainwashing of USAF Crews', *Air Defence Herald*, Moscow, July 1981.
Clark, A., *Barbarossa* (London: Hutchinson, 1972).
——, *Father's Old Army Tunic* (Moscow: Children's Publishers, 1973).
Dolgikh and Kuraniov, *Communist Ideals and the Atheistic Indoctrination of the Troops* (Moscow: Military Publishing House, 1976).
Dubrovin, B., *The Scholar's Calendar* (Moscow: Political Publishing House, 1981).
Gabriel, R., *The New Red Legions* (New York: Greenwood, 1981).
——, *General Regulations for the Soviet Armed Forces*, Articles 107 and 119.
Gaidar, A., *Tale of the Military Secret* (Moscow: Novosti Publishers, 1978).
Gilmore, E., *Me and My Russian Wife* (Slough: Foulsham, 1950).
Goldhamer, H., *The Soviet Soldier* (New York: Crane, Russack, 1975).
Grant, N., *Soviet Education* (Harmondsworth, Middx: Penguin, 1967; (new edn, 1983).
——, *Great Soviet Encyclopaedia* (vol. 8), (Moscow, 1970–79).
Grechko, A. A., *The Armed Forces of the Soviet States* (Moscow: Military Publishing House, 1975).
Inkeles, A., *Public Opinion in Soviet Russia* (Harvard University Press, 1950).
Ilinskiy, I., *What Is the KOMSOMOL?* (Moscow: Novosti Publishers, 1978).
Inozhevskiy, *Red Pilot* (London: Cassell, 1938).
Ivanov, A., 'The Spiritual "Ration" of the Bundeswehr', *Red Star*, 20 May 1982.
Kalachnikov, A. V., *The Inculcation of Vigilance in Soviet Troops* (Moscow: Military Publishing House, 1978).
Kilmarx, R. A., *A History of Soviet Air Power* (London: Faber & Faber, 1962).
Kassoff, A., *The Soviet Youth Programme* (Harvard University Press, 1965).
Kolkowicz, R.. *The Soviet Military and the Communist Party* (Princetown University Press, 1967).
Khourizhkin, 'Combat demands Coordination', *Red Star*, 10 November 1983.

Korotov, V. M., *Developing the Educational Function of the Collective* (Moscow: Pedagogic Publishers, 1980).

Kostikov, N. A., *A Complete Approach to the Training of Pre-call up youth* (Moscow: DOSAAF Publishers, 1980).

Kozlov, S. N., *The Officer's Handbook* (Moscow: Military Publishing House, 1971).

Lenin, V. I., *Collected Works* (Moscow: Political Publishing House).

Levin and Kamsyuk, *Bourgeois Culture in the Service of Reaction* (Moscow: Central Club of the Soviet Army, 1975).

Meade, M., *Soviet Attitudes towards Authority* (London: Tavistock Publications, 1955).

Mellenthin, F. W. von, *Panzer Battles* (University of Oklahoma Press, 1956).

Migolyatev, 'The Stark Reality of our Times', *Red Star*, 8 January 1982.

Monoszona, E. I., *The Formation of a Communist World Outlook in Children* (Moscow: Pedagogic Press, 1978).

Mosyaikin, V. V., 'The DOSAAF Organisation – Programme of Action', (Moscow: DOSAAF Publishers, 1978).

Myagkov, A., *Inside the KGB* (New York: Ballantine Books, 1981).

Nemzer, L., *Basic Patterns of Political and Propaganda Operations in the Soviet Armed Forces* (New York: Johns Hopkins University Press, 1953).

Novikov, V. P., *The Inculcation of Traditions* (Moscow: Military Publishing House, 1979).

Novikov, Y., 'Lack of Imagination and Innovation are Incompatible', *Aviation and Cosmonautics*, Moscow, November 1983.

Pesterev, L., 'The Combat Examination', *Military Knowledge*, Moscow, June 1974.

Pesterev, L., 'ORYLONOK is no Picnic', *Military Knowledge*, Moscow, April 1975.

Pinchyuk, 'The Business of All the People', *Aviation and Cosmonautics*, August 1983.

Polyaakov, Y., *A History of Soviet Society* (Moscow: Progress Publishers, 1977).

——, 'Ready for Labour and Defence', *Red Star*, 26 April 1972.

Reid, J., *Ten Days that Shook the World* (Harmondsworth, Middx: Penguin, 1981).

Rumyantisev, A. M., *Dictionary of Scientific Communism* (Moscow: Political Publishing House, 1980).

Sheehy, A., 'Language Problems in the Soviet Armed Forces', Radio Liberty Research Paper, RL 196/78.

Shnitzler, J. H., *Secret History of the Court and Government of Russia* (London: Richard Bentley, 1849).

Scott, W. F., and Scott, H. F., *Armed Forces of the USSR* (New York: Westview, 1983).

Skirdo, M. P., *The People, the Army, the Commander* (Moscow: Military Publishing House, 1970).

Smith, H., *The Russians* (London: Sphere Books, 1976).

Smorigo, N. I., *Towards More Effective Propaganda and Agitation* (Moscow: Military Publishing House, 1979).

Snezhko, V., 'The Code of Military Law', *Agitator of the Army and the Fleet*, no. 18, Moscow, 1984.

Suvorov, V., *The Liberators* (London: Hamish Hamilton, 1981).

Svechin, A., *Military Strategy* (Moscow: Military Publishing House, 1926).
——, 'USA – Latin America', *Izvestia*, 16 May 1982.
Vasilyev, G., *The Green and the Orange* (Moscow: Military Press, 1981).
Vernon, G. D., 'Soviet Combat Operations in WW2 – Lessons for Today', *Military Review* March and April 1980.
Vladimirov, L. V., The Russians (Pall Mall, London, 1968).
Volkov, Y., *The Truth about Afghanistan* (Moscow: Novosti Publishers, 1980).
Volkogonov, D. A., *Handbook for Propagandists and Agitators in the Army and the Fleet* (Moscow: Military Publishing House, 1978).
Volodin, O., *Bringing up Defenders of the Homeland* (Moscow: National Education, 1978).
Voskresenskaya, L. A., *A Word About a Great Matter* (Moscow: Children's Press. 1981).
——, 'What They Teach Tommy', *Red Star*, 24 January 1977.
——, 'Who Would Like to Become an Officer', *Red Star*, 19 January 1982.
Wimbush, F. E. and Alexiev, A., 'The Ethnic Factor in the Soviet Armed Forces', Paper 2787–1, Rand Corporation, March 1982.
Yakovlev, A., *The Aim of a Lifetime* (Moscow: Progress Publishers, 1972).
Yefimov, M., *The USSR Constitution* (Moscow: Novosti Publishers, 1979).
Yepishev, A. A., 'Address to KOMSOMOL Conference', *Red Star*, 20 May 1982.
——, *True to the Ideas of the Party* (Moscow: Military Publishing House, 1972).
Zaitsev, A., *Communist of the Armed Forces*, Moscow, December 1976.
Zhilin and Bayul, *The Military Block Alliance Policies and Imperialism* (Moscow: Military Publishing House, 1980).
Zyryanov, A., 'Let's Discuss the New Military Regulations', *Military Knowledge* no. 11, (Moscow, 1975).

Index